BIBLE-BASED DICTIONARY

OF PROPHETIC SYMBOLS FOR EVERY CHRISTIAN

BIBLE-BASED DICTIONARY

OF PROPHETIC SYMBOLS

FOR EVERY CHRISTIAN

Bridging the Gap Between
Revelation and Application

PLUS THE EXPANDED VERSION OF THE
ILLUSTRATED BIBLE-BASED DICTIONARY OF DREAM SYMBOLS

DR. JOE IBOJIE

CROSS HOUSE BOOKS
Christian Book Publishers
245 Midstocket Road
Aberdeen
AB15 5PH, UK

"The entrance of Your Word brings light."

Cover, Text Design and Typesetting by Jeffrey M. Hall, www.iongdw.com

ISBN: 978-0-9564008-2-6

For Worldwide Distribution, Printed in U.S.A.

1 2 3 4 5 6 7 8 / 13 12 11 10 09

To order products by Dr. Joe Ibojie & other Cross House Books,
contact sales@crosshousebooks.co.uk.

Other correspondence: info@crosshousebooks.co.uk.
Visit www.crosshousebooks.co.uk.

DEDICATION

I DEDICATE THIS BOOK to my first son, Eje Ibojie. You are the fruit of my youthful vigor and the strength and might of my beginning. You will surely become the excellence of dignity and excel in power! You are a determined, resilient, and resourceful son, the delight of any father. You have had your share of life's challenges but have emerged on top of them all!

I remain your biggest fan, as I am convinced that it will be as the Lord has shown me concerning you.

With love,
Dad

ACKNOWLEDGMENTS

I WISH TO ACKNOWLEDGE Angela Rickabaugh Shears for her excellent editorial services on this book. It has been a pleasure to work with her on this and many other projects. Her painstaking and superb attention to details have been invaluable in making this book what it is.

Thank God for my connection with Jeff Hall. Jeff's commitment to ensure a quality book is laudable, and I am highly indebted. He is a gift to the Body of Christ.

I would like to thank Dawn Maclean for enduring the pains of reading my handwriting and typing most of the manuscripts. Also, thanks to Dawn Williams for reading through the manuscripts.

PRAISE FOR
THE FIRST EDITION OF THE ILLUSTRATED
BIBLE-BASED DICTIONARY OF DREAM SYMBOLS

God has given Joe wisdom to open a door for us to understand the symbolic nature of our dreams.

This book will help you gain depth and breadth of understanding in what these symbols mean. When Joe teaches, he often asks questions like, "What do you think it means?" and what it means to you may be different from what it means for someone else.

We have a tool in our hands that can help take away the frustration of not knowing what our dreams mean and also remove the danger of misinterpretation. I thank God and the Holy Spirit for my friend Joe Ibojie and for the many gifts and talents he has.

Out of Joe's anointing God has led him to write these books in order that we may grow in our understanding. I pray as you read that God will bless you and give you wisdom as you use these wonderful tools.

—Pastor Joseph Ewen
Founder and Leader of Riverside Church Network
Banff, Scotland, UK

The Illustrated Bible-Based Dictionary of Dream Symbols and *Dreams & Visions: How to Receive, Interpret and Apply Your Dreams* are mighty tools in the hands of those in the Body of Christ who are seeking to recognize the voice of God in their lives. God has blessed Dr. Ibojie not only with a powerful anointing and gift himself, but also with the grace to help others unlock the inner potential within themselves through powerful keys of wisdom and insight. These books are treasure chests, loaded down with revelation and the hidden mysteries of God that have been waiting since before the foundation of the earth to be uncovered. *The Illustrated Bible-Based Dictionary of Dream Symbols* shall bless, strengthen, and guide any believer who is in search for the purpose, promise, and destiny of God for their lives. Thank God for this Christ-centred, Bible-based message that will restore the awareness that God is continually longing to communicate His love, desires, and will to His children. *"He that keeps Israel never sleeps or slumbers."* While you are sleeping, He is still speaking. Let he who has an ear (the desire to hear) hear what the Spirit is saying to the Church.

—Bishop Ron Scott Jr.
President, Kingdom Coalition International
Hagerstown, Maryland

The Illustrated Bible-Based Dictionary of Dream Symbols is much more than just a handbook for dream symbols; it has also added richness to our reading of God's Word. This book has many great God-inspired strategies to understand the symbols in the ever-increasing dreams and visions the Lord is using to speak to His people. Whether you use this book to assist in interpreting your dreams or as a resource for your study of the Word of God, you will find Dr. Joe's book to be a welcome companion.

—Robert & Joyce Ricciardelli
Directors, Visionary Advancement Strategies
Seattle, Washington

On our flight from Amsterdam to Florida, I sat beside Joe Ibojie. Joe obviously thought he would opt for the reading method of passing time, as he had a few books tucked under his arm. One of these books was his draft of a dictionary of dream symbolism. He was going through it, cross-referencing each definition with the Bible and adding annotations where necessary. In no time at all the conversation turned to dreams and all books were put to the side. The next eight hours passed so quickly that we could hardly believe it when we landed in Miami. In fact, throughout the following two weeks, as Joe and I shared a room and ministered together, the conversation would always turn to dreams and visions. Little did I know that the content of most of our friendly chats since then would make it to the pages of his wonderful book. Not that my contribution was anything more than asking Joe difficult questions, but I was pleased to see that his answers to these questions are contained in this book.

I have been privileged to minister with Joe on a frequent basis, but I am more privileged to know him not just as a person with Daniel-type anointing or as a prophetic voice (although he is frequently both these things to me) but as one of my closest friends. He is a true servant of God and a man with a passion to see God's Kingdom extend to wherever he goes and whomever he meets. Writing this book is simply an extension of this passion and has come out of years of experience—of working it out on a practical level, of seeing people transformed and set free to a life of liberty and purpose in the Holy Spirit, and of seeing people built up, encouraged, and edified, because they have come to a clearer understanding of God's purposes and plans in their life through a godly and, I believe, biblical interpretation of their dreams.

—Pastor Phil Sanderson
Third Day Church
Aberdeen, Scotland UK

This is a wonderful resource to assist the reader in understanding the symbolic language of dreams. Dr. Ibojie uses the Scripture extensively to reveal spiritual truth and has compiled an extremely thorough resource for interpreting the significance of the different aspects of our dreams. God's gift on his life for understanding dreams is evident as he gives insight to the subject. This is a must-add to your personal library as an active member of the Body of Christ.

—Emmanuel Ziga, President
Grace For All Nations Ministries International
Seattle, Washington

...Write down the revelation and make it plain on tablets so that a herald may run with it. For the revelation awaits an appointed time; it speaks of the end and will not prove false. Though it linger, wait for it; it will certainly come and will not delay (Habakkuk 2:2-3).

The first time I met Dr. Joe Ibojie was in Aberdeen city on an extremely cold evening when the sky was dark with impending snow. By contrast, Joe's countenance was bright and sunny and in all of our ensuing dialogue, whether in person, by telephone or email, I have found Joe's love for Christ and for life to be a constant source of joy.

Joe and his wife, Cynthia, and their four delightful children warmly welcomed me into their hearts and their home. It was at their family home that I had my first taste of African food—delicious! As a medical practitioner, Joe's life is full and busy. Not only this, but he and Cynthia have recently become pastors of The Father's House, a Christian fellowship in Aberdeen. I believe in "meeting the man behind the ministry," and I am delighted to commend Dr. Joe Ibojie to you as a loving husband, father, doctor, teacher, brother, and friend, as well as a gifted Christian writer. He is a genuine and humble Christian leader. I am sure you will be blessed by his character and desire to serve the Lord.

I have enjoyed ministering with Joe. He is enthusiastic and energetic and is an anointed teacher on the subject of dreams and their interpretation. Joe's inspiration is ever our Lord Jesus Christ.

About the Book

Over the last year it has been a wonderful experience to journey with Joe as he has worked on his first two books, *The **Illustrated** Bible-Based Dictionary of Dream Symbols* being the companion to *Dreams & Visions: How to Receive, Interpret and Apply Your Dreams*. I have thoroughly enjoyed learning more about dreams and their interpretation as we have fellowshipped, studied the Scriptures, and prayed together. Joe's teaching is motivational.

*The **Illustrated** Bible-Based Dictionary of Dream Symbols* is written in clear language, with detailed descriptions throughout its narrative that assist the reader on the journey of discovering the gift of interpretation. Dr. Joe enables the reader to become conversant with the parabolic language of symbols through Holy Spirit-inspired articulation. We rejoice that our Lord in His infinite grace and mercy chooses to communicate with His children. Ultimately, the gift of God's revelation ought to draw us deeper into a loving relationship with Christ, His Church, and those who do not yet know Him.

*The **Illustrated** Bible-Based Dictionary of Dream Symbols* is not intended to be a stand-alone resource; in other words, interpretation of symbols is not to be seen as a prescriptive exercise. Without prayerful application and understanding, our attempts at interpretation would be little more than presumptive. We may rest in the reality that interpretations belong to God (see Gen. 40:8). Joe encourages the reader to approach dream interpretation from a worshipful posture, giving careful consideration to the context and content of each dream or revelatory experience (such as a vision). Interpretation cannot be seen as a formula, but rather we ought to receive it as a gift from God, whereby the Holy Spirit imparts wisdom and understanding, fusing them with our faith, and opens our surrendered hearts and minds to receive Divine Counsel in a way that we can readily apply the interpretation of the dream symbols to our modern lifestyles.

*The **Illustrated** Bible-Based Dictionary of Dream Symbols* is a useful resource to help train and equip the Church to demonstrate God's love to the many who have not yet received salvation.

Jesus spoke in the language of parables and symbols to His disciples and to the multitudes who followed Him. Our Lord used numerous images to describe what the Kingdom of Heaven is like, such as a field (see Mt. 13:24), a mustard seed (see Mt. 13:31), treasure hidden in a field (Mt. 13:44), and a net let down into the lake that catches all kinds of fish (see Mt. 13:47). Jesus asked His disciples, "Have you understood all these things?" They replied "yes." Jesus then responded, "Therefore every teacher of the law who has been instructed about the kingdom of heaven is like the owner of a house who brings out of his storeroom new treasures as well as old" (Mt. 13:52).

My prayer for you, dear reader, is that you will gain understanding by the Holy Spirit from *The **Illustrated** Bible-Based Dictionary of Dream Symbols* and that you will enjoy this new treasure that the Lord has poured out from Heaven's storeroom through his servant, Dr. Joe Ibojie.

We live to glorify our heavenly Father. Don't be disappointed if it takes a little time and effort to grow in your gifting. Jesus is patient and gracious as He trains us in His ways. Be blessed!

—Catherine Brown
Gatekeeper Prayer & Mission
Glasgow, UK

TABLE OF CONTENTS

FOREWORD

THIS IS A UNIQUE AND EXHAUSTIVE collection of biblical and prophetic terms in one authoritative volume, by a true practitioner—Dr. Joe
Ibojie—who has written from his wealth of experience as a Bible and prophetic
teacher. This is one of the most comprehensive dictionaries of prophetic symbols
ever compiled, a masterpiece, and a seminal work. Dr. Joe Ibojie has established
himself as one of the voices that God has raised to give clear direction to us in the
contemporary world.

Many everyday Christians and prophets today are looking for a helpful resource
written in plain language, not scholarly jargon. This book provides that link, a vital
tool for the Body of Christ. This book brings rare insight, understanding, wisdom,
balance, and joy to bridging the gap between revelation and application that have
eluded many for so long.

Bible-Based Dictionary of Prophetic Symbols will bless you and change your life
as it helps you gain insightful knowledge about what God is saying to you. Joe has
skillfully put together biblical imagery as they relate to how God speaks to you. *God
expresses spiritual truth in spiritual words.* When you use this book by the help of the
Holy Spirit, it will save you the frustration of not knowing what God is saying. The
eyes of your understanding will be enlightened, and God will open the doors that
have been closed in your life.

Whether you want help for personal study or a resource for teaching purposes,
you will find this work not only fascinating but thoroughly educative and enjoyable.

This book will bless, empower, and guide all those who want to fulfill their purpose and destiny in life.

—Bishop John Francis
Senior Pastor
Ruach Ministries, London, UK

PREFACE

SYMBOLS ARE USED throughout the Bible. A cursory look at the myriad of symbols and the infinite permutation of the ways they are used demonstrate the glory and majesty of God. Symbolism is when one thing represents another or something stands for something else, or is used to typify something else, either by association, resemblance, or convention.

A symbol can also mean a material object used to represent something invisible, such as an idea (the dove as a symbol of peace). Therefore, a symbol is an image that stands for something but has a dual advantage of having its own literal meaning. Symbols carry more meaning than just their simple literal meaning in the natural run of things. Symbols are not real entities but representations of the real.

Symbols may include details we can sometimes find difficult to understand. Patience and due diligence are required to unravel the depth and scope of each symbol's meaning. Only God has the sovereign choice of symbol selection in divine revelation; nevertheless, all symbols seem to be drawn from a background that bears relevance to the life of the recipient. Therefore, symbol language remains not only infinite, but also rich and deeply personal in its application. Because the language of the spirit is rich with symbolism, understanding the symbolic language of God is an essential component of our walk in the spirit.

From the Old to the New Testament, we see symbols and metaphors that were drawn not only from the history, but also from the knowledge and culture of the people. In a vision, God showed Ezekiel the valley of dry bones. In this case, no one would imagine that God was referring to literal bones. But instead, God explained later that these bones refer to the house of Israel (see Ezek. 37:11). When Jesus Christ said, *"Out of your belly will flow rivers of living water"* (see John 7:38 NASB), He did not mean actual water, but referred to the Holy Spirit.

Symbols help us to see things from God's perspective because they reflect God's thoughts on the matter. The striking features of symbols also help with the impartation and remembrance of the message, or its interpretation. The fact that symbols can have hidden meaning allows God to clarify things in stages so He may reveal different aspects at chosen times. Humility is an essential key in our walk with God. Symbolism is one way to ensure our dependence on guidance from the Holy Spirit. A symbol makes us want to search out the meaning, and in the process of our searching, we increase our dependence on God's Word and on the Holy Spirit.

As apostle Paul explained:

> *To keep me from becoming conceited because of these surpassingly great revelations, there was given me a thorn in my flesh, a messenger of Satan, to torment me. Three times I pleaded with the Lord to take it away from me. But He said to me, "My grace is sufficient for you, for My power is made perfect in weakness." Therefore I will boast all the more gladly about my weaknesses, so that Christ's power may rest on me* (2 Corinthians 12:7-9).

Paul tells how a thorn was given to afflict his flesh to keep him humble. Like for apostle Paul, symbolism can help to keep us humble and dependent on God.

Symbols are used extensively in parables, so the two often go together. A parable is an allegorical representation of something that often embodies a moral or a lesson. No wonder, then, that God uses symbols and parables extensively to speak to us.

Symbolism is also the language of three godheads.

1. Let us look at God, the Father:

    God said of Himself:

> *O my people hear My teaching; listen to the words of My mouth. I* **will open My mouth in parables,** *I will utter hidden things, things from of old* (Psalm 78:1-2).

And again in the Book of Hosea, He said:

*I spoke to the prophets, gave them many visions **and told parables through them*** (Hosea 12:10).

On the other hand, God does not always speak in symbols or parables. God Himself described His pattern of speech to the prophets in Numbers;

he said, "Listen to my words: When a prophet of the Lord is among you, I reveal Myself to him in visions, I speak to him in dreams. But this is not true of My servant Moses; he is faithful in all My house. With him I speak face to face, clearly and not in riddles; he sees the form of the Lord. Why then were you not afraid to speak against My servant Moses?" (Numbers 12:6-8)

Lessons from this passage are:
- God does not speak to everyone the same way.
- He speaks in dreams and visions.
- He speaks in clear language.
- He speaks in riddles or parables.
- He speaks in dark speeches.
- He speaks in similitude.

However, we can broaden our perspectives if we are open to receive from God in whatever way He may chose to communicate with us. On the other hand, we limit our perception if we stereotype the way God speaks to His people. When we are limited this way, sadly we limit God and His messages to us on vital issues. Each one of us has a dominant way of receiving from God, and we should learn to master this dominant way while keeping all other options open as well. Unfortunately, some people master their dominant way of receiving from God but close the door to other options. This is often tantamount to a tragic error of presumption.

Pictorial revelations need interpretation because a picture speaks more than a thousand words. Some people receive mainly by pictorial revelations. Such people should master the use of their natural and spiritual eyes as their dominant way of receiving from God. However, many others receive mostly by hearing and should master hearing as their major mode of receiving from God. Additionally, some receive mainly by discernment, and yet a few others receive from God mainly by feeling. Those who receive from God by feeling are often referred to as "feelers." Nevertheless, everyone should strive to sharpen all the methods by which man receives from God, while gaining the mastery of the dominant way he or she receives from God. When we avoid stereotyping how we can receive from God in this way, we open great potentials to hear from God.

2. *Now let us look at God, the Son:*

    The teachings of Jesus were full of parables. Jesus taught in parables and used symbols to illustrate His message:

    *With many similar parables Jesus spoke the word to them, as much as they could understand. **He did not say anything to them without using a parable.** But when He was alone with His own disciples, He explained everything* (Mark 4:33-34).

    *The disciples came to Him and asked, "Why do you speak to the people in parables?" He replied, "The knowledge of the secrets of the kingdom of heaven has been given to you, but not to them. Whoever has will be given more, and he will have an abundance. Whoever does not have, even what he has will be taken from him. This is why I speak to them in parables: **Though seeing, they do not see; though hearing, they do not hear or understand"** (Matthew 13:10-13).*

Notice from this passage that just as it was in those days when Jesus taught in parables but explained privately to His disciples, today the parable language of God is available to everyone, but the heathen will "see and hear" without gaining understanding. In the same way as Jesus explained the meaning privately to His disciples, so the Holy Spirit explains the meaning of parable language (dreams and visions) to the believers these days often using the Scriptures.

3. *Last, let us look at God, the Holy Spirit:*

    The Holy Spirit also speaks in the language that words cannot express:

*In the same way, the Spirit helps us in our weakness. We do not know what we ought to pray for, **but the Spirit Himself intercedes for us with groans that words cannot express.** And He who searches our hearts knows the mind of the Spirit, because the Spirit intercedes for the saints in accordance with God's will* (Romans 8:26-27).

Also, the Holy Spirit helps us to understand the spiritual truth in spiritual language (often parable illustration):

*We have not received the spirit of the world but the Spirit who is from God, that we may understand what God has freely given us. This is what we speak, not in words taught us by human wisdom **but in words taught by the Spirit, expressing spiritual truths in spiritual words*** (1 Corinthians 2:12-13).

In summary, God, the Father; God, the Son; and God, the Holy Spirit can speak to us in a variety of ways, including symbolism and parable language. The onus is on us to learn how to decipher these coded messages.

PERSONAL RELEVANCE OF SYMBOLISM IN REVELATIONS

In the revelatory realm there exists a great degree of personal symbolism in God's communication. There are symbols that God incorporates in His revelations to us that only the person receiving the revelation will fully understand. Perhaps this is the real reason behind the sovereign choice of the symbol.

Introduction

THE LANGUAGE
OF SYMBOLS

THE NATURE OF SYMBOLS

THROUGH SYMBOLISM GOD also brings His message to bear on us at individual levels; the Lord will relate to a person in symbolism that has meaning to that person. Symbolism helps secure the message from the enemies, as a symbol's true meaning can only be revealed to the intended recipient because of the deep individual traits embedded in symbolic communication. In many ways, the personal traits in the symbolism allow the person to whom the message is intended to relate to its particular importance or relevance.

The language of symbols is deep and powerful; at the same time, it is the most elementary language of men and available to all ages. God can express His message to children as well as to adults. Symbolism also helps with man's conceptualization (the ability to form mental imagery), as the human mind understands or processes information in pictures. In this way, symbolic thinking helps broaden our different ways of thinking.

The following are key points worthy of note:

- To interpret a symbolic revelation one must think symbolically.
- The choice of symbols in revelations is the prerogative of God.

- Even the most literal revelation may contain some degree of symbolism.

- One meaning of a symbol is not necessarily the meaning for all times.

- The meaning of symbols must be drawn for each time one receives a revelation and may be different on different occasions, even though some symbols may be used repeatedly for some people.

- One should not get fixed on a single meaning of a symbol as it may change as the person grows in relationship and walk with God.

- As a person studies the Word of God, he or she will draw less and less from life experiences and more and more from the biblical reservoir of examples.

- One must interpret symbols from the life with which the recipient of the revelation is familiar.

- Each symbol may have a unique association drawn from the person's own experience.

- Symbols are not used haphazardly; their use is specific and purposeful.

- As symbols are chosen for very specific purposes, it is necessary to first identify what God's purpose is for using a particular symbol.

- Symbols or symbolic actions come out of the setting of the person's life, especially the immediate life circumstance.

- Remember, the true meaning of a symbol in a revelation does not come from human reasoning or intellectualism, but by allowing the meaning to flow into our hearts or subconscious mind from the Holy Spirit.

- This flow occurs more easily by being quiet and still in our heart.

- A symbolic revelation addresses the issue more frankly than human illustration because the symbolic representation allows emphasis to be placed in the way God sees it.

- Symbols are not real entities; they are simply representations of the real entities.

HOW SYMBOLS DERIVE THEIR MEANING
IN DIVINE REVELATIONS

A message that is given in symbols automatically switches your thinking to symbolism. Every parable needs to be symbolically interpreted and the meaning should be drawn at the major symbols in the revelation. The meaning of a symbol is drawn first of all from the reservoir of the Word of God, then from the inherent meaning of the symbol (that is the basic meaning as would be contained in a good dictionary) or its association to the dreamer's experience, or from the culture and colloquial expressions in society.

In general terms, interpretation is the process of bringing meaning (deciphering of) to symbolism or a parable language, and it involves three key points:

1. Deriving meaning

    A. Bringing meaning to the symbols in the dream or parable.

    B. Gaining understanding of the message in the dream or parable.

    C. Bringing understanding to the symbolic actions in the dream or parable.

    D. Deriving the meanings for symbols should first of all be hinged on the Word of God and should be drawn in the following order:

        1. The Scriptures

        2. The inherent meaning of the symbol

        3. The dreamer's personal experience

        4. The social influences of the dreamer (the culture and the colloquial expressions the dreamer is used to)

Exercise: *Give meaning to the following symbols:*

- A bottle of clear water
- Armored car coming against a group of people
- Microwave in front of you

2. Expounding

    A. Relating the understanding of the symbols and events to the person or dreamer's personal experience.

    B. Expounding on the relevance of the symbols to the person's life circumstance.

    C. Declaring the essence of the symbolic language or parable as it relates to the person's life circumstance.

Exercise: *Give meaning to the following:*

- *Playing with a friendly snake*
- *Bleeding nose*
- *Broken tooth requiring a dentist*

3. *Bringing Them Together*

    A. The deriving of the meaning for the symbols and the exposition of the symbolic actions must go together to truly interpret a symbolic revelation or parable.

    B. Therefore, the true and complete interpretation must incorporate the two phases.

Exercise: *Give meaning to the following:*

- Daniel 5:25-30

THE POWER OF THE LANGUAGE OF SYMBOLS

Those who have understood the tremendous power of symbols have gained incredible insight into the mysteries of God. As human beings, we think in pictures and may need visual appreciation in order to grasp the essence of a concept. Symbols evoke powerful emotion and passion. From generation to generation, politicians, philosophers, and religious leaders have used symbols to illustrate their points. For example, national commitment is symbolized in the pride and honor that is accorded to the national symbol of a flag. Many would be outraged to see their flag dishonored, and public hatred is often demonstrated by the burning of an enemy's national flag. These are highly significant symbolic gestures.

David—A Biblical Example

Symbolism brought the seriousness of David's adulterous act to him. Nathan's message to King David could have easily been a perfect setting for the plot or good storyline for a dream, and God could have chosen to send King David the same message through a dream. Nathan narrated the message to David in a dream format, in parable, to bring home the gravity of the sin.

> *The Lord sent Nathan to David. When he came to him, he said, "There were two men in a certain town, one rich and the other poor. The rich man had a very large number of sheep and cattle, but the poor man had nothing except one little ewe lamb he had bought. He raised it, and it grew up with him and his children. It shared his food, drank from his cup and even slept in his arms. It was like a daughter to him. Now a traveler came to the rich man, but the rich man refrained from taking one of his own sheep or cattle to prepare a meal for the traveler who had come to him. Instead, he took the ewe lamb that belonged to the poor man and prepared it for the one who had come to him." David burned with anger against the man and said to Nathan, "As surely as the Lord lives, the man who did this deserves to die! He must pay for that lamb four times over, because he did such a thing and had no pity." Then Nathan said to David, "You are the man! This is what the Lord, the God of Israel, says: 'I anointed you king over Israel, and I delivered you from the hand of Saul. I gave your master's house to you, and your master's wives into your arms. I gave you the house of Israel and Judah. And if all this had been too little, I would have given you even more. Why did you despise the word of the Lord by doing what is evil in his eyes? You struck down Uriah the Hittite with the sword and took his wife to be your own. You killed him with the sword of the Ammonites'"* (2 Samuel 12:1-9).

ANATOMY OF NATHAN'S STATEMENT TO DAVID

Symbol/Action	Meaning	Inspired Interpretation/ Comment
Poor man.	Uriah.	A person who is vulnerable because he lacks the necessities of life.
Little ewe, like a daughter.	Uriah's wife— precious to him.	Something precious to the dreamer.
Arrival of traveler.	A need arises.	A potential need is imminent or at hand.
Refrain from using his own.	Selfishness.	Spirit of self-centeredness, or beings inconsiderate of others.
David's anger burned against the injustice of the man in Nathan's story.	David's realization that the sin was his, therefore realizing the true gravity of the sin.	Holy anger stirred by spirit of righteousness or coming to one's senses after a period of attack of carnality.

HOW TO CREATE A PERSONAL SYMBOL VOCABULARY

It is important to build up a personal symbol vocabulary. A personal symbol vocabulary reflects the uniquely personal traits that God may use in revelatory communication. It also helps build up the person's confidence in the art of understanding one's revelations. A personal symbol vocabulary should be built from the person's real life revelatory experiences that ideally emanate from a reservoir of the imagery of the Bible. The meaning of symbols could be derived from personal experiences or from the symbols used in other people's revelatory experiences contained in the Bible (Bible imagery). I have found that the meaning of symbols derived from personal experiences and the meaning derived from biblical imagery nearly always agree, provided both are correctly interpreted. It is important that deriving meaning of revelatory symbols is carefully done to avoid error and misunderstanding.

Incorrectly derived meaning for symbols can be dangerously misleading and may lead to bondage. Most superstitious beliefs about the meaning of dreams and visions emanate from erroneously derived meanings of symbols devoid of biblical relevance.

This is how to derive the meaning of symbols as used in the revelatory experiences contained in the Bible (from Bible imagery). The gospel according to Matthew contains many parable illustrations used by Jesus when teaching His disciples. In these parables Jesus also gave their interpretation and the meaning of the symbols in the parables. These parables and their stated biblical meanings constitute an unequivocal reservoir from which the meaning of symbols used in our contemporary revelations can be understood. I found that studying the parables of Jesus Christ is a good place to start understanding the meaning of symbols.

Jesus' teaching during His earthly ministry was mainly through parables, so much so that the Bible says He said nothing except in parables. A parable is a symbolic illustration of a principle, a divine truth or a moral lesson. It is also an allegorical representation of something or a story.

> *With many similar parables Jesus spoke the word to them, as much as they could understand. He did not say anything to them without using a parable. But when He was alone with His own disciples, He explained everything* (Mark 4:33-34).

> *The disciples came to Him and asked, "Why do you speak to the people in parables?" He replied, "The knowledge of the secrets of the kingdom of heaven has been given to you, but not to them"* (Matthew 13:10-11).

> *To you it has been granted to know the mysteries of the kingdom of heaven, but to them* [those without the Holy Spirit] *it has been not been granted* (Matthew 13:11 NASB).

> *Therefore I speak to them in parables, because while seeing they do not see, and while hearing they do not hear, nor do they understand* (Matthew 13:13 NASB).

A study of the parable of the lost sheep:

What do you think? If a man owns a hundred sheep, and one of them wanders away, will he not leave the ninety-nine on the hills and go to look for the one that wandered off? And if he finds it, I tell you the truth, he is happier about that one sheep than about the ninety-nine that did not wander off (Matthew 18:12-13).

Interpretation

In the same way your Father in heaven is not willing that any of these little ones should be lost (Matthew 18:14).

Symbol/Action	Meaning	Inspired Interpretation/ Comment
A man owns one hundred sheep.	Father in Heaven.	God Himself, the man of God, the Pastor.
One sheep wanders away.	Lost soul.	The unsaved people, area of uncertainties or indecision in the dreamer's life whether he is a believer or not.
Look for the one that wandered off.	Not willing that any of these little ones should be lost.	God always brings light to areas of darkness.
He is happier about that one sheep than about the ninety-nine that did not wander off.	There is rejoicing in Heaven over a lost soul that is saved.	To reach the lost should be our goal and happiness.

Conclusion

Whenever the meaning of a symbol derived from personal experiences conflicts with a correctly derived Bible meaning, the Bible meaning of the symbol supersedes. This is because the Bible-derived meaning of symbols is timeless, whereas meaning derived from the dreamer's personal dream experience is time restricted. It can change as the situation and awareness of the dreamer change. As a dreamer grows more intimately with God, he will draw more from the scriptural examples and less from non-biblical personal experiences because God expresses spiritual truth in spiritual words (see 1 Cor. 2:12-13).

How to Use a Dictionary of Prophetic Symbols

The purpose of a personal vocabulary should be to assist in broadening our thinking and preventing the tendency to become fixed on the meaning of a symbol. If we become fixed on the meaning of a symbol, we become limited in the benefits that can be obtained from the revelation.

Symbolic thinking broadens our appreciation of the symbol's true meaning. The main purpose is to remove restricted perspectives of the symbol or the symbolic message. Man thinks in pictures, and picture language automatically switches a person to symbolic thinking. Many elements in revelation will remain unravelled and largely unexpressed until we are able to understand their symbolic connotations or overtones. It is only then that we are able to appreciate the true meaning, which may lie beneath the obvious literal or ordinary meaning. This process consists of knowing their ordinary meaning as well as knowing what they may generally evoke in the minds of others. Valuable information is lost if we fail to understand the symbolic meaning of the elements, persons, and actions in a revelation.

An image is any object or action that can be pictured. Understanding an image, therefore, requires that we appreciate the image in the literal sense, that is, what it means in ordinary usage. Then we must capture what it evokes, through connotations or overtones, in the minds of the general public. What a symbol connotes may not be immediately obvious to our natural senses, and we may therefore have to search for it.

When someone comes across an image, two questions should arise in the person's mind:

1. What is the literal meaning of the image? (This is usually the most obvious or common meaning.)
2. What does the image evoke? (This is the overtone.)

If either of these two aspects is not well understood, the understanding of pictorial language is limited.

Examples:

The word *husband*

1. Ordinarily understood to mean—male, man
2. The word also evokes some lateral thinking—father, head of a home; provider or Jesus Christ as the Husband of the Church.

The word *wife*

1. Ordinarily understood to mean—female, woman
2. The word also evokes some lateral thinking—mother, home keeper; the Church as the Bride of Christ.

The following points are important to bear in mind when using the personal vocabulary of symbols:

- Interpretation belongs to God. Therefore, attempting to use a personal vocabulary without the help of the Holy Spirit is a futile exercise.

- A personal vocabulary is not a carte blanche for dream interpretation.

- The true meaning of a symbol must be drawn within the context of each dream; do not be fixed on the meaning of a symbol as it could vary from dream to dream and from person to person.

- The Bible says that God expresses spiritual truth in spiritual words; the derived meaning for a symbol must therefore be largely dependent on the Word of God.

- The reader must bear in mind at all times that what is personally descriptive should not be taken as generally prescriptive. God deals with each one of us uniquely.

It is also important that you realize that there are many types of symbols.

A *metaphor* is a symbol with implied comparison (for example, the tongue as the pen of a ready writer or Jesus, the Lion of the tribe of Judah). A *simile,* on the other hand, compares one thing to another and it makes the comparison explicit by using formula "like" or "as." For example, "As the deer pants for water, so my soul pants for You." A *motif* is a pattern that appears in written text or a mental picture that has emerged from a written text. We allow the motif to develop wherever the Bible says, "Selah," to pause and think.

To illustrate the difference between literal (ordinary dictionary meaning) and inspired interpretation of dreams and revelations, let's look at the mysterious hand writing on the wall in the Book of Daniel.

> *This is the inscription that was written: Mene, Mene, Tekel, Parsin*
> *This is what these words mean: Mene: God has numbered the days*
> *of your reign and brought it to an end. Tekel: You have been weighed*
> *on the scales and found wanting. Peres: Your kingdom is divided and*
> *given to the Medes and Persians. Then at Belshazzar's command,*
> *Daniel was clothed in purple, a gold chain was placed around his*
> *neck, and he was proclaimed the third highest ruler in the kingdom.*
> *That very night Belshazzar, king of the Babylonians, was slain* (Daniel 5:25-30).

Symbol	Literal Meaning or Ordinary Dictionary Compilation (*)	Inspired Meaning (Interpretation) Based on the Holy Spirit (**)
Mene	Numbered	God has numbered the days of the king's reign and brought it to an end.
Tekel	Weighed	You (the king) have been weighed on the scales and have been found wanting.
Peres	Divided	The kingdom is divided and given to the Medo-Persians.

(*) Characteristics of ordinary compilations of meaning of symbols—interpretations not inspired by the Holy Spirit:

1. Lack divine strength

2. Do not have Holy Spirit prompting

3. Do not tap into the mind of God

4. Do not meet the yearning of the dreamer

5. Do not have wisdom of God necessary to make it relevant to the dreamer's situation

6. May cause confusion

(**) Characteristics of inspired interpretation:

1. Inspired by the Holy Spirit

2. Have divine strength to break the sealed instruction in the dreamer's spirit and release its meaning to the dreamer's mind

3. Contain the wisdom and the mind of God for the situation

4. Satisfy the dreamer's yearning

5. Resonate with the dreamer's inner witness

6. Drive the dreamer closer to God

The question that must be asked is: Why were all the wise men, the magicians, the soothsayers, and the astrologers unable to translate a few simple words, especially when Daniel—who was educated in same language—had no difficulty translating them. The answer is that as King Nebuchadnezzar recognized Daniel as a man who was filled with the Spirit of God, Daniel alone was enabled by God to gain the secret of that mystery. In the New Testament, Jesus Christ echoed this, telling His disciples, *"the secret of the kingdom of God has been given to you..."* (Mark 4:11). Those who by reasoning of the indwelling presence of the Holy Spirit are able to gain this understanding. Apostle Paul said:

> *"And we are setting these truths forth in words not taught by human wisdom but taught by the [Holy] Spirit, combining and interpreting Spiritual truths with Spiritual language [to those who possess the Holy Spirit]"* (1 Corinthians 2:13 AMP).

The following diagram illustrates how all the steps in deriving the meaning of symbols and the exposition of the symbolic action must go together to bring complete and true meaning to a parable or dream:

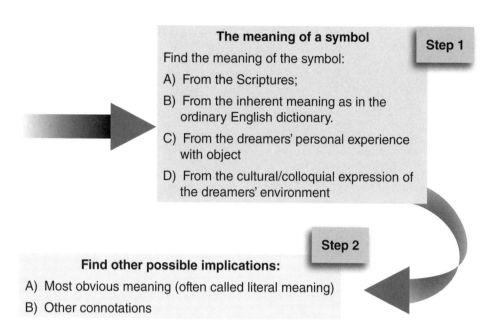

The meaning of a symbol

Step 1

Find the meaning of the symbol:

A) From the Scriptures;

B) From the inherent meaning as in the ordinary English dictionary.

C) From the dreamers' personal experience with object

D) From the cultural/colloquial expression of the dreamers' environment

Step 2

Find other possible implications:

A) Most obvious meaning (often called literal meaning)

B) Other connotations

Expositions on the symbolic actions

A) Hinges predominantly on the dreamers' personal experience

B) Brings the derived meaning of the symbols into direct relevance in the dreamers' life and circumstances

Steps 1 and 2 must go together to bring full meaning to a message in symbols

PART I

ILLUSTRATED
BIBLE-BASED
DICTIONARY
OF PROPHETIC SYMBOLS
AND SYMBOLIC ACTIONS

A

ACID: Something that eats from within. Keeping offense or hatred or malice.

Symbolic Actions

1. ***Seeing acid in a container:*** Potentially dangerous situation, something to be handled with care.

2. ***Acid smeared on the skin:*** Challenging situation, something that could be dangerous and corrosive.

See to it that no one misses the grace of God and that no bitter root grows up to cause trouble and defile many (Hebrews 12:15).

ADULTERY: Unfaithfulness regarding things of the spirit or of the natural, or actual adultery; lust for the pleasures of this world; sin.

Symbolic Actions

1. ***When a married person dreams of having extra-marital affairs:*** May indicate dreamer unfaithful in things of God, or may be literal or tempting situation, divided loyalty, wavering between options.

2. ***When a married man dreams of looking for a person to marry:*** May indicate the need to fully identify one's calling in God; the dreamer is not completely settled into the marriage relation; the need to be more intimate with one's spouse.

3. ***When the dreamer suspects spouse is in extra-marital affair.*** This may commonly indicate that one's spouse is paying too much attention to things like business

or profession. From my experience, however, this may only occasionally be literal.

The acts of the sinful nature are obvious: sexual immorality, impurity and debauchery; idolatry and witchcraft; hatred, discord, jealousy, fits of rage, selfish ambition, dissensions, factions (Galatians 5:19-20).

You adulterous people, don't you know that friendship with the world is hatred toward God? Anyone who chooses to be a friend of the world becomes an enemy of God (James 4:4).

AIRPLANE: A personal ministry or a church; capable of moving in the Holy Spirit. Flowing in high spiritual power. Holy spirit-powered ministry.

Symbolic Actions

1. ***Crashing:*** The end of one phase or change of direction.

2. ***High Flying:*** Fully-powered in the Spirit.

3. ***Low Flying:*** Only partially operative in the Spirit.

4. ***Aircraft Soaring:*** Deep in the Spirit or moving in the deep things of God.

5. ***Warplane:*** Call to intercessory ministry; things of present or spiritual warfare.

AIRPORT: This often refers to the minis- try that sends out missionaries; high-powered spiritual church capable of equipping and sending out ministries; ministry in preparation or capable of providing or nourishing others in readiness for service.

Types:

1. A ministry capable of influencing many people or groups.
2. An aspect of the ministry that is a major resource and should be guarded carefully, or a ministry that is itself a major gate in the area or region.
3. The major means of resources in the ministry.

ALLIGATOR: Large-mouthed enemy; verbal attacks; situation or person from which or whom verbal attack will emanate.

Other animals with similar meaning:

1. *Crocodile:* Large mouth—very dangerous at all times, to be avoided.
2. *Whale:* Large mouth—care is needed to avoid danger.

ALTAR: A place set apart for spiritual rituals or prayers/worship; place of sacrifice; call to repentance; place for meeting with God or the devil.

Symbolic Actions

1. *Taken to or being compelled to go to an altar:* Issue concerning the person is being taken to place of spiritual importance either

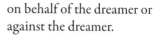

on behalf of the dreamer or against the dreamer.

2. *Worshiping at an altar:* May indicate true worship of God (if holy) or willing participation in idolatry (if unholy—whether innocent or not).

3. *Non-participatory observance of activities at an altar:* May indicate a spiritual glimpse of things being done in place of spiritual importance.

4. *Hear pronouncements/incantations being issued at an altar against one:* May indicate blessings or curses being issued against the person by people in high spiritual places.

David built an altar to the Lord there and sacrificed burnt offerings and fellowship offerings. Then the Lord answered prayer in behalf of the land, and the plague on Israel was stopped (2 Samuel 24:25).

Then Noah built an altar to the Lord, taking some of all the clean animals and clean birds, he sacrificed burnt offerings on it (Genesis 8:20).

There he built an altar, and he called the place El Bethel, because it was there that God revealed Himself to him when he was fleeing from his brother (Genesis 35:7).

Destroy completely all the places on the high mountains and on the hills and under every spreading tree where the nations you are dispossessing worship their gods. Break down their altars, smash their sacred stones and burn their Asherah poles in the fire; cut down the idols of their gods and wipe out their names from those places (Deuteronomy 12:2-3).

ANCHOR: The pillar that something or person hangs on; something that hope is built on.

Symbolic Actions

1. *Trying to secure an anchor:* Realizing the need to put things in order or making things more secure.

2. *Broken anchor:* Losing firmness or security.

3. *Strong/firm anchor:* Confirmation that security is in place.

4. *Weak/shaking anchor:* Indicates the need to strengthen existing security.

We have this hope as an anchor for the soul, firm and secure. It enters the inner sanctuary behind the curtain (Hebrews 6:19).

ANKLES: Little faith, early stages.

Symbolic Actions

1. *Water up to the ankle:* Faith in God, little faith.

2. *Chains on the ankle:* Bondage, slavery.

3. *Jewelry on ankle:* Vanity; seduction; beautiful; wrong emphasis.

As the man went eastward with a measuring line in his hand, he measured off a thousand cubits and then led me through water that was ankle-deep (Ezekiel 47:3).

ANOINT: Equipping with the Holy Spirit for service. The power of Holy Spirit to do something; sanctification; setting apart for something; a call to a particular responsibility.

Symbolic Actions

1. *Being anointed in a church service:* May indicate a new level of anointing imminent.

2. *Being anointed by a person who is wrongly dressed or by a person saying things that are not in consonance with the Word of God, or when there are doubts in the mind of dreamer regarding the purity of the minister:* May indicate the need to be mindful of who lays hands on the dreamer. Prayers to avoid corrupt doctrines, impartation or contamination from polluted spiritual influences.

Is any one of you sick? He should call the elders of the church to pray over him and anoint him with oil in the name of the Lord (James 5:14).

Also, anoint Jehu son of Nimshi king over Israel, and anoint Elisha son of Shaphat from Abel Meholah to succeed you as prophet (1 Kings 19:16).

How God has anointed Jesus of Nazareth with the Holy Spirit and power, and how He went around doing good and healing all who were under the power of the devil, because God was with him (Acts 10:38).

Then the men of Judah came to Hebron and there they anointed David king over the house of Judah... (2 Samuel 2:4).

ANT: Industrious, ability to plan ahead; conscious of seasons of life; unwanted guest, nuisance.

Symbolic Actions

1. ***Invasion of large number of ants:*** May commonly refer to challenging situations.

2. ***Stung or bitten by ants:*** Dangerous situations/attacks of the enemy—to be avoided by prayers.

Go to the ant, you sluggard; consider its ways and be wise! It has no commander, no overseer or ruler, yet it stores its provisions in summer and gathers its food at harvest (Proverbs 6:6-8).

Ants are creatures of little strength, yet they store up their food in the summer (Proverbs 30:25).

ANTIQUES: Something relating to the past; an inherited thing.

Symbolic Actions

1. ***Receiving or discovering antiques:*** There are things in the past (usually valuables) to be discovered or yet to be revealed.

2. ***Many antiques in the house or on display in the house:*** Valuables from the past, potential, from in the bloodline; may also indicate need to make things more relevant to the time and season.

This is what the Lord says: "Stand at the crossroads and look; ask for the ancient paths, ask where the good way is, and walk in it, and you will find rest for your souls." But you said, "We will not walk in it" (Jeremiah 6:16).

APPLES: Spiritual fruit, something precious like the apple of God's eyes, something dear to God.

Symbolic Actions

1. ***Spoiled apple:*** Corrupt wisdom or wasted giftedness.

2. ***Unripe apple:*** Time and season is yet to come for manifestation of the promise or gift/potential.

3. ***Overripe apple:*** Danger of missing the divine timing; or, if unused, the gift may become irrelevant with time.

4. ***Enticing apple:*** Tempting situation.

5. ***Difficulty in reaching an apple:*** Not fully equipped to reach a promise fulfillment. If apple is precious in the dream—something valuable to the dreamer or apple of God's eyes.

When the woman saw that the fruit of the tree was good for food and pleasing to the eye, and also desirable for gaining wisdom, she took some and ate it. She also gave some to her husband, who was with her, and he ate it (Genesis 3:6).

In a desert land he found him, in a barren and howling waste. He shielded him and cared for him; He guarded him as the apple of His eye (Deuteronomy 32:10).

For this is what the Lord Almighty says: "After he has honored Me and has sent Me against the nations that have plundered you—for whoever touches you touches the apple of his eye" (Zechariah 2:8).

ARK: Something relating to God's presence. Something of strength or a symbol of God's authority.

A

Symbolic Actions

1. *Large ark:* Something for rescuing people (Noah's ark).

2. *Building an ark:* Obedience or preparing for future event or rainy day.

Place the cover on top of the ark and put in the ark the Testimony, which I will give you. There, above the cover between the two cherubim that are over the ark of the Testimony, I will meet with you and give you all my commands for the Israelites (Exodus 25:21-22).

ARM: Power and strength whether for or against the dreamer; superior assistance, the spirit of might.

Symbolic Actions

1. *A display of arm:* A threatening situation; boastfulness; warning from a superior power.

2. *An arm coming against the dreamer:* A dangerous situation may be approaching; a call for additional wisdom, strength, or prayers.

But his bow remained steady, his strong arms stayed limber, because of the hand of the Mighty One of Jacob, because of the Shepherd, the Rock of Israel (Genesis 49:24).

Therefore, say to the Israelites: "I am the Lord, and I will bring you out from under the yoke of the Egyptians. I will free you from being slaves to them, and I will redeem you with an outstretched arm and with mighty acts of judgment" (Exodus 6:6).

With him is only the arm of flesh, but with us is the Lord our God to help us

and to fight our battles. And the people gained confidence from what Hezekiah the king of Judah said (2 Chronicles 32:8).

Who has believed our message and to whom has the arm of the Lord been revealed? (Isaiah 53:1).

ARMIES: Spiritual warriors—good or bad; sudden declaration of hostility; call to intercessory prayers; call to be in war mode.

Types:

One's own army:

1. *Well-equipped and dressed:* In a state of adequate readiness.

2. *Disorderly /confused:* Need to re-strategize to avoid defeat in warfare.

3. *Wounded soldiers:* Need to avoid casualties, prayers need to be intensified.

Enemy army:

1. *Coming against the dreamer:* May indicate a challenge from the enemy and the need for intercession.

2. *Running away from the dreamer:* Victory at hand for the dreamer.

3. *Overpowered by the enemy army:* Call for prayer to avoid defeat or the need to avoid presumptions that may lead to defeat.

4. *In a well-organized formation:* Well-structured enemy opposition.

ARMOR: Spiritual covering that protects the dreamer. Divine protection. The truth of God.

Types:

1. *Good, well-fitting armor:* Well-prepared for spiritual warfare.

2. *Defective/incomplete armor:* Protection is not adequate.

Finally, be strong in the Lord and in His mighty power. Put on the full armor of God so that you can take your stand against the devil's schemes (Ephesians 6:10-11).

ARROWS: Powerful words whether for or against the dreamer. Word of God or curses from the devil. Spiritual children. Good or bad intentions. Arrows with poisonous tip equals words capable of much damage. Modern sign for direction.

Sons are a heritage from the Lord, children a reward from Him. Like arrows in the hands of a warrior are sons born in one's youth (Psalm 127:3-4).

They sharpen their tongues like swords and aim their words like deadly arrows (Psalm 64:3).

Like a club or a sword or a sharp arrow is the man who gives false testimony against his neighbor (Proverbs 25:18).

"Open the east window," he said, and he opened it. "Shoot!" Elisha said, and he shot. "The Lord's arrow of victory, the arrow of victory over Aram!" Elisha declared. "You will completely destroy the Arameans at Aphek" (2 Kings 13:17).

He made my mouth like a sharpened sword, in the shadow of His hand He hid me; He made me into a polished arrow and concealed me in His quiver (Isaiah 49:2).

ASHES: Signs of repentance or sorrow. To humble oneself. A memorial. Aftermath of God's consuming fire (see Ezek. 28:18; 2 Pet. 2:6).

Your maxims are proverbs of ashes; your defenses are defenses of clay (Job 13:12).

My ears had heard of you but now my eyes have seen you. Therefore I despise myself and repent in dust and ashes (Job 42:5-6).

Tamar put ashes on her head and tore the ornamented robe she was wearing. She put her hand on her head and went away, weeping aloud as she went (2 Samuel 13:19).

ATOM BOMB: Something capable of great destruction. Something of great suddenness or quick in occurring.

ATTIC: The mind-zone; thought process. The spirit realm. Memories/past issues/stored up materials.

Symbolic Actions

1. *Dream takes place in the attic:* Relating to the mind or spiritual realm, or something that is happening or is about to happen.

2. *Memorabilia in the attic:* Things from the past that are stored up in the mind.

3. *Leaking attic:* Defect in the mind-zone, no adequate spiritual coverage.

A

About noon the following day as they were on their journey and approaching the city, Peter went up on the roof to pray. He became hungry and wanted something to eat, and while the meal was being prepared, he fell into a trance. He saw heaven opened and something like a large sheet being let down to earth by its four corners (Acts 10:9-11).

AUTOGRAPH: Prominence or fame.

Symbolic Actions

1. ***Being asked for an autograph:*** May mean the person will become famous or will come to a place of prominence.

2. ***Obtaining an autograph:*** Favor or approval from people in high places.

3. ***Unable to obtain an autograph:*** Pray for more favor or for hindrances to be removed so that favor from high places can flow in; the need to avoid presumptuous action.

AUTUMN: Transition. The close of harvest season or entering difficult times. End of something and beginning of another.

Symbolic Actions

1. Seasons and timing are relevant in the situation.

2. Warning to prepare for difficult times ahead.

They do not say to themselves, "Let us fear the Lord our God, who gives autumn and spring rains in season, who assures us of the regular weeks of harvest" (Jeremiah 5:24).

AUTOBIKE: A spirit-powered ministry that has either one or two-person involvement. Single man ministry with a lot of exhibitionism.

AUTOMOBILE: Means of getting to a destination or achieving the desired goal.

Symbolic Actions

1. ***Air-conditioning:*** If in good working condition, indicates adequate comfort for situation; if not working, indicates faulty provision for comfort.

2. ***Brakes:*** Slowing down; to stop; compelled to stop; hindrance.

3. ***Convertible:*** Capable of open-heaven ministration; indicative of revelatory ministry.

4. ***Driver's seat:*** Indicates leadership.

5. ***Engine:*** Holy Spirit power, supernatural empowerment

6. ***Four-wheel drive:*** A powerful ministry; ground breaking; capable of global influence.

7. ***Junkyard:*** Ministries that are abandoned or in need of repairs.

8. ***Rear-view mirror:*** Looking back, focusing on things in the past; warning to look ahead; warning to watch your back.

9. ***Seatbelt:*** Something that ensures safety; fastened means prepared/prayers; unfastened means prayerlessness/carelessness.

10. **Steering:** The controlling and leading part, the means by which leadership is affected.

11. **Tires:** Symbolic of the spiritual conditions of the ministry; flat means needing spiritual enabling, needing more prayers; full means powered by the Spirit.

12. **Topless van:** Not having adequate anointing for the occasion; vulnerable or transparent.

13. **Van:** Goods—delivering, group-ministering.

14. **Vehicle key:** Authority in the ministry.

15. **Wreck:** Crashing, clash, end of one phase, change of direction. Danger. Contention or confrontation or offense.

The chariots storm through the streets, rushing back and forth through the squares. They look like flaming torches; they dart about like lightning (Nahum 2:4).

AWAKENING: To be alert/watchfulness; to be stirred into action. Rousing the dreamer or being aroused in order to take action. Aroused from passivity and vulnerability to initiatives and progression or aggression (see Isa. 52).

Then the Lord awoke as from sleep, as a man wakes from the stupor of wine (Psalm 78:65).

Awake, awake! Clothe yourself with strength, O arm of the Lord; awake, as in days gone by, as in generations of old. Was it not you who cut Rahab to pieces, who pierced that monster through? (Isaiah 51:9).

"Awake, O sword, against My shepherd, against the man who is close to Me!" declares the Lord Almighty. "Strike the shepherd, and the sheep will be scattered, and I will turn My hand against the little ones" (Zechariah 13:7).

Wake up, wake up Deborah! Wake up wake up, break out in song! Arise, O Barak! Take captive your captives, O son of Abinoam (Judges 5:12).

AX: The Word of God. To encourage by kind word. Issue that needs to be settled.

Symbolic Actions

1. **Ax at the foot of the tree:** Judgment has come; the time to give account, especially for those who have been given responsibilities.

2. **To ax:** Forceful determination of an outcome.

3. **Ax-head:** The cutting edge or the sharp point of something or anointing.

4. **Ax-head floating:** Miraculous event is coming.

The ax is already at the root of the trees, and every tree that does not produce good fruit will be cut down and thrown into the fire (Matthew 3:10).

BABY: The beginning of something new. Beginning to be productive. New Christians. Something in its infancy or early stages. Honor from God; something to celebrate, a gift from God.

Symbolic Actions

1. **Caring for other people's babies:** Helping others to nurture other

ministries; interceding for others; scene common with intercessors.

2. ***Having or giving birth to a baby:*** Something new is about to break forth, or the birth of new ministry.

3. ***Deformed baby:*** Need to pray against corrupted or perverted gift beginning.

4. ***Stolen baby:*** Guard against hindrances or delay to the manifestation of gift or potentials.

Like newborn babies, crave pure spiritual milk, so that by it you may grow up in your salvation (1 Peter 2:2).

Brothers, I could not address you as spiritual but as worldly—mere infants in Christ. I gave you milk, not solid food, for you were not yet ready for it. Indeed, you are still not ready (1 Corinthians 3:1-2).

BACK: Pertaining to the past. Something behind or hidden; out of view. Concealed thing.

Symbolic Actions

1. ***Watching the back:*** There may be something not yet visible to the dreamer.

2. ***Looking at the back:*** Paying attention to things in the past or out of immediate view.

Answer me, O Lord, answer me, so these people will know that You, O Lord, are God, and that You are turning their hearts back again (1 Kings 18:37).

Let no one in the field go back to get his cloak (Mark 13:16).

Jesus replied, "No one who puts his hand to the plow and looks back is

fit for service in the kingdom of God" (Luke 9:62).

BACKSIDE: Something in the past or behind the dreamer. Something concealed from view or understanding. Evocative image for rejection, a time of pruning, e.g., Moses at the backside of desert.

BADGER: Underground dwellers.

BAKER: One who instigates or originates something.

Symbolic Actions

1. ***Watching a baker or dreamer baking as a baker:*** The dreamer may be potentially gifted in forming concepts or will be especially good in architecture.

BAKING: Making provision for feeding people. Preparation for welfare ministry; God's provision; hospitality; preparing for tomorrow.

BALANCES: Something reflecting both sides of the matter. Something waiting to tilt one way or the other. Judgment. Need to objectively look at things.

BALD HEAD: Lacking wisdom, emblem of shame, mockery. To shave one's hair signifies mourning (see Jer. 16:6).

Types:

1. ***Bald head on youth:*** May indicate the lack of wisdom.

2. ***Bald head on a female:*** May indicate lack of glory, attraction, honor; or being too masculine.

B

B

3. ***Bald head on an old man:*** Sign of maturity or mourning.

4. ***Compelled to shave the hair:*** Humiliation, sign of bereavement.

From there Elisha went up to Bethel. As he was walking along the road, some youths came out of the town and jeered at him, "Go on up, you baldhead!" (2 Kings 2:23).

Both high and low will die in this land. They will not he buried or mourned, and no one will cut himself or shave his head for them (Jeremiah 16:6).

Shave your heads in mourning for children in whom you delight; make yourselves as bald as the vulture, for they will go from you into exile (Micah 1:16).

BALM: Healing, anointing; something to relieve pain, stress, or agony.

Types:

1. ***Apply balm:*** To comfort; to help with restoration; to bring healing to the situation.

2. ***To receive balm:*** To be imparted with healing anointing; to receive encouragement.

Is there no balm in Gilead? Is there no physician there? Why then is there no healing for the wound of My people? (Jeremiah 8:22).

Babylon will suddenly fall and be broken. Wail over her! Get balm for her pain; perhaps she can be healed (Jeremiah 51:8).

Judah and Israel traded with you; they exchanged wheat from Minnith and confections, honey, oil and balm for your wares (Ezekiel 27:17).

BANK: Heavenly account. God's favor for a future season. A place of safety/ security. A dependable place or source; God's provision.

Symbolic Actions

1. ***Withdraw money from a bank:*** Favor as a result of one's effort; reward of labor; time of favor has come.

2. ***Deposit money in a bank:*** Saving for a future time.

3. ***Robbing a bank:*** Attempting to obtain what is not rightfully yours or forcefully obtaining favor, maybe good or bad, depending on the context of entire dream!

Not that I am looking for a gift, but I am looking for what may be credited to your account (Philippians 4:17).

But store up for yourselves treasures in heaven, where moth and rust do not destroy, and where thieves do not break in and steal (Matthew 6:20).

BANNER OR FLAG: The covering to which everyone belongs or is committed to. Something that brings unity, love, or purpose; a unifying object or circumstance; victory.

Symbolic Actions

1. ***Carrying a banner:*** To act as the unifying agent, or agent of love; demonstration of commitment.

2. ***Burning a banner:*** Protesting against the organization or country the banner represents.

3. ***Waving a banner:*** Sign of victory; sign of surrender; sign of pride in the group.

B

Moses built an altar and called it The Lord is my Banner (Exodus 17:15).

BANQUET: God's provision. A full cup. Plentiful/affluence/abundance. Satisfaction. Blessing. Celebrations. Structured teaching of the Word of God. An evil banquet means decadence, idolatry, indulgence/judgment (see Dan. 5:1-6).

He has taken me to the banquet hall, and his banner over me is love (Song of Solomon 2:4).

King Belshazzar gave a great banquet for a thousand of his nobles and drank wine with them…As they drank the wine, they praised the gods of gold and silver, of bronze, iron, wood and stone. Suddenly the fingers of a human hand appeared and wrote on the plaster of the wall, near the lampstand in the royal palace. The king watched the hand as it wrote (Daniel 5:1,4-5).

His face turned pale and he was so frightened that his knees knocked together and his legs gave way (Daniel 5:6).

BAPTIZING: A change in spiritual life; transformation from the natural to Christ-likeness. A change from the natural to the spiritual. Dying to self, expression of the new man.

He went into all the country around the Jordan, preaching a baptism of repentance for the forgiveness of sins (Luke 3:3).

We were therefore buried with him through baptism into death in order that, just as Christ was raised from the dead through the glory of the Father, we too may live a new life (Romans 6:4).

Having been buried with Him in baptism and raised with Him through your

faith in the power of God, who raised Him from the dead (Colossians 2:12).

BARBERSHOP: Time, place, period of changing beliefs or customs or habits. A church where these can take place; a place of correction.

Types:

1. A place where beliefs could be changed, a place for instructions.

2. A place of gathering for gossip or training.

3. A place of impartation for good or bad cultures.

BARENESS: Unproductive, difficult time or period, need for supernatural, divine intervention. Sign of vulnerability, exposure, and shame.

BARN: A place of provision. A church. Stored spiritual wealth.

Symbolic Actions

1. ***Finding yourself in a barn:*** May indicate a place of restoration or reward is imminent.

2. ***Receiving from a barn:*** Indicating benefiting from the storehouse of God.

Let both grow together until the harvest. At that time I will tell the harvesters: First collect the weeds and tie them in bundles to be burned; then gather the wheat and bring it into my barn (Matthew 13:30).

Is there yet any seed left in the barn? Until now, the vine and the fig tree, the pomegranate and the olive tree have not borne fruit. From this day on I will bless you (Haggai 2:19).

BASEMENT: The unseen part of something. Storage zone. Related to the foundation. Hidden. Bloodline-related issue.

Symbolic Actions

1. *Valuables in the basement:* May mean inherited giftedness, or great potentials are yet to be revealed or manifested.

2. *Fault in the basement:* May indicate the need for repairs or may indicate broken foundation or something in the bloodline that needs repentance or repair.

BASKET: A measure of something; A measure of God's provision. A measure of judgment.

Symbolic Actions

1. *Receiving a basket of fruits:* A measure of impartation of the gift of the Holy Spirit.

2. *A basket of ripe fruits:* Time for something, no more delay.

3. *A basket of bad fruit:* That which is not usable for God's purpose.

4. *A basket covered or sealed with a lid:* May mean a measure or reward or punishment that will be revealed at a future date.

5. *A basket of bread:* Life-giving resources.

6. *A basket of flowers:* A measure of appreciation; to be honored or recognized; a show of love.

This is what the Sovereign Lord showed me: a basket of ripe fruit. "What do you see, Amos?" He asked. "A basket of ripe fruit," I answered. Then the Lord said to me, "The time is ripe for My people Israel; I will spare them no longer" (Amos 8:1-2).

Then the angel who was speaking to me came forward and said to me, "Look up and see what this is that is appearing." I asked, "What is it?" He replied, "It is a measuring basket." And he added, "This is the iniquity of the people throughout the land." Then the cover of lead was raised, and there in the basket sat a woman! He said, "This is wickedness," and he pushed her back into the basket and pushed the lead cover down over its mouth. Then I looked up—and there before me were two women, with the wind in their wings! They had wings like those of a stork, and they lifted up the basket between Heaven and earth. "Where are they taking the basket?" I asked the angel who was speaking to me. He replied, "To the country of Babylonia to build a house for it. When it is ready, the basket will be set there in its place" (Zechariah 5:5-11).

BAT: Creature of darkness. Satanic instrument, related to witchcraft. A nighttime creature. Could represent association with the dark side of life.

Symbolic Actions

1. *Flying bats:* Challenges from the enemy are imminent.

2. *Sounds from bats:* The boastfulness of the enemy, satan—ignore and walk in faith.

BATHING: What you do on the outside or outwardly to prevent unclean or unholy attitude from sticking to you; outward repentance.

Symbolic Actions

1. ***Preparing for a bath:*** Contemplating how to rid oneself of surrounding evil practices.

2. ***Having a bath:*** What the dreamer does to resist the influences of the vile things in the world.

3. ***Not having enough water for a bath:*** Need for more prayers and the need to move more in the Holy Spirit; some areas of indulgence may be hindering the desire for holiness.

4. ***Bathing in public places:*** Not ashamed to disassociate oneself from evil practices.

5. ***Bathing with dirty water:*** Desire for good, but care not to go about it in a corrupted or ungodly way.

6. ***Bathing in shrine:*** Worshiping an idol, putting your faith in an idol or man.

BATHROOM: A period of cleansing/ entering a time of repentance. A place of voluntary nakedness or vulnerability or facing reality in one's life.

Symbolic Actions

1. ***Clean bathroom:*** Conducive atmosphere for resisting the influences of the evil one; the right frame of mind to resist the devil.

2. ***Unable to get into or use the bathroom:*** A place or season that may not be helpful in resisting evil practices; prideful attitude not allowing true repentance.

3. ***Attack in the bathroom:*** To be watchful of challenges at the area of vulnerability.

BEAM: Power or illumination coming from God or the heavenly. A time of exposure or spotlight. A supporting frame. God is the Father of lights and Christians are the children of lights.

BEAR: Danger; wicked person or spirit; vindictiveness. Evil, something that is after what you possess.

Symbolic Actions

1. ***Being attacked by a bear:*** Impending dangerous challenge or attack from wicked person.

2. ***Being pursued by a bear:*** Watch also for any spirit of vindictiveness in the dreamer himself or from others.

But David said to Saul, "Your servant has been keeping his father's sheep. When a lion or a bear came and carried off a sheep from the flock, I went after it, struck it and rescued the sheep from its mouth. When it turned on me, I seized it by its hair, struck it and killed it. Your servant has killed both the lion and the bear; this uncircumcised Philistine will be like one of them, because he has defied the armies of the living God. The Lord who delivered me from the paw of the lion and the paw of the bear will deliver me from the hand of this Philistine." Saul said to David, "Go, and the Lord be with you" (1 Samuel 17:34-37).

You know your father and his men; they are fighters, and as fierce as a wild bear robbed of her cubs. Besides, your father is an experienced fighter; he will not spend the night with the troops (2 Samuel 17:8).

It will be as though a man fled from a lion only to meet a bear, as though he entered his house and rested his hand on the wall only to have a snake bite him (Amos 5:19).

BEARD: To have respect for authority.

Symbolic Actions

1. *Messy:* Insane.

2. *Trimmed:* Sane.

3. *Having a long and well-kept beard:* A symbol of wisdom, authority, or prophetic anointing.

4. *To shave one's beard:* To mourn or to be humiliated.

BEAUTY SHOP: A place of preparation with emphasis on outward appearance, tending toward vanity. See also *Barber's Shop.*

BED: Revelations, rest, contentment. Becoming relaxed or lax. Final place of rest means death.

Symbolic Actions

1. *House or place with many beds:* May mean a person with prophetic gift, particularly great capacity to receive dreams/visions.

2. *Happening on the bed:* Something likely to happen or refers to something happening in an intimate place.

BEDROOM: A place of intimacy. A place of rest, sleep, or dreams. A place of covenant, a place of revelation.

BEES: That which makes offensive noise. More noisy than effective. A double-edged situation capable of going bad or producing sweetness. Stinging words, gossip.

Some time later, when he went back to marry her, he turned aside to look at the lion's carcass. In it was a swarm of bees and some honey (Judges 14:8).

BELLS: Call to attention or action. To bring to alertness. To say it loudly; public warning.

Symbolic Actions

1. *To hear the sound of a bell:* Means time for something has come.

2. *The sound of an alarm bell:* Something of great importance is happening or *about to happen. A warning to get ready!*

BELLY: Feelings, desires, spiritual well-being, sentiment.

Types:

1. *As mind/sour:* See Jeremiah 4:19, Luke 10:33; Job 15:35.

2. *As greed:* See Philippians 3:19.

3. *As words:* See Job 10:15.

4. *As a place/pains:* See Jonah 2:2.

Their destiny is destruction, their god is their stomach (belly) and their glory is in their shame (Philippians 3:19).

BICYCLE: A ministry depending on much human effort. One-man ministry. A ministry with much exposure—may be a good thing, but could increase vulnerability. Limited capacity to influence many people at one time.

BINOCULARS: Looking ahead, looking into the future. Prophetic ministry.

BIRD: Symbol of leader, evil or good at different levels. Agents of authority.

Symbolic Actions

1. *As food or divine provision of food.* See First Kings 4:23.
2. *As a symbol for escape into freedom/safety.*
3. *As faithful observers of the season.*
4. *As an emblem of trust in the Lord's provision.*

Types:

1. *Dove:* Holy Spirit, peace, a seal of approval from Heaven. May mean spiritual naivety.
2. *Eagle:* Personality or spirit capable of soaring in the Spirit. Good focus/swiftness powerful. A prophet of God.
3. *Owl:* A watchful eye that monitors; spirit of craftiness.
4. *Raven:* Symbol of unclean spirit.
5. *Sparrow:* Divine provision and food. Symbol of God's desire to provide for us.
6. *Vulture:* Evil spirit, opportunistic person. Night creature or something that preys on dead things (human weaknesses). Unclean spirit. A loner.
7. *Feathers:* A protective covering, a shield or instrument for flying or moving in the spirit.
8. *Wings:* A place of refuge. God's presence. Safety/something that provides escape from danger.
9. *Fowler:* A person or spirit that entraps. Fowler's net.

Leave here, turn eastward and hide in the Kerith Ravine, east of the Jordan. You will drink from the brook, and I have ordered the ravens to feed you there (1 Kings 17:3-4).

I said, "Oh, that I had the wings of a dove! I would fly away and be at rest— I would flee far away and stay in the desert, I would hurry to my place of shelter, far from the tempest and storm" (Psalm 55:6-8).

Even the stork in the sky knows her appointed seasons, and the dove, the swift and the thrush observe the time of their migration (Jeremiah 8:7).

Then Jesus said to His disciples, "Therefore do not worry about your life, what you will eat; or about your body, what you will wear. Life is more than food, and the body more than clothes. Consider the ravens: They do not sow or reap, they have no storeroom or barn; yet God feeds them. And how much more valuable you are than birds!" (Luke 12:22-24).

Ephraim is like a dove, easily deceived and senseless (Hosea 7:11).

BLACK: Lack, famine. Evil, demonic spirit. Darkness.

May darkness and deep shadow claim it once more; may a cloud settle over it; may blackness overwhelm its light (Job 3:5).

They are wild waves of the sea, foaming up their shame; wandering stars, for whom blackest darkness has been reserved forever (Jude 1:13).

I clothe the sky with darkness and make sackcloth its covering (Isaiah 50:3).

BLEEDING: Hurting. To lose spiritually; verbal accusation. Traumatic.

1. *Injury with much bleeding:* A situation that will drain the person of much spirituality.

2. *Persistent bleeding:* Situation that may cause repeated irritation and so continue to drain spirituality.

BLIND: Lack of understanding, ignorance. Not able to see into the spirit world.

1. *To be blindfolded:* Beware of deceptive situation.

BLOOD: Atonement, to appease. Something that testifies, or warning.

Symbolic Actions

1. *Blood often indicates the blood of Christ.*

2. *Blood may mean a warning of danger.*

BLOOD TRANSFUSION: Getting new life, rescuing situation.

Symbolic Actions

1. *Receiving a pure blood transfusion:* A rescuing process or getting new life in Christ.

2. *Receiving any other intravenous infusion:* May indicate the need for caution; to avoid dangerous indoctrination that could persist for a life time.

BLUE: Heaven-related or something related to the Holy Spirit. Spiritual. Depends on the shade of blue.

Types:

1. *Light blue:* Usually of the Spirit.

2. *Ocean blue:* Also of the Spirit, but huge/massive.

3. *Dark blue:* Possible lowliness in mood or depression.

BOAT: A ministry that is capable of influencing many people. Depends on the type of boat.

Types:

1. *Rescue boat:* Intercessory ministry.

2. *Fishing boat:* Ministry involving evangelism; soul-saving mission.

3. *Rowing boat:* Exercise in the Spirit (prayers).

4. *Speed boat:* Acceleration phase is at hand; the need for acceleration.

BODY ODOR: Unclean spirit, aftereffect of fleshy actions.

Symbolic Actions

1. *Repulsive body odor:* May indicate revelation of character defect that is unacceptable to others.

2. *Sweat smell:* May indicate action that will show efforts not of the Holy Spirit.

BONES: The substance or essence of something; power or importance of something. The main issue. Long-lasting. Something without flesh/substance. Something without details.

Types:

1. **Dry bone:** Lack of Holy Spirit in life (see Ezek. 37).

2. **Crushed bones:** To remove hope.

The man said, "This is now bone of my bones and flesh of my flesh; she shall be called 'woman' for she was taken out of man" (Genesis 2:23).

Once while some Israelites were burying a man, suddenly they saw a band of raiders; so they threw the man's body into Elisha's tomb. When the body touched Elisha's bones, the man came to life and stood up on his feet (2 Kings 13:21).

Moses took the bones of Joseph with him because Joseph had made the sons of Israel sear an oath. He had said, "God will surely come to your aid, and then you must carry my bones up with you from this place" (Exodus 13:19).

BOOK: Gaining understanding/knowledge. Scriptures. Revelation. Promise from God. Message based on the title of the book.

Symbolic Actions

1. **Reading a book:** Gaining knowledge/revelation and information.

2. **The topic or title of the book:** May indicate the main message.

3. **Unable or difficulty in reading a book:** Issues in the life of the

person or circumstances around that are not conducive to gaining knowledge.

BOTTLE: A vessel, a measure, something relating to the body. As the container of anointing.

Symbolic Actions

1. **A bottle of clear water:** May be symbolic of the prophetic anointing; a certain move of the Holy Spirit.

2. **A bottle of dirty water:** Beware of wrong or contaminated doctrines.

3. **Drinking from a bottle of dirty water:** May be receiving from contaminated doctrine.

BOW: Source from which attacks come. The heart from which issues of life come, the power of a nation or person. Verbal attacks. The tongue. Arrow or gun. A power source.

But his bow remained steady, his strong arms stayed limber, because of the hand of the Mighty One of Jacob, because of the Shepherd, the Rock of Israel (Genesis 49:24).

"They make ready their tongue like a bow, to shoot lies; it is not by truth that they triumph in the land. They go from one sin to another; they do not acknowledge Me," declares the Lord (Jeremiah 9:3).

This is what the Lord Almighty says: "See, I will break the bow of Elam, the mainstay of their might" (Jeremiah 49:35).

BOWL: A container; measure of something.

His offering was one silver plate weighing a hundred and thirty shekels, and one silver sprinkling bowl weighing seventy shekels, both according to the sanctuary shekel, each filled with fine flour mixed with oil as a grain offering (Numbers 7:13).

You drink wine by the bowlful and use the finest lotions, but you do not grieve over the ruin of Joseph (Amos 6:6).

And the Lord Almighty will shield them. They will destroy and overcome with slingstones. They will drink and roar as with wine; they will be full like a bowl used for sprinkling the corners of the altar (Zechariah 9:15).

And that is what happened. Gideon rose early the next day; he squeezed the fleece and wrung out the dew—a bowlful of water (Judges 6:38).

BRACELET: Pertaining to pride. Valuable but of the world, means identity if it has a name.

BRANCHES: God's people, churches. Church split, or offshoot of something.

I am the vine; you are the branches. If a man remains in Me and I in him, he will bear much fruit; apart from Me you can do nothing (John 15:5).

I am the true vine, and my Father is the gardener. He cuts off every branch in Me that bears no fruit, while every branch that does bear fruit He prunes so that it will be even more fruitful (John 15:1-2).

BRASS: Hardness, hard covering. Judgment/captivity/hard to break out from. Strength. Negative stronghold. Resistance.

Do I have the strength of stone? Is my flesh bronze? (Job 6:12).

The sky over your head will be bronze, the ground beneath you iron (Deuteronomy 28:23).

They killed the sons of Zedekiah before his eyes. Then they put out his eyes, bound him with bronze shackles and took him to Babylon (2 Kings 25:7).

I will break down your stubborn pride and make the sky above you like iron and the ground beneath you like bronze (Leviticus 26:19).

BREAD: Jesus Christ; Bread of life; Word of God; source of nourishment; God's provision.

Types:

1. **Fresh:** New word from God.

2. **Moldy:** Something that is not new. Unclean.

3. **Yeast:** Deceptive teaching.

4. **Unleavened:** Showing lack of sin, something prepared in haste.

Then she arose with her daughters-in-law that she might return from the country of Moab: for she had heard in the country of Moab that the Lord had visited His people by giving them bread (Ruth 1:6 NKJV).

At this the Jews began to grumble about him because He said, "I am the bread that came down from Heaven" (John 6:41).

Then at last they understood that He wasn't telling them to guard against the yeast used in bread, but against the teaching of the Pharisees and Sadducees (Matthew 16:12).

A man ought to examine himself before he eats of the bread and drinks of the cup (1 Corinthians 11:28).

Give us today our daily bread (Matthew 6:11).

BREAST: Source of milk for new Christians. Object of enticement. Source of sustenance.

Because of your father's God, who helps you, because of the Almighty, who blesses you with blessings of the heavens above, blessings of the deep that lies below, blessings of the breast and womb (Genesis 49:25).

Why were there knees to receive me and breasts that I might be nursed? (Job 3:12).

A loving doe, a graceful deer—may her breasts satisfy you always, may you ever be captivated by her love (Proverbs 5:19).

BREASTPLATE: God's protective shield. Covering or the anointing which covers one. Preparing to give judgment. Protective of vital human organs or issues.

He put on righteousness as his breastplate, and the helmet of salvation on his head; he put on the garments of vengeance and wrapped himself in zeal as in a cloak (Isaiah 59:17).

He placed the breastpiece on him and put the Urim and Thummim in the breastpiece (Leviticus 8:8).

Stand firm then, with the belt of truth buckled around your waist, with the breastplate of righteousness in place (Ephesians 6:14).

BREATH: Means Spirit; spirit of man. Breath of life. Sign of life. Revive to life.

The Lord God formed the man from the dust of the ground and breathed into his nostrils the breath of life, and the man became a living being (Genesis 2:7).

His breath sets coals ablaze, and flames dart from His mouth (Job 41:21).

Topheth has long been prepared; it has been made ready for the king. Its fire pit has been made deep and wide, with an abundance of fire and wood; the breath of the Lord, like a stream of burning sulphur, sets it ablaze (Isaiah 30:33).

Then he said to me, "Prophesy to the breath; prophesy, son of man, and say to it, 'This is what the Sovereign Lord says: Come from the four winds, O breath, and breathe into these slain, that they may live'" (Ezekiel 37:9).

BRICK: A building unit. Something that is man-made or designed to be durable. Something used for personality building.

They said to each other, "Come, let's make bricks and bake them thoroughly." They used brick instead of stone, and tar for mortar (Genesis 11:3).

The bricks have fallen down, but we will rebuild with dressed stone; the fig trees have been felled, but we will replace them with cedars (Isaiah 9:10).

A people who continually provoke Me to My very face, offering sacrifices in gardens and burning incense on altars of brick (Isaiah 65:3).

BRIDE/BRIDEGROOM: The Church relationship to Jesus. Special to Jesus. Covenant or relationship.

Symbolic Actions

1. **Bride:** Special to Jesus.

2. **Bridegroom:** Christ, the actual standing of person from God's viewpoint.

3. **Wedding:** The beginning of fruitful union; new level of intimacy with Jesus Christ; end of certain things, such as dependence on earthly support and youthful exuberance; beginning of certain things, such as spiritual life responsibility; parenthood.

4. **Wedding dress:** The state of preparation for the union.

5. **Stained wedding dress:** Past issues that should be dealt with so as not to bring strain.

6. **Holes in the dress:** Faulty preparation, needs to be corrected.

7. **Wedding Cake:** God's provision for the new union; God's provision that will overflow to others. Means of joyous celebration.

8. **Wedding Wine:** Holy Spirit empowerment; God's miraculous provision. Drinks, avoid overindulgence.

9. **Absence of key people in wedding ceremony:** Eager to grow in the Lord, but have not totally put key things in place; need to carry along some people.

"Lift up your eyes and look around; all your sons gather and come to you. As surely as I live," declares the Lord, "you will wear them all as ornaments; you

will put them on, like a bride" (Isaiah 49:18).

The bride belongs to the bridegroom. The friend who attends the bridegroom waits and listens for him, and is full of joy when he hears the bridegroom's voice. That joy is mine, and it is now complete (John 3:29).

One of the seven angels who had the seven bowls full of the seven last plagues came and said to me, "Come, I will show you the bride, the wife of the Lamb" (Revelation 21:9).

BRIDGE: Something that takes you across an obstacle, e.g., faith. The connection between two things/circumstances. Something that holds you up in times of difficulty.

Types:

1. **Broken bridge:** Lack of faith, lack of communication, or obstacle to unity exists.

2. **Weak/shaking bridge:** Weak faith, need for more trust in God. There is need to pray.

BRIDLE: Put control over, e.g., self-control over the use of the tongue. Something imposed by some higher authority to affect control

A whip for the horse, a bridle for the ass, and a rod for the fool's back (Proverbs 26:3 KJV).

If anyone among you thinks he is religious, and does not bridle his tongue but deceives his own heart, this one's religion is useless (James 1:26 NKJV).

I said, "I will watch my ways and keep my tongue from sin; I will put a muz-

B

zle on my mouth as long as the wicked are in my presence" (Psalm 39:1).

Because your rage against Me and your tumult have come up to My ears, Therefore I will put My hook in your nose and My bridle in your lips, and I will turn you back by the way which you came (Isaiah 37:29 NKJV).

BRIERS: Something "wild and thorny" that needs to be trimmed. Something uncultivated or false.

BRIGHTNESS: Presence of God. Revelation. Solution. End of difficult period.

Symbolic Actions

1. ***Sudden appearance of brightness:*** May indicate God's light to the situation; better understanding is imminent.

I looked, and I saw a figure like that of a man. From what appeared to be His waist down He was like fire, and from there up His appearance was as bright as glowing metal (Ezekiel 8:2).

Those who are wise will shine like the brightness of the heavens, and those who lead many to righteousness, like the stars for ever and ever (Daniel 12:3).

You looked, O king, and there before you stood a large statue—an enormous, dazzling statue, awesome in appearance (Daniel 2:31).

The Son is the radiance of God's glory and the exact representation of His being, sustaining all things by His powerful word. After He had provided purification for sins, He sat down at the right hand of the Majesty in heaven (Hebrews 1:3).

BRIMSTONE: Judgment of God. Punishment. Trial period. Burning stone.

BROKEN: Loss of strength, authority, or influence. Open. Heart; wounded. Watch out for any break in unity. Break in bond between people. Broken chain commonly indicates deliverance from evil, bondage, or curse.

Like a city whose walls are broken down is a man who lacks self-control (Proverbs 25:28).

I will seek what was lost and bring back what was driven away, bind up the broken and strengthen what was sick; but I will destroy the fat and the strong, and feed them in judgment (Ezekiel 34:16 NKJV).

BROOK: A provision of God. Something that brings refreshment, wisdom, prosperity from God. If dirty, means corrupted or contaminated. A source of defense.

The rivers will turn foul; the brooks of defense will be emptied and dried up; the reeds and rushes will wither (Isaiah 19:6 NKJV).

Get away from here and turn eastward, and hide by the Brook Cherith, which flows into the Jordan. And it will be that you shall drink from the brook, and I have commanded the ravens to feed you there (1 Kings 17:3-4 NKJV).

My brothers have dealt deceitfully like a brook, like the streams of the brooks that pass away (Job 6:15 NKJV).

BROOM: Something, or in the process of, getting rid of sins. Symbol of witchcraft.

Symbolic Actions

1. **Sweeping:** Get rid of sin/obstacles/weaknesses.

2. **Flying on the broom:** May be symbolic of spirit of control or manipulation.

"Though many people talk about spiritual warfare, only few people grasp the true concept of what it means. In simple terms, it is the process of handling invisible events and circumstances to achieve the desired results in the visible world. Spiritual warfare is a special form of prayers and intercession in which the believers pray, intercede, and set in motion that which will activate things in the spiritual realm to influence and determine the outcome of things in the natural realm."

More information about spiritual warfare is found in my book, *The Final Frontiers.*[1]

BROTHER: Christian brother (spiritual brother); biological brother. Someone with similar qualities.

Whoever does God's will is My brother and sister and mother (Mark 3:35).

BROTHER-IN-LAW: Same as a brother, but under special obligation. Spiritual brother without in-depth love. A person of another church who is also Christian. Actual brother-in-law. Someone with similar qualities.

BROWN/TAN: Life; change of season; born again.

BRUISE: Event or circumstance that leaves a hurt feeling with one. In need

of healing. Suffering of Jesus on our behalf. Inner hurting of spirit.

This is what the Lord says:"Your wound is incurable, your injury beyond healing"(Jeremiah 30:12).

But He was wounded for our transgressions, He was bruised for our iniquities; The chastisement for our peace was upon Him, and by His stripes we are healed (Isaiah 53:5 NKJV).

BUCKET: A measure of something. Used for service. Supplies life.

Symbolic Actions

1. **A bucket of clear water:** A certain move of the Holy Spirit, a measure of provision.

2. **Difficulty in getting a bucket of water:** Hindrances to obtaining a flow in the Holy Spirit, or receiving needed provision.

3. **A bucket of dirty water:** A certain move of the spirit, not of the Holy Spirit.

Surely the nations are like a drop in a bucket; they are regarded as dust on the scales; he weighs the islands as though they were fine dust (Isaiah 40:15).

Water will flow from their buckets; their seed will have abundant water. Their king will be greater than Agag; their kingdom will be exalted (Numbers 24:7).

BUILDING: Symbolic of the spiritual and emotional being of the place, person, or church. Life of the person, church, or office.

Symbolic Actions

1. *A building under construction:* Undergoing some form of personality transformation.

2. *A fallen building:* Prayer for good health is needed.

3. *A flooded building:* Major challenges imminent.

And I tell you that you are Peter, and on this rock I will build My church, and the gates of Hades will not overcome it (Matthew 16:18).

He is like a man building a house, who dug down deep and laid the foundation on rock. When a flood came, the torrent struck that house but could not shake it, because it was well built (Luke 6:48).

Therefore everyone who hears these words of Mine and puts them into practice is like a wise man who built his house on the rock. The rain came down, the streams rose, and the winds blew and beat against that house; yet it did not fall, because it had its foundation on the rock. But everyone who hears these words of Mine and does not put them into practice is like a foolish man who built his house on sand (Matthew 7:24-26).

BULL: Threatening situation. Warfare. Opposition. May also mean a source of economy.

Symbolic Actions

1. *Fighting with a bull:* May indicate a major opposition or the need to do self-check to ascertain there are no inner issues (within the person) that may constitute opposition to the will of God in the person's life (internal component of dream).

2. *Bulls grazing in a field:* A major source of wealth.

BUNDLE: Measure of harvest. Grouping for judgment or reward. Fullness.

Types:

1. *A bundle of flowers:* Expression of love, appreciation, or a measure of God's glory is coming.

2. *A bundle of money:* May mean wealth, or a move that will bring money, or a certain measure of favor.

Then it happened as they emptied their sacks, that surprisingly each man's bundle of money was in his sack; and when they and their father saw the bundles of money, they were afraid (Genesis 42:35 NKJV).

Even though someone is pursuing you to take your life, the life of my master will be bound securely in the bundle of the living by the Lord your God. But the lives of your enemies He will hurl away as from the pocket of a sling (1 Samuel 25:29).

BURIAL: Memorial to mark the end of something.

Symbolic Action

1. *Attending a burial ceremony:* At the end of certain phase/a final change or witnessing the end of something.

2. *Digging up burial place:* Recovery of generational gifts or potentials, or bringing up old issues

Uzziah rested with his fathers and was buried near them in a field for burial that belonged to the kings, for people

said, *"He had leprosy." And Jotham his son succeeded him as king"* (2 Chronicles 26:23).

He will have the burial of a donkey— dragged away and thrown outside the gates of Jerusalem (Jeremiah 22:19).

When she poured this perfume on My body, she did it to prepare Me for burial (Matthew 26:12).

BURIED: A permanent end to something. To bring to final end.

We were therefore buried with Him through baptism into death in order that, just as Christ was raised from the dead through the glory of the Father, we too may live a new life (Romans 6:4).

having been buried with Him in baptism and raised with Him through your faith in the power of God, who raised Him from the dead (Colossians 2:12).

BURN: To consume. To heat up or stir up. To set aflame. To kindle. Sign of fervency. Total change of something by a drastic action.

Now the people complained about their hardships in the hearing of the Lord, and when he heard them his anger was aroused. Then fire from the Lord burned among them and consumed some of the outskirts of the camp (Numbers 11:1).

I will enslave you to your enemies in a land you do not know, for My anger will kindle a fire that will burn against you (Jeremiah 15:14).

Command the Israelites to bring you clear oil of pressed olives for the light so that the lamps may be kept burning (Exodus 27:20).

BUS: A big ministry.

Symbolic Actions

1. ***School bus:*** A teaching ministry.

2. ***To miss the bus:*** May indicate likelihood of missing divine appointment—a call for prayers.

3. ***To board the wrong bus:*** Watch out for misdirection/misplaced priorities.

4. ***To leave the bus at the wrong bus station:*** Watch against wrong timing or wrong decisions or preoccupation.

BUTTER: Something that brings soothing, smooth words. Encouragement.

Symbolic Actions

1. ***To butter a slice of bread:*** To make it easier, or to increase the comfort or joy, or to provide encouragement.

He will eat curds [butter] and honey when he knows enough to reject the wrong and choose the right (Isaiah 7:15).

His speech is smooth as butter, yet war is in his heart; his words are more soothing than oil, yet they are drawn swords (Psalm 55:21).

BUY: To prepare, take, acquire, or obtain something good or bad.

"Fields will be bought for silver, and deeds will be signed, sealed and witnessed in the territory of Benjamin, in the villages around Jerusalem, in the towns of Judah and in the towns of the hill country, of the western foothills and of the Negev, because I will restore their fortunes," declares the Lord (Jeremiah 32:44).

Buy the truth and do not sell it; get wisdom, discipline and understanding (Proverbs 23:23).

For a hundred pieces of silver, he bought from the sons of Hamor, the father of Shechem, the plot of ground where he pitched his tent (Genesis 33:19).

CAFETERIA: A place or period of spiritual nourishment—good or bad. A church. Structural teaching of the Word of God. Celebration.

CAGE: To restrict. Limited mobility. Negatively—captivity. Positively—to guard or watch.

Symbolic Actions

1. ***To put something in a cage:*** To limit the freedom or to put in bondage.

2. ***To help get out of a cage:*** To break the bondage or remove limitations.

Like cages full of birds, their houses are full of deceit; they have become rich and powerful (Jeremiah 5:27).

CAKE: Provisions from Heaven. Nourishment from God.

Symbolic Actions

1. ***To bake a cake:*** To help bring about joy/celebration.

2. ***A birthday cake:*** Major celebration, an important day.

3. ***A wedding cake:*** Joy from fruitful relationship with Jesus Christ.

4. ***Baking a cake and running out of ingredients.*** Preparations are not adequate.

The people went around gathering it, and then ground it in a hand mill or crushed it in a mortar. They cooked it in a pot or made it into cakes. And it tasted like something made with olive oil (Numbers 11:8).

CALF: A young cow or bull. Increase in prosperity. Suggestive of youthfulness, abounding in energy. Fatted calf indicates hospitality and celebrations.

And kill the calf we have been fattening. We must celebrate with a feast (Luke 15:23).

CAMEL: Having a servant heart. Capable of bearing other people's burdens. Intercessory spirit.

Symbolic Actions

1. ***A camel load:*** Abundance/plentiful.

CAMP: Temporary settlement; a transit situation. Something intended for traveling or for temporary residence, not permanent building.

Symbolic Actions

1. ***A camp of angels:*** Major divine encounter or help.

2. ***A camp of friends:*** Divinely appointed help on the way.

3. ***A camp of enemies:*** Major challenge or opposition.

Jacob also went on his way, and the angels of God met him. When Jacob saw them, he said, "This is the camp of God!" So he named that place Mahanaim (Genesis 32:1-2).

They left the Red Sea and camped in the Desert of Sin. They left the Desert of Sin and camped at Dophkah. They left Dophkah and camped at Alush. They left Alush and camped at Rephidim, where there was no water for the people to drink. They left Rephidim and camped in the Desert of Sinai. They left the Desert of Sinai and camped at Kibroth Hattaavah. They left Kibroth Hattaavah and camped at Hazeroth. They left Hazeroth and camped at Rithmah (Numbers 33:11-18).

CANDLE: Word of God. Symbolic of man's spirit. If not lit, could mean lack of God's presence. Jesus is also source of light. Conscience.

Types:

1. Lamp

2. Electricity

The lamp of the Lord searches the spirit of a man; it searches out his inmost being (Proverbs 20:27).

At that time I will search Jerusalem with lamps and punish those who are complacent, who are like wine left on its dregs, who think, "The Lord will do nothing, either good or bad" (Zephaniah 1:12).

CANDLESTICK: People who carry the light of God. The lamp stand, Spirit of God. Church.

CARPENTER: Jesus. Someone who makes or amends things. A preacher.

CAT: Deceptive situation/person. Something or a person who is self-willed. Not a teachable spirit. A sneaky, crafty, and deceptive spirit. Witchcraft, waiting to attack. A personal pet. A precious habit that could be dangerous.

CAVE: Safe hiding place. Secret place of encountering God.

Symbolic Actions

1. *Hiding in a cave:* Fear, lack of faith.

2. *Putting valuables in a cave:* A place that may not be easily seen by enemies.

CHAIN: Bondage or captivity. To be bound in the spirit or in the natural.

CHAIR: Authority over something; coming to position of authority or a place of respite; throne of God.

Symbolic Actions

1. *Difficulty in finding one's chair:* Hindrances to obtaining one's place of authority.

2. *Sitting on a chair:* A place of authority/power/respite.

3. *Stolen chair:* Watchfulness needed to maintain one's authority or designated place or position.

CHANNEL: A way out. A process of time. Difficult period leading to the next stage.

Symbolic Actions

1. *Passing through channel:* The dreamer is the process of going through something.

2. *Dark channel:* Difficult period.

CHASE: Cause to flee. Get rid of something. To pursue. To go after something.

Symbolic Actions

1. *To be chased by a mad person:* A great challenge to mental stability; prayers should be of-

fered against insanity or insane decisions.

2. ***To be chased by dangerous animals:*** Major challenges or attacks, but also requires self examination to resist tendency to go toward the spirit represented by the animal during waking hours, e.g., excessive anger or violence (may be symbolized by a tiger).

CHECK/CHEQUE: The seal of promise. Promise that is guaranteed.

Symbolic Actions

1. ***To cash a check:*** Time of maturity of divine promise has come.

2. ***A bounced check:*** Fake promises.

3. ***To be given a check:*** A promise for a future date.

CHEEK: Vulnerable part, beauty.

CHEESE: To comfort. To soothe.

 CHEETAH: A spirit that is capable of quick overcoming. Unclean spirit.

CHEW: To meditate. To ruminate. To cut off.

Symbolic Actions

1. ***To be chewing something:*** In the process of gaining better understanding.

2. ***Difficult to chew:*** Hard to comprehend, lacking in detail.

CHICKEN: An evangelist. Gifting, caring spirit. Gathering

Symbolic Actions

1. ***Rooster:*** Boasting.

2. ***Chick:*** Defenseless.

O Jerusalem, Jerusalem, you who kill the prophets and stone those sent to you, how often I have longed to gather your children together, as a hen gathers her chicks under her wings, but you were not willing (Matthew 23:37; Luke 13:34).

CHILDHOOD HOME: Influence from the distant past, whether good or bad.

CHOKING: Biting more than you can chew. Too fast, too much in the wrong way.

Symbolic Actions

1. ***Choking:*** Action that will drain one of spiritual strength.

CHRISTMAS: New thing in Christ. Tradition of men. Spiritual gift. Season of gifts/love. A period of joy and humanitarianism. Celebration of Christ. False or pretend celebration or hypocrisy.

CIRCLE: Something endless signifies agreement or covenant. If making a circle, relating to the universe; Ring, round.

Symbolic Actions

1. ***Something in circles:*** May indicate something that will seemingly continue without end.

He sits enthroned above the circle of the earth, and its people are like grasshoppers. He stretches out the heavens like a canopy, and spreads them out like a tent to live in (Isaiah 40:22).

CIRCUMCISION: Cutting off fleshy things/coming to liberty. Covenanting with God. Blood relationship. New levels of spiritual walk, born again. New level of maturity.

You are to undergo circumcision, and it will be the sign of the covenant between Me and you (Genesis 17:11).

Circumcise yourselves to the Lord, circumcise your hearts, you men of Judah and people of Jerusalem, or My wrath will break out and burn like fire because of the evil you have done—burn with no one to quench it (Jeremiah 4:4).

Then He gave Abraham the covenant of circumcision. And Abraham became the father of Isaac and circumcised him eight days after his birth. Later Isaac became the father of Jacob, and Jacob became the father of the twelve patriarchs (Acts 7:8).

CITY: The makeup of the person. All that has been inputted in the person or people. The city or what the city is known for. Group or church.

1. *Las Vegas:* Gambling.

2. *Los Angeles:* Hollywood, immorality.

3. *Paris:* Love.

CLASSROOM: A time of spiritual preparation. A person with a gifting to teach others.

Symbolic Actions

1. *Difficulty in finding one's classroom:* May mean hindrances to getting proper training.

2. *In a childhood classroom:* New foundational teaching/knowledge imminent.

CLAY: Something that refers to frailty of man; delicate and fragile; not secure.

Symbolic Actions

1. *To mold a pot with clay:* God's power of restoration or creation.

I am just like you before God; I too have been taken from clay (Job 33:6).

Its legs of iron, its feet partly of iron and partly of baked clay. While you were watching, a rock was cut out, but not by human hands. It struck the statue on its feet of iron and clay and smashed them. …As the toes were partly iron and partly clay, so this kingdom will be partly strong and partly brittle (Daniel 2:33-34,42).

CLEAN: To make holy, pure; to make righteous; to make ready and acceptable.

CLEANSE: To put right something. To put away what is bad.

CLEAR: To bring light to the situation; to bring understanding. To be set free from something.

Symbolic Actions

1. *Something becoming clear:* The end of confusion; to bring enlightenment or clarification to a situation.

CLOCK: Timing is important in the situation. Time to do something is revealed. May refer to Bible passages. Running out of time.

CLOSE: To shut up, to keep silent, or to be hedged or walled up.

For the Lord has poured out on you the spirit of deep sleep, and has closed your eyes, namely, the prophets; and He has covered your heads, namely, the seers (Isaiah 29:10 NKJV).

For this people's heart has become calloused; they hardly hear with their ears, and they have closed their eyes. Otherwise they might see with their eyes, hear with their ears, understand with their hearts and turn, and I would heal them (Matthew 13:15).

CLOSET: Hidden, confidential, personal, or exclusive. A place of prayer. A place of fellowship with God.

Gather the people, sanctify the congregation, assemble the elders, gather the children, and those that suck the breasts: let the bridegroom go forth of his chamber, and the bride out of her closet (Joel 2:16 KJV).

But thou, when thou prayest, enter into thy closet, and when thou hast shut thy door, pray to thy Father which is in secret; and thy Father which seeth in secret shall reward thee openly (Matthew 6:6 KJV).

Therefore whatsoever ye have spoken in darkness shall be heard in the light; and that which ye have spoken in the ear in closets shall be proclaimed upon the housetops (Luke 12:3 KJV).

CLOTHING: Covering whether pure or impure. Your standing or authority in a situation. Covering God is providing to us.

Symbolic Actions

1. ***Wearing national clothing:*** Indicates special anointing to teach or minister to the people of that nation.

2. ***Wearing rich clothing:*** Moving in rich anointing/mantle.

3. ***Wearing torn clothing:*** Defects in the manifestation of the anointing.

4. ***Tearing cloths:*** Signifies grief, sorrow.

On the third day a man arrived from Saul's army camp, with his clothes torn and with dust on his head… (2 Samuel 1:2).

5. ***Torn on one's body:*** Mourning.

Then David and all the men with him took hold of their clothes and tore them. They mourned and wept and fasted till evening for Saul and his son Jonathan, and for the army of the Lord and the house of Israel, because they had fallen by the sword (2 Samuel 1:11-12).

CLOUDS: Heavenly manifestation; glory, presence of God. Dark time of travel, fear, trouble, or storms of life. Hiddenness of God.

Types:

1. ***Dark clouds:*** A time of storm or difficulty.

2. ***White clouds:*** Glory of God; time of joy/abundance.

By day the Lord went ahead of them in a pillar of cloud to guide them on their way and by night in a pillar of fire to give them light, so that they could travel by day or night (Exodus 13:21).

The Lord said to Moses: "Tell your brother Aaron not to come whenever he chooses into the Most Holy Place behind the curtain in front of the atonement cover on the ark, or else he will die, because I appear in the cloud over the atonement cover" (Leviticus 16:2).

At that time the sign of the Son of Man will appear in the sky, and all the nations of the earth will mourn. They will see the Son of Man coming on the clouds of the sky, with power and great glory (Matthew 24:30).

CLOWN: Not a serious person. Not taking God seriously. Childish.

Symbolic Actions

1. ***To be in the presence of a clown:*** May indicate the presence of a person or surrounding not to be taken seriously; a need to put away childish tendencies.

COAT: Protective, covering, mantle.

Symbolic Actions

1. ***Clean:*** Righteousness.

2. ***Dirty:*** Not righteous, unclean.

The Lord God made garments [coat] of skin for Adam and his wife and clothed them (Genesis 3:21).

He is to put on the sacred linen tunic, with linen undergarments next to his body; he is to tie the linen sash around him and put on the linen turban. These are sacred garments [coats]; so he must bathe himself with water before he puts them on (Leviticus 16:4).

Take the garments [coats] and dress Aaron with the tunic, the robe of the ephod, the ephod itself and the breast-piece. Fasten the ephod on him by its skillfully woven waistband (Exodus 29:5).

COLLEGE: Promotion in the Spirit. Pertaining to the equipping season.

COLUMNS: Spirit of control and manipulation; obsessive or orderliness.

Symbolic Actions

1. ***To run into a column of people:*** Challenge may be at hand that will be obsessive or manipulative.

2. ***To run into a column of soldiers:*** A well-organized opposition likely.

CONCEIVE: In process of preparation. To add. To multiply.

CONGREGATION: An appointed meeting. An assembly. Called together.

Symbolic Actions

1. ***Preaching to a congregation:*** A manifestation of one's gift is imminent.

2. ***Talking to a large congregation:*** Influence likely to affect many people.

CORD: Something that holds things together. Enhances unity/love; or something that binds to cause restriction or bondage.

COUCH: Rest, relaxation, peace.

Symbolic Actions

1. ***To be seated on a couch:*** A place of rest or comfort; one's place of authority.

2. ***To be seduced on a couch:*** Watch out for challenges from the spirit of Jezebel.

COUNTRYSIDE: A time of peace/tranquillity. A potential that is yet unexplored. A place of fertility and abundance. A place or privacy or escape from noise. A place or spiritual retreat or romance.

COURTHOUSE: Time of being judged or persecuted; trial.

COW: Food/source of enrichment; potential source of sin.

CRAB: Moving sideways; potential to hurt; self-centered.

CRAWLING: Humility or to be humiliated; sign of judgment.

So both of them showed themselves to the Philistine outpost. "Look!" said the Philistines. "The Hebrews are crawling out of the holes they were hiding in" (1 Samuel 14:11).

So I went in and looked, and I saw portrayed all over the walls all kinds of crawling things and detestable animals… (Ezekiel 8:10).

So the Lord God said to the serpent, "Because you have done this, cursed are you above all the livestock and all the wild animals! You will crawl on your belly and you will eat dust all the days of your life" (Genesis 3:14).

CROOKED: Distorted, not straight. Wickedness, not upright. Not of God. Crooked mind means a perverse mind.

Every valley shall be raised up, every mountain and hill made low; the rough ground [crooked] shall become level [straight], the rugged places a plain (Isaiah 40:4).

But those who turn to crooked ways the Lord will banish with the evildoers. Peace be upon Israel (Psalm 125:5).

They have left the straight way and wandered off to follow the way of Balaam son of Beor, who loved the wages of wickedness (2 Peter 2:15).

Good and upright is the Lord; therefore He instructs sinners in His ways (Psalm 25:8).

A man of perverse heart does not prosper; he whose tongue is deceitful falls into trouble (Proverbs 17:20).

With many other words he warned them; and he pleaded with them, "Save yourselves from this corrupt generation" (Acts 2:40).

CROSSING STREET: Changing perspective.

CROSSROADS: Vital choice to make or change in position. Options.

Symbolic Actions

1. ***Coming to a crossroad:*** Will come to a place to make a choice, or there will be the need to make a decision.

CROWN: Symbol of authority. Seal of power. Jesus Christ. To reign. To be honored.

Symbolic Actions

1. ***To be crowned:*** To be rewarded; to come to a place of honor or a place of authority.

2. ***To be given a crown:*** To be given power.

3. ***A crown of thorns:*** Humiliation or ridicule.

CRYING: Actual crying. A period of grief, outburst of sadness. Intense emotional expression.

CULTURAL CLOTHES: A call to the people of that culture; call to nation or that cultural affiliation.

CUP: Your portion in life; provision or responsibility.

Symbolic Actions

1. ***To receive a cup:*** May mean to bear your portion; assume your responsibility.

CURTAIN: Separation. Concealed. Hidden. End of something.

Symbolic Actions

1. ***Separated by a curtain:*** Unrevealed; not exposed.

2. ***Torn curtain:*** Barrier broken; limitation removed; exposed; no longer hidden.

Behind the second curtain was a room called the Most Holy Place (Hebrews 9:3).

CYMBALS: Instrument to praise God with. Could be used without genuine love.

DAM: Deliberate hold to generate the power of unity or gathering resources. Obstacle to flow. Reserve sustenance. An obstacle to the move of God. Temporary or deliberate holding back of some moves of God. Stillness.

DANCING: Worshiping God or idol.

Symbolic Actions

1. ***Worshiping:*** A time of joy or rejoicing.

DARKNESS: Lack of light. Without spiritual direction.

Symbolic Actions

1. ***Appearance of darkness:*** A place without the revelation of God, or where evil is celebrated.

2. ***A place of darkness:*** Coming to difficult time or season.

DAUGHTER: Gift of God. Ministry that is your child in the Spirit. The child herself. Someone with similar qualities.

DAYTIME: The opportune time. A time of light. Season of good deeds. Season when things are revealed or understanding is gained.

1. ***Dawn:*** The beginning of good times; the beginning of enlightening period; the beginning of better understanding.

DEAF: Not spiritually attentive. Not paying attention.

Symbolic Actions

1. ***Difficulty in hearing:*** May indicate issues in the person or around the person that hinders hearing in the Spirit.

2. ***To be completely deaf:*** The loss of ability to hear in the Spirit.

DEATH: What the Bible says more frequently about death is dying to self. Some measure of dying to self in an area. Separation from things of evil; actual physical death. The end of life on earth. Death is also overcoming the work of the flesh to resume communion with God.

DEER: Spiritual longing; symbol of hunger for the things of God; ability to take great strides; grace. Divine enabling. A deer is noted for swiftness, agility, and sure-footedness. Picture of graceful beauty.

As the deer pants for streams of water, so my soul pants for You, O God. My soul thirsts for God, for the living God. When can I go and meet with God? (Psalm 42:1-2).

A loving doe, a graceful deer—may her breasts satisfy you always, may you ever be captivated by her love (Proverbs 5:19).

The Sovereign Lord is my strength; He makes my feet like the feet of a deer, He enables me to go on the heights. For the director of music. On my stringed instruments (Habakkuk 3:19).

DEN: Busy doing the wrong thing.

DESERT: Training; lack; testing. A place of reliance on God.

DEW: Blessings of God for all seasons. Condensed, moisturized air formed in drops during still, cloudless night indicates divine blessing on the earth. The Word of God.

May God give you of heaven's dew and of earth's richness—an abundance of grain and new wine (Genesis 27:28).

It is as if the dew of Hermon were falling on Mount Zion. For there the Lord bestows His blessing, even life forevermore (Psalm 133:3).

Let my teaching fall like rain and my words descend like dew, like showers on new grass, like abundant rain on tender plants (Deuteronomy 32:2).

Therefore, because of you the heavens have withheld their dew and the earth its crops (Haggai 1:10).

DIAMOND: Something to engrave with, something hard; stubbornness. Diamond as a pen nib. Valuable, precious, gift, majesty, beauty.

DIARY: A record of something or record of encounters with God.

DIFFICULT WALKING: Difficult times of life. Facing opposition.

DINING ROOM: Feeding on the Word of God. A place of spiritual food. Table of the Lord.

DINOSAUR: Something in the distant past. Something big and terrible, but it has been dealt with by God. What used to be a major issue or hindrance in the past generation, but which no longer exists.

DIRTY CLOTH: False doctrine. Of a sinful nature.

Now Joshua was dressed in filthy clothes as he stood before the angel. The angel said to those who were standing before him, "Take off his filthy clothes." Then he said to Joshua, "See, I have taken away your sin, and I will put rich garments on you." Then I said, "Put a clean turban on his head." So they put a clean turban on his head and clothed him, while the angel of the Lord stood by (Zechariah 3:3-5).

DIRTY/DRY: Not pure spiritual things.

DIRTY/NEGLECTED: A place in need of attention.

DISEASE: Emotional upset, or it may be literal; bondage from the devil.

DITCH: Deception, a trap; fleshy desire.

DOCTOR: Jesus the healer. A person with healing anointing. Someone with caring service, minister. Symbol of healing anointing.

DOG: A gift that could be harnessed to do good, but may not be trusted. Could be versatile in function, but unpredictable. Man's best friend. A pet sin.

DONKEY: An enduring spirit, usable by the Lord. A gift that God could use if surrendered to Him.

DOOR: An opening. Jesus Christ. The way, a possibility, grace. Something to do with Jesus. Transition.

Symbolic Actions

1. *Closed door:* Hidden activities, or obstacle to progress.

2. *Open door:* Opportunity, grace for progress.

3. *Door keys:* Authority to create opportunity, power over the obstacle.

Set a guard over my mouth, O Lord; keep watch over the door of my lips (Psalm 141:3).

Therefore Jesus said again, "I tell you the truth, I am the gate [door] for the sheep. All who ever came before Me were thieves and robbers, but the sheep did not listen to them. I am the gate [door]; whoever enters through Me will be saved. He will come in and go out, and find pasture" (John 10:7-9).

After this I looked, and there before me was a door standing open in heaven. And the voice I had first heard speaking to me like a trumpet said, "Come up here, and I will show you what must take place after this" (Revelation 4:1).

DOWN: Spiritual descent/backslide. Falling away. Humiliation. Failure. Repositioning.

DRAGON: Satan. High demonic spirit. Great level of wickedness. Antichrist.

Then another sign appeared in heaven: an enormous red dragon with seven heads and ten horns and seven crowns on his heads (Revelation 12:3).

The great dragon was hurled down — that ancient serpent called the devil, or Satan, who leads the whole world astray. He was hurled to the earth, and his angels with him (Revelation 12:9).

DRAWING: Conceptualization. A means or method of illustration. To be fluent in expression. Doctrine, truth; deception.

DREAMING: To dream of dreaming means receiving a deeply spiritual message, or a much more futuristic message.

DRINKING: Receiving from the spiritual realm, whether good or bad. Receiving your portion in life; bearing your cross.

DRIVER: The one in command or control. The one who makes the decisions.

DRIVING IN REVERSE: Not going in correct direction with anointing.

DROUGHT: A period of lack without God.

DROWNING: Overcome by situation leading to depression. Overwhelmed to the point of self-pity.

DRUGS: Medication. Illicit drugs may mean counterfeit anointing.

DRUNKARD: Influenced by counterfeit source of

anointing. Self-indulgence or error. Uncontrolled lust.

DUST: Temporary nature of humanity. Frailty of man. Curse. Symbolically may refer to humiliation. Dust may often mean a large number of something.

Symbolic Actions

1. *Dust on the head:* Grief.
2. *Sitting in dust:* Repentance.
3. *Lying in dust:* Humiliation.
4. *Lying down in dust:* Death.
5. *Enemies licking the dust:* Defeat to the enemy.
6. *Shaking dust off the feet:* Rejection of a place.
7. *Throwing dust in the air:* Expression of shock.

The Lord God formed the man from the dust of the ground and breathed into his nostrils the breath of life, and the man became a living being (Genesis 2:7).

Your descendants will be like the dust of the earth, and you will spread out to the west and to the east, to the north and to the south. All peoples on earth will be blessed through you and your offspring (Genesis 28:14).

Shake off your dust; rise up, sit enthroned, O Jerusalem. Free yourself from the chains on your neck, O captive Daughter of Zion (Isaiah 52:2).

DYNAMITE: Holy Spirit "dynamus." Power/great spiritual power, whether good or bad.

Symbolic Actions

1. *Having dynamite in a car:* Ministry with great potential.

EAR: Symbolic of the prophet. Hearing spiritual things that either build up or tear down. Need to be paying more attention.

Symbolic Actions

1. *The ear that is listening:* Able to receive from God good instruction; eavesdropping; gossiper.
2. *The ear eager to listen:* Understanding the things of the Spirit.
3. *The ear that is dull or even deaf:* Not paying attention to what is being said by God or by man.
4. *A closed ear:* Deliberate refusal to listen even though the ear is capable of hearing; depending on what is closing the ear, being hindered by extraneous influence.
5. *The ear itching to hear:* Mind is not yielded to Jesus and prone to being deceived.

EARTHQUAKE: Sudden release of great power. Judgment. Ground-shaking changes. Great shock. A time of trial. Release from prison.

As when fire sets twigs ablaze and causes water to boil, come down to make Your name known to Your enemies and cause the nations to quake before You! For when You did awesome things that we did not expect, You came down, and the mountains trembled before You. Since ancient times no one has heard, no ear has perceived, no eye has seen any God besides You, who acts on behalf of those who wait for Him (Isaiah 64:2-4).

EAST: God's glory—the sun rising. East wind brings judgment/hardship.

EATING: Feeding on something, e.g. Word of God, or may be on something evil. Meditation and gaining greater understanding.

ECHO: Word coming back. Word sphere against living revealed. Repercussions.

EGG, SEED: Sustenance. The possibility for growth—potential and development in any manner, revelation. Delicate seed or promise.

EGYPT: Bondage/slavery. Refuge—Egypt was refuge for Jesus. Old sin. Pre-Christian life.

EIGHT: A new beginning. Circumcision of flesh.

EIGHTEEN: Bondage. God gave Israelites to Philistine for eighteen years.

He became angry with them. He sold them into the hands of the Philistines and the Ammonites, who that year shattered and crushed them. For eighteen years they oppressed all the Israelites on the east side of the Jordan in Gilead, the land of the Amorites (Judges 10:7-8).

And a woman was there who had been crippled by a spirit for eighteen years. She was bent over and could not straighten up at all. When Jesus saw her, He called her forward and said to her, "Woman, you are set free from your infirmity." Then He put His hands on her, and immediately she straightened up and praised God. Indignant because Jesus had healed on the Sabbath, the synagogue ruler said to the people, "There are six days for work. So come and be healed on those days, not on the Sabbath." The Lord answered him, "You hypocrites! Doesn't each of you on the Sabbath untie his ox or donkey from the stall and lead it out to give it water? Then should not this woman, a daughter of Abraham, whom Satan has kept bound for eighteen long years, be set free on the Sabbath day from what bound her?" (Luke 13:11-16).

Getting the Ammonites and Amelikites to join him, Eglon came and attacked Israel and they took possession of the City of Palms. The Israelites were subject to Eglon King of Moab for eighteen years (Judges 3:13-14).

ELECTRICITY: Spiritual power; potential for God's flow.

Symbolic Actions

1. ***Outlet for electricity:*** Possibility of being connected into the flow of the Holy Spirit.

2. ***Unplugged cord:*** Not connected to the power of the Spirit.

ELEMENTARY: The infant stage, not yet mature.

ELEVATOR: Moving up and down in levels of godly authority.

ELEVEN: Disorder confusion, lawlessness.

EMPLOYEE/SERVANTS: The one who is submitted to the authority. The actual person.

EMPLOYER/MASTER: Jesus. The authority, good or bad. Pastor. Evil leadership.

EXPLOSION: Quick outburst, generally positive. Sudden expansion or increase. Quick work or devastating change.

EYES: Seer's anointing. To desire; to eye something; lust of the eyes; to watch out. You are being watched.

Symbolic Actions

1. *Opened or enlightened eyes:* Knowledge or increase in knowledge.
2. *Bright eyes:* Intelligence or highly knowledgeable.
3. *Dim eyes:* Grief or lack of knowledge.
4. *Winking eyes:* Mockery or perversity; concealed intention or cunning person.
5. *Dissatisfied eyes:* Greed; lack of agreement or sign of disapproval.
6. *Closed eyes:* Ignorance; spiritually blind, mostly self-imposed.
7. *Steering eyes:* Being watched by someone, whether God or evil agent.
8. *Eyes in focus:* Thinking, thoughtfulness, no distraction.
9. *The eye of God:* God's omniscience and God's ability to watch over us.

FACE: Identity or characteristics. Image expression.

Symbolic Actions

1. *Angry-looking face:* Disagreement/hatred.
2. *Smiling face:* Agreement/friendship.
3. *Seductive face*: Temptation likely.

4. *The face of something:* The public image given to something.
5. *A person with the face of an animal:* A person with hidden characteristics of that animal.
6. *Animal with human face:* Spirit working through humans.

FACTORY: Structured service in God's vineyard.

Symbolic Actions

1. *Working in a factory:* To be useful in the corporate plan.
2. *Factory not working well:* Set-up not in order.
3. *Flooded factory:* Challenging situation.
4. *Factory on fire:* End of one phase; a significant change.

FALLING: Loss of support. Falling out of favor. Entering a time of trial/darkness/sin.

FAMILY: The Christian or spiritual family. Group of people in covenant or spirit of oneness; unified fellowship.

Symbolic Actions

1. *Family reunion:* A time of reconciliation; a time of love.
2. *Family home:* Something from the past, a place of love, security.
3. *Family feud:* Issues of the past concerning the family that have not been resolved. Needs prayers.

FAN: Stirring up of gifting. Something that brings relief or comfort. Make fire hotter. Increasing circulation.

Symbolic Actions

1. ***Fan not put on, though environment is hot:*** Not using all the resources at one's disposal; not tapping into the help of the Holy Spirit.

2. ***Faulty fan:*** Issues in the life of the dreamer hindering the flow of the Holy Spirit.

FARMER: One who plants, nurtures, cares for new Christians. Pastor capable of sowing and reaping harvest. Jesus Christ.

FATHER: Father God, supplier of needs. Natural father of the bloodline. One who provides. The head of home or place.

Symbolic Actions

1. ***Dreaming of abusive father:*** May indicate the need to forgive abuse of the past or someone presently in authority over the dreamer, may have the same spirit as the abusive father! You may have the same spirit of abusive father.

2. ***Dreaming of a caring and loving father:*** Someone like a loving father is around you or God's provision for you.

FATHER-IN-LAW: Father figure within the organization. An advisor, spirit of delegation, head of another organization.

FEATHERS: Protective spiritual covering. Weightless. Something with which to move in the spiritual realm. Presence of God.

He will cover you with His feathers, and under His wings you will find refuge; His faithfulness will be your shield and rampart (Psalm 91:4).

Say to them, "This is what the Sovereign Lord says: A great eagle with powerful wings, long feathers and full plumage of varied colors came to Lebanon. Taking hold of the top of a cedar, he broke off its topmost shoot and carried it away to a land of merchants, where he planted it in a city of traders. He took some of the seed of your land and put it in fertile soil. He planted it like a willow by abundant water, and it sprouted and became a low, spreading vine. Its branches turned toward him, but its roots remained under it. So it became a vine and produced branches and put out leafy boughs. But there was another great eagle with powerful wings and full plumage. The vine now sent out its roots toward him from the plot where it was planted and stretched out its branches to him for water" (Ezekiel 17:3-7).

FEEDING: To partake in a spiritual provision, good or evil.

Symbolic Actions

1. ***Feeding on good food:*** Good spiritual nourishment.

2. ***Feeding of food (not quite right):*** Nourishment that may not be of the right doctrine—watch out.

3. ***Bread with spider web within:*** Something that may look good, but has a trap at the end—'do not take the bribe'.

FEET: A spiritual walk, heart attitude.

F

Symbolic Actions

1. **Barefoot:** Humble before the presence of God. One inner state—spiritual poverty. Reverence to God.

2. **Diseased:** Spirit of offense.

3. **Kicking:** Not under authority or working against authority.

4. **Lame:** Crippled with unbelief, mindset, negative stronghold.

5. **Washing:** Humble; duty of Christians.

6. **Overgrown nails:** Lack of care, not in proper order.

7. **Washing feet:** Cleansing; sign of courtesy, repentance, and of servanthood.

8. **Cutting off feet:** Punishment.

Other Actions

1. **Everything under feet:** Dominion.

2. **Feet on solid rock:** Security.

3. **Falling down at one's feet:** Gratitude or submission.

4. **Trampling underfoot/placing feet on the neck:** Enemies as one's footstool; victory.

5. **Shaking dust off one's feet:** Rejection.

6. **As a lamp to our feet:** God's Word.

Therefore, I will mourn and lament, I will walk around barefoot and naked… (Micah 1:8).

at that time the Lord spoke through Isaiah son of Amoz. He said to him, "Take off the sackcloth from your body and the sandals from your feet." And

he did so, going around stripped and barefoot. Then the Lord said, "Just as my servant Isaiah has gone stripped and barefoot for three years, as a sign and portent against Egypt and Cush, so the king of Assyria will lead away stripped and barefoot the Egyptian captives and Cushite exiles, young and old, with buttocks bared—to Egypt's shame (Isaiah 20:2-4).

"Do not come any closer," the Lord warned, "Take off your sandals, for you are standing on holy ground" (Exodus 3:5).

The commander of the Lord's army replied, "Take off your sandals, for the place where you are standing is holy." And Joshua did so (Joshua 5:15).

FENCE: Protection. Security. Self-imposed. Limitation, stronghold.

How long will you assault a man? Would all of you throw him down—this leaning wall, this tottering fence? (Psalm 62:3).

Then the king of the North will come and build up siege ramps and will capture a fortified [fenced] city. The forces of the South will be powerless to resist; even their best troops will not have the strength to stand (Daniel 11:15).

FIELD: Life situation, things to do and accomplish. (Depends on the field and context.)

He gives rain on the earth, and sends waters on the fields (Job 5:10 NKJV).

FIFTEEN: Mercy, grace, liberty, rest, freedom.

FIFTY: Period or time of outpouring, such as Pentecost. Number of Holy Spirit/jubilee/freedom/liberty.

FIGHT: To struggle with, to agonize, to war or resist something.

Symbolic Actions

1. ***Fighting with a mad person:*** Prayers against issues that may result in troubled mind; struggle with situations which are difficult to resolve.

2. ***Fighting with an animal:*** Internal struggle with tendencies toward the characteristics of the animal, e.g., violence. May also mean the characteristics of the evil spirit coming against the dreamer.

Contend, O Lord, with those who contend with me; fight against those who fight against me (Psalm 35:1).

Fight the good fight of the faith. Take hold of the eternal life to which you were called when you made your good confession in the presence of many witnesses (1 Timothy 6:12).

Remember those earlier days after you had received the light, when you stood your ground in a great contest [fight] in the face of suffering (Hebrews 10:32).

FINGER: Means of discernment. Spiritual sensitivity, feelings.

Symbolic Actions

1. ***Pointed finger:*** Accusations, persecution, instructions, direction.

2. ***Finger of God:*** Work of God, authority of God.

3. ***Clenched:*** Pride.

4. ***Thumb:*** Apostle.

5. ***Index:*** Prophet.

6. ***Middle:*** Evangelist.

7. ***Small:*** Pastor.

FIRE: God's presence. Trial, persecution, burning fervency, emotion, longing, aching and craving. Power. Holy Spirit. Anger or judgment/punishment. Lake of fire, very different from tongue of fire.

Then the Lord rained down burning sulphur on Sodom and Gomorrah—from the Lord out of the heavens (Genesis 19:24).

FISH: New converts to the Lord. Newly recreated spirit of man. Miraculous provision of food.

"Come, follow me," Jesus said, "and I will make you fishers of men" (Mark 1:17).

FIVE: Grace related to the fivefold ministry.

FLASH: Revelation or insight.

FLEA: Not plentiful. Inconvenience. Subtlety.

FLOOD: Judgment on those who use whatever power they have to inflict violence on others. Sin judged. Overcome. To be overcome and unable to recover. That which the Holy Spirit will use as a standard.

From the west, men will fear the name of the Lord, and from the rising of the sun, they will revere His glory. For He will come like a pent-up flood that the breath of the Lord drives along (Isaiah 59:19).

I am going to bring floodwaters on the earth to destroy all life under the heavens, every creature that has the breath of life in it. Everything on earth will perish (Genesis 6:17).

F

FLOWERS: Man's glory of the flesh that is passing away. An offering. Glory of God. Beautiful expression of love. Renewal. Spring.

Symbolic Actions

1. *Lily of the valley:* Jesus.
2. *Rose:* Love, courtship, romance.

That fading flower, his glorious beauty, set on the head of a fertile valley, will be like a fig ripe before harvest—as soon as someone sees it and takes it in his hand, he swallows it (Isaiah 28:4).

But the one who is rich should take pride in his low position, because he will pass away like a wild flower (James 1:10).

For, "All men are like grass, and all their glory is like the flowers of the field; the grass withers and the flowers fall" (1 Peter 1:24).

FLY (A FLY): Evil spirits. Corruption. To be possessed by evil spirit. Results of unclean actions.

Symbolic Actions

1. *Something or place covered by flies:* Corruption that will breed unclean spirit and that will be exposed.

As dead flies give perfume a bad smell, so a little folly outweighs wisdom and honor (Ecclesiastes 10:1).

In that day the Lord will whistle for flies from the distant streams of Egypt and for bees from the land of Assyria (Isaiah 7:18).

FLYING: Highly powered by the Holy Spirit.

Symbolic Actions

1. *Repeated dreams of flying:* May indicate times in the dreamer's life that he experienced intervention of the Holy Spirit; constant flow of the Holy Spirit in the person's life; sign of potentials to move in the Spirit.

Who are these that fly along like clouds, like doves to their nests? (Isaiah 60:8).

Like birds hovering overhead, the Lord Almighty will shield Jerusalem; He will shield it and deliver it, He will "pass over" it and will rescue it (Isaiah 31:5).

He mounted the cherubim and flew; He soared on the wings of the wind (Psalm 18:10, 2 Samuel 22:11).

FOG: Not clear, uncertainty, concealed, vagueness. Wrath of God.

Symbolic Actions

1. *Driving into a fog:* Coming to a situation in the person's life that may challenge; a place where there may be uncertainties.

FOOD: Spiritual and physical nourishment, good or evil. To bring increase.

They should collect all the food of these good years that are coming and store up the grain under the authority of Pharaoh, to be kept in the cities for food (Genesis 41:35).

FOREIGNER: A person outside the Christian faith (not a citizen of Heaven). Someone to be taught and cared for, and brought into the covenant.

FOREHEAD: Thought process and reasoning. Revelations. Retaining and recalling ability. Commitment to God.

FOREST: Growth in life (depending on the context). Place of danger and darkness where one can be easily lost and harmed. Confusion and lack of direction, uncultivated. A land covered with trees that are naturally planted is different from a park where man's hand is more evident.

The battle spread out over the whole countryside, and the forest claimed more lives that day than the sword (2 Samuel 18:8).

FORTY: Testing period, season of trial.

Moses was there with the Lord forty days and forty nights without eating bread or drinking water. And he wrote on the tablets the words of the covenant—the Ten Commandments (Exodus 34:28).

I brought you up out of Egypt, and I led you forty years in the desert to give you the land of the Amorites (Amos 2:10).

Where for forty days he was tempted by the devil. He ate nothing during those days, and at the end of them He was hungry (Luke 4:2).

FOUR: Worldly creation; four corners of the world; four seasons. Global implication or the four Gospels.

FOURTEEN: Double anointing. Recreation. Reproduction. Passover.

FOX: A cunning spirit. Craftiness, secretly, or counter-productive.

Tobiah the Ammonite, who was at his side, said, "What they are building—if even a fox climbed up on it, he would break down their wall of stones!" (Nehemiah 4:3).

Catch for us the foxes, the little foxes that ruin the vineyards, our vineyards that are in bloom (Song of Solomon 2:15).

Your prophets, O Israel, are like jackals [foxes] among ruins (Ezekiel 13:4).

He replied, "Go tell that fox, 'I will drive out demons and heal people today and tomorrow, and on the third day I will reach my goal'" (Luke 13:32).

FREEZER: Storing spiritual food for future time.

Symbolic Actions

1. ***Rotten food in freezer:*** May indicate the need to forget and forgive hurts and pains of the past.

2. ***Discovering food and frozen food in the freezer:*** Recovering the reward of one's labor.

FRIEND: Brother or sister in Christ. Yourself. Showing to have similar qualities. Faithful person.

FROG: Evil spirit. Makes a lot of noise, boastful. Sorcery. Lying nature. Issuing curses.

If you refuse to let them go, I will plague your whole country with frogs (Exodus 8:2).

He sent swarms of flies that devoured them, and frogs that devastated them (Psalm 78:45).

Then I saw three evil spirits that looked like frogs; they came out of the mouth of the dragon, out of the mouth of the beast and out of the mouth of the false prophet (Revelation 16:13).

FRONT SIDE: Looking ahead, something in the future.

F

FRUITS: Source of nourishment. Means of increase. Reward of labor. To bear something or child. Harvest. Come to fullness. Gifts of the Spirit. Fruit of our labor. Fruit of the womb. Fruit of the Holy Spirit, consisting of all the Christian virtues.

FUEL: Source of energy. Source of food for the Spirit. Capable of reviving.

FURNACE: Source of heat, the heart, heated and painful experiences. Period of trial. Source of pruning. Center of holy activities.

Whoever does not fall down and worship will immediately be thrown into a blazing furnace (Daniel 3:6).

But as for you, the Lord took you and brought you out of the iron-smelting furnace, out of Egypt, to be the people of His inheritance, as you now are (Deuteronomy 4:20).

See, I have refined you, though not as silver; I have tested you in the furnace of affliction (Isaiah 48:10).

GALLOWS: A place of severe punishment. A place of nemesis or a place of death.

 So they hanged Haman on the gallows he had prepared for Mordecai. Then the king's fury subsided (Esther 7:10).

GAP: Breach. A break in continuity; weak spot. A loophole. An opening.

You have not gone up to the breaks in the wall to repair it for the house of Israel so that it will stand firm in the battle on the day of the Lord (Ezekiel 13:5).

I looked for a man among them who would build up the wall and stand before Me in the gap on behalf of the land so I would not have to destroy it, but I found none (Ezekiel 22:30).

GARAGE: Symbolic of storage. Potential or protection.

GARBAGE: Abandoned things. Corruption. Reprobate or unclean. Unclean spirit; departure from all that is godly. Something that is thrown away. Opinion of life without Jesus.

Symbolic Actions

1. *Getting something from garbage:* Time of lack, or poverty, pray to avoid; may mean lack of refreshment and resorting to the things of the past.

2. *Eating from the garbage:* Experiencing severe famine; period of insanity.

GARDEN: A piece of land that is cultivated, signifying the life situation as planned by God. Field of labor in life. Place of increase, fruitfulness, and productivity. A place of rest or romance. Life of believer as a garden watered by the Holy Spirit.

Now the Lord God had planted a garden in the east, in Eden; and there He put the man He had formed (Genesis 2:8).

The Lord will guide you always; He will satisfy your needs in a sun-scorched land and will strengthen your frame. You will be like a well-watered garden, like a spring whose waters never fail (Isaiah 58:11).

The woman said to the serpent, "We may eat fruit from the trees in the garden" (Genesis 3:2).

Then the man and his wife heard the sound of the Lord God as He was walking in the garden in the cool of the day, and they hid from the Lord God among the trees of the garden (Genesis 3:8).

GARDENING: An area of labor. A place of reward, increase, or harvest. Putting things in order.

"Satan and his cohorts draw inspirations from and worship the elements of the earth, but as Christians we must only relate to these elements from the place of dominion given to Adam by God and redeemed to us by the precious blood of Jesus Christ. Many religions are already in this grave error—the error of worshiping the elements of nature. Imagery and scenes of the monumental celebration of worshiping rivers and other elements abound in our days. Joshua and Moses both spoke from the place of dominion; Moses commanded the ground and it obeyed him, and Joshua spoke to the sun and it stood still. Jesus Christ in His humanity rebuked the wind and punished the fig tree. These instances represent the correct and proper engagement of the elements of nature in spiritual warfare. We should always operate from the place of dominion rather than from the place servitude to nature."

More information about the relational consequences of the curse is found in my book, *The Final Frontiers.*[2]

GARMENT: Covering.

<u>Symbolic Actions</u>

1. ***Clean:*** Honor or mantle. The glory of God upon a person.

2. ***Dirty:*** Mantle stained with sin.

3. ***To put on the garment of praise:*** A time of joy and thanksgiving.

Now Joshua was dressed in filthy clothes as he stood before the angel. The angel said to those who were standing before him, "Take off his filthy clothes." Then he said to Joshua, "See, I have taken away your sin and I will put rich garments on you" (Zechariah 3:3-4).

...a garment of praise instead of the Spirit of despair... (Isaiah 61:3).

GASOLINE: Source of energy. Faith-filled/prayer. Danger if not handled correctly, inflammable or potential for sudden explosion.

GATE: Doors, opening. Salvation. Entrance to something, such as building, grounds, or cities. In biblical days, business bargaining negotiations were conducted at the gates. Passage into or out of a place.

All these cities were fortified with high walls and with gates and bars, and there were also a great many unwalled villages (Deuteronomy 3:5).

For he breaks down gates of bronze and cuts through bars of iron (Psalm 107:16).

I will go before you and will level the mountains; I will break down gates of bronze and cut through bars of iron (Isaiah 45:2).

G

The twelve gates were twelve pearls, each gate made of a single pearl. The great street of the city was of pure gold, like transparent glass (Revelation 21:21).

The Lord loves the gates of Zion more than all the dwellings of Jacob (Psalm 87:2).

GAZELLE: To be sure-footed. Grace.

The three sons of Zeruiah were there: Joab, Abishai and Asahel. Now Asahel was as fleet-footed as a wild gazelle. He chased Abner, turning neither to the right nor to the left as he pursued him (2 Samuel 2:18-19).

GIANT: A powerful spiritual being, e.g., an angel or demon. A challenging situation. Something that arouses fear.

We saw the Nephilim there (the descendants of Anak come from the Nephilim). We seemed like grasshoppers in our own eyes, and we looked the same to them (Numbers 13:33).

GIRDLE: To prepare for use; might or potency. To be made ready to show strength; gathering together of the strength within you.

GLOVES: Something that protects the means of service. Something that fits into another thing; protects the means of productivity.

GOAT: Pertaining to foolishness. Carnal, fleshly. Not submitting to authority. Walking into sin. Need for repentance. Miscarriage of judgment, e.g., scapegoat.

GOLD: Of God. Seal of divinity. Honorable. God's glory. Faithful; endurance; holiness that endures. Symbol of honor

and high valor. Something valuable that endures.

I turned around to see the voice that was speaking to me. And when I turned I saw seven golden lampstands (Revelation 1:12).

Overlay it with pure gold, both inside and out, and make a gold molding around it (Exodus 25:11).

Make a table of acacia wood—two cubits long, a cubit wide and a cubit and a half high. Overlay it with pure gold and make a gold molding around it. Also make around it a rim a handbreadth wide and put a gold molding on the rim. Make four gold rings for the table and fasten them to the four corners, where the four legs are. The rings are to be close to the rim to hold the poles used in carrying the table. Make the poles of acacia wood, overlay them with gold and carry the table with them. And make its plates and dishes of pure gold, as well as its pitchers and bowls for the pouring out of offerings. Put the bread of the Presence on this table to be before Me at all times (Exodus 25:23-30).

In a large house there are articles not only of gold and silver, but also of wood and clay; some are for noble purposes and some for ignoble (2 Timothy 2:20).

GOVERNOR: The person who has the power in the place. Spiritual leader in the church, or of a geographical region or an evil principality. Authority; rulership; reigning.

Symbolic Actions

1. ***Governor's statement or order:*** The statement from a person of high spiritual standing (power

and authority), either of God or demonic power.

For our struggle is not against flesh and blood, but against the rulers, against the authorities, against the powers of this dark world and against the spiritual forces of evil in the heavenly realms (Ephesians 6:12).

GRANDCHILD: Blessing passed on from previous generation. Spirit passed on from the past generation. Generation inheritance, good or bad. Heir. Spiritual offspring of your ministry.

GRANDMOTHER: Generational authority over the person. Spiritual inheritance. Past wisdom or gifting. Parent church of a church plant.

GRAPES: Fruit of the Promised Land. Successful agriculture or success in life. Pleasant to the eyes. Evidence of fertility.

Symbolic Actions

1. *Carry grapes:* Evidence of rich inheritance or future prosperity.

2. *Spoilt grapes:* Corrupted promises/wisdom.

When I found Israel, it was like finding grapes in the desert; when I saw your fathers, it was like seeing the early fruit on the fig tree. But when they came to Baal Peor, they consecrated themselves to that shameful idol and became as vile as the thing they loved (Hosea 9:10).

"The days are coming," declares the Lord, "when the reaper will be overtaken by the plowman and the planter by the one treading grapes. New wine will drip from the mountains and flow from all the hills" (Amos 9:13).

Still another angel, who had charge of the fire, came from the altar and called in a loud voice to him who had the sharp sickle, "Take your sharp sickle and gather the clusters of grapes from the earth's vine, because its grapes are ripe" (Revelation 14:18).

When they reached the Valley of Eshcol, they cut off a branch bearing a single cluster of grapes. Two of them carried it on a pole between them, along with some pomegranates and figs (Numbers 13:23).

GRASS: Divinely provided; something meant to be maintained. Life. God's Word in seed form. Word of God; sustenance for animals.

Symbolic Actions

1. *Dried:* Death to the flesh through repentance.

2. *Mowed:* Disciplined obedience.

GRASSHOPPER/LOCUST: A devastating situation. Instrument of God's judgment. Low self-esteem.

Symbolic Actions

1. *A swarm of locust:* Destroyer of harvestable income; destruction of livelihood.

GRAVEYARD/GRAVE: Old tradition. Cultural reserve. Death. Demonic influence from the past. Buried potentials. Darkness, hell.

Symbolic Actions

1. *Digging the grave:* Discovering the hidden from ancient past.

2. *Burying something in the graveyard:* The end

of one phase or putting an end to something.

Let's swallow them alive, like the grave, and whole, like those who go down to the pit (Proverbs 1:12).

All your pomp has been brought down to the grave, along with the noise of your harps; maggots are spread out beneath you and worms cover you (Isaiah 14:11).

They came out of the tombs, and after Jesus' resurrection they went into the holy city and appeared to many people (Matthew 27:53).

GREY: Uncertainty, compromise, consisting of good and bad mixture.

Symbolic Actions

1. ***Coming to a grey zone:*** Coming to a time or place of uncertainty.

GREEN: Life, good or evil. Provision. Rest and peace.

Symbolic Actions

1. ***Green vegetation:*** Richness of life.

2. ***Green light:*** Time to proceed— obstruction has been removed.

GROOM: Christ. Marriage. Headship.

Symbolic Actions

1. ***Appearance or arrival of a groom:*** The manifestation of the work of Christ.

2. ***Waiting for a groom:*** The waiting for the manifestation of the words of Jesus in one's life, in the process of intimating with Jesus.

3. ***Delayed arrival of a groom:*** Hindrances to the work of Jesus

in a person's life, issues hindering the ability to intimate with God.

GUARD: Ability to keep on the right path. Spirit of protection/to be vigilant.

Symbolic Actions

1. ***Faceless and protective guard:*** Holy Spirit.

2. ***Forceful and frustrating guard:*** Situation or something with the power to limit the person.

GUEST: Spiritual messenger. An angel or evil presence.

Symbolic Actions

1. ***Arrival of a guest:*** New situation, new demand, or new challenge.

2. ***Unwanted guest:*** Difficult and unpleasant challenges.

3. ***Forceful guest:*** Situation that may try to impose itself on the person.

GUN: Instrument of demonic affliction. Spoken words that wound. Power of words in prayer. Dominion through speaking the Word of God.

Symbolic Actions

1. ***To be shot with a gun:*** Powerful force/words coming against the person, curses or attacks that may be difficult to neutralize or reverse.

2. ***Holding a gun:*** Equipped with the power to face the challenge.

HAIL: Means of judgment against God's enemies. Something that can cause considerable damage to crops, property, and life. Means of punishment for the wicked.

Symbolic Actions

1. ***Falling hail:*** Time of punishment/judgment or destruction.

Therefore, at this time tomorrow I will send the worst hailstorm that has ever fallen on Egypt, from the day it was founded till now (Exodus 9:18).

When Moses stretched out his staff toward the sky, the Lord sent thunder and hail, and lightning flashed down to the ground. So the Lord rained hail on the land of Egypt; hail fell and lightning flashed back and forth. It was the worst storm in all the land of Egypt since it had become a nation (Exodus 9:23-24).

I will execute judgment upon him with plague and bloodshed; I will pour down torrents of rain, hailstones and burning sulphur on him and on his troops and on the many nations with him (Ezekiel 38:22).

HAMMER: Living Word. Preaching the Word hard and fast. Capable of breaking something to pieces. Something that smoothes strong things such as metal or rocks. For building.

Symbolic Actions

1. ***To hammer something:*** To bring to bear a power force into a situation.

2. ***Hammer coming against one:*** Powerful words or challenges coming against a person.

The craftsman encourages the goldsmith, and he who smoothes with the hammer spurs on him who strikes the anvil. He says of the welding, "It is good." He nails down the idol so it will not topple (Isaiah 41:7).

"Is not My word like fire," declares the Lord, "and like a hammer that breaks a rock in pieces?" (Jeremiah 23:29).

HANDS: Means of service. Means of expressing strength.

Symbolic Actions

1. ***Clapping:*** Joy and worship.
2. ***Fist:*** Pride in one's strength; anger.
3. ***Hands covering face:*** Guilt or shame.
4. ***Holding hands:*** In agreement.
5. ***Left hand:*** Something spiritual.
6. ***Raised hands:*** Surrender or worshiping.
7. ***Right hand:*** Oath of allegiance. Means of power, of honor. Natural strengths.
8. ***Shaking hands:*** Coming to an agreement.
9. ***Stretched out hands:*** Surrender.
10. ***Trembling:*** To fear, spirit of fear; anxiety. Awe at God's presence.
11. ***Under thighs:*** In oaths.
12. ***Washing:*** Declaring innocence; to dissociate oneself.

HARLOT: Prostitute. A tempting situation. Something that appeals to your flesh. Worldly desire. Pre-Christian habit that wants to resurrect. Enticement.

Symbolic Actions

1. ***Appearance of a harlot:*** A tempting situation likely; enticement likely.
2. ***Affairs with a harlot:*** To fall or succumb to one's fleshy desires, sexual and non-sexual.

3. *Negotiating with a harlot:* Handling situation that would be enticing; being seduced by evil spirit.

4. *Repeated dreams of scenes involving harlot:* Unbroken root of sexual lust in person's life; undue preoccupation with sexual desires.

HARP: If used for God, praise and worship in Heaven and on the earth. Instrument for praise and worship. Could be used for idolatry.

Symbolic Actions

1. *Playing harp:* Praise or worship of God; thanksgiving situation.

2. *Hanging a harp:* Situation that causes one to not be able to praise God (see Ps. 137:1-2).

HARVEST: Seasons of grace. Opportunities to share the gospel. Fruitfulness. Reward of labor and action.

Symbolic Actions

1. *A time of harvest:* The season of reward; times of opportunity.

2. *Poor harvest:* Things falling short of expectation.

HAT: Covering, protection, mantle, crown. Protection of the head.

Symbolic Actions

1. *Putting on a new hat:* New mantle or a new level of protection or a new wave of vanity to be avoided.

2. *To remove one's hat:* To demonstrate or show respect to another person, or a sign of submission.

HEAD: Lordship, authority. Jesus/God. Husband. Pastor. Boss. Mind, thoughts.

Symbolic Actions

1. *Anointed:* Set apart for God's service.

2. *Hands on:* Signifying sorrow.

3. *Laying on of hands:* To be imparted with anointing.

*"Strange or bizarre events are common to the manifestation of the seer's anointing. Some of the dramatization of the prophecies given to Ezekiel were weird, and Ezekiel's life was obviously complicated by these unusual requirements. Not only did God require him to deliver a very unpopular message, but He also instructed Ezekiel to dramatize the messages in bizarre ways—such as shaving his **head,** cooking with cow manure, and lying outside beside a model of Jerusalem and on one side for 390 days."*

Additional interesting information about this and other topics are shared in my book, *The Watchman.*[3]

HEDGE: God's safeguard, security, safety. Literally means loose stonewall without mortar. Protection. Supernatural or prophetic protection. God as hedge around His people. Where the very poor find shelter.

Symbolic Actions

1. *A broken or fallen hedge:* Fault in the protection.

2. *Snake on the hedge:* Possible enemy infiltration of one's defenses.

Why have you broken down its walls [hedge] so that all who pass by pick its grapes? (Psalm 80:12).

He then began to speak to them in parables: "A man planted a vineyard. He put a wall around it, dug a pit for the winepress and built a watchtower. Then he rented the vineyard to some farmers and went away on a journey" (Mark 12:1).

HEEL: The crushing power.

HELICOPTER: Spirit-powered for spiritual warfare. One-man ministry.

Symbolic Actions

1. *Military helicopter:* Powerful or effective prayer life, or challenging enemy attack.

2. *Attacking war helicopters:* Forces coming against one.

3. *Military helicopters fighting for the dreamer:* Powerful intercessor on dreamer's behalf.

HELMET: The awareness and inner assurance of salvation. God's promise.

Symbolic Actions

1. *Putting on a helmet:* Protection of vital part of one's life/evidence and protection of the salvation.

2. *Walking around in construction site without helmet:* Not adequately protected for possible danger.

HIGH SCHOOL: Moving into a higher level of walk with God; high level of training/equipping. Capable of giving the same to others.

HIGHWAY: Holy way; the path of life. Truth of God, Christ; Predetermined path of life, or path of life that enjoys high volume usage. May lead to good or evil destinations.

Symbolic Actions

1. *Dead end:* A course of action that will lead to nothing, that which will not persist.

2. *Gravel (stony ground):* Difficult path, a course that is not straight.

3. *Muddy:* Difficult path; not clear, uncertain path.

4. *Construction:* In preparation, change, not ready.

HILLS: A place of exaltation. Uplift high above the natural. Throne of God. Mount Zion. An obstacle.

Symbolic Actions

1. *Ascending a hill:* Coming to a place of prayers or spiritual exaltation.

2. *Descending a hill:* Be watchful not to lose ground spiritually.

HIPS: Reproduction. Relating to reproduction or supporting structure. May indicate seduction.

Symbolic Actions

1. *Exposed hips:* Enticement or seduction.

2. *Water up to hip level:* Faith to impart the next generation/spiritual offspring.

HONEY: Sweet; strength; wisdom. Spirit of God. The abiding anointing. The sweet Word of our Lord. Standard of measure for pleasant things. The best product of the land. Abundance. A land flowing with milk and honey. Food in times of scarcity.

Then their father Israel said to them, "If it must be, then do this: Put some of the best products of the land in your bags and take them down to the man as a gift—a little balm and a little honey, some spices and myrrh, some pistachio nuts and almonds" (Genesis 43:11).

He will not enjoy the streams, the rivers flowing with honey and cream (Job 20:17).

So I have come down to rescue them from the hand of the Egyptians and to bring them up out of that land into a good and spacious land, a land flowing with milk and honey—the home of the Canaanites, Hittites, Amorites, Perizzites, Hivites and Jebusites (Exodus 3:8).

Honey and curds, sheep, and cheese from cows' milk for David and his people to eat. For they said, the people have become hungry and tired and thirsty in the desert (2 Samuel 17:29).

HORNS: The source of anointed power. The power of a king, evil power.

Symbolic Actions

1. ***Horns anointed:*** Powerful authority.

2. ***Horns against one:*** Powers coming against one.

HORSE: Of great strength, powerful in warfare. Spirit of tenaciousness, not double-minded. A ministry that is powerful and capable of competing. Strength under control, such as meekness. God's judgment.

Symbolic Actions

1. ***Horse that kicks:*** Threatening, or opposition to the agreed terms.

2. ***Black:*** Lack.

3. ***Bay (flame-colored):*** Power, fire.

4. ***Pale:*** Spirit of death.

5. ***Red:*** Danger; passion; blood of Jesus.

6. ***White:*** Purity or righteousness.

7. ***Blue:*** Spiritual.

8. ***Brown:*** Repented, born-again.

9. ***Green:*** Life, mortal.

10. ***Grey:*** In between black and white. Vague, hazy.

11. ***Orange:*** Danger, evil.

12. ***Pink:*** Flesh. Relating to desire and decision based on the mind.

13. ***Purple:*** Something related to royalty. Noble in character. Riches.

14. ***Yellow:*** Gift from God; cowardliness, fear.

HOSPITAL: A gift of healing/anointing or caring or love. Edifying others. A place for treatment.

Symbolic Actions

1. ***Visiting a hospital:*** Possible welfare or healing anointing in the person's life.

2. ***As patient in a hospital:*** Pray against physical afflictions; needing some assistance.

3. *As a patient in a mental hospital:* Situation that may challenge one's emotional or mental stability; needing help to resolve mental conflict.

HOTEL: A place of gathering, a temporary place of meeting. A transit place of meeting, church; a transit situation.

Symbolic Actions

1. *Lodging in a five star hotel:* Place of elevation, an exalted place imminent.

HOUSE: One's spiritual and emotional house. Personality. Church.

Symbolic Actions

1. *Parents' house:* Influences from the past or parents.

2. *Cracked walls:* Faulty defenses, physical afflictions.

3. *Leaking roof:* Not adequately covered spiritually.

HUSBAND: Jesus Christ. Actual spouse.

Symbolic Actions

1. *Dreaming of a husband:* Someone with authority over the dreamer/may mean the literal husband.

2. *Being pursued by a husband who is loving/kind in real life:* Jesus Christ reaching out to the person.

3. *Ex-husband:* Previous head over the dreamer; something that had control over dreamer in the past.

INCENSE: Prayer, worship, praises. Acceptable unto God.

Symbolic Actions

1. *Burning incense:* Prayers.

IRON: Something of strength, powerful; strict rules; powerful strongholds.

1. *Broken iron bars:* Broken limitation/deliverance.

IRONING: The process of correction by instructions, teaching. To talk things over. Working out problem relationships. Turning from sin.

ISLAND: Something related to the island. What the island is known for, or its name.

ISRAEL: The nation of Israel. The Christian community; the redeemed ones; authority that comes from God over men; people of God.

JERUSALEM: The establishment of peace. Chosen place by God. The city of God.

JEWELRY: Valuable possessions. God's people. Gifted person who has received abilities from the Lord. Something or person valued by the dreamer. Not to be given to those who will not value it.

JOINT: Difficult to separate except by the Word of God.

For the Word of God is living and active, sharper that any double-edged sword, it penetrates even to dividing soul and spirit, joints and marrow; it judges the thoughts and attitudes of the heart (Hebrews 4:12).

H
I
J

JUDGE: Father God. Authority. Anointed to make decisions. Jesus Christ. Unjust ruler.

Symbolic Actions

1. *A just and fair judge:* The rule of God.

2. *Before unfair judge:* Evil powers influencing one's situation.

KANGAROO: Something that is not based on the truth. Prejudiced. Rushing to conclusion.

Symbolic Actions

1. *Before a kangaroo court:* Unfair judgment may be at hand or imminent.

KEY: The authority to something, claim to ownership. Prophetic authority. Kingdom authority.

Symbolic Actions

1. *Given keys:* Power and authority, e.g., the keys of David.

2. *To lose one's keys:* To be watchful over the authority given to one so as not to lose it.

KISS: Coming to agreement, covenant. Seductive process. Enticement; deception or betrayal; betrayal from a trusted friend or brother/sister in Christ.

Symbolic Actions

1. *To be kissed:* A time of agreement/a time of romance. Beware of a possible time of enticement.

KITCHEN: A place of preparing spiritual food. Hunger for the work of God. A place of spiritual nourishment.

KNEELING: Surrender; praying; art of submission.

Symbolic Actions

1. *Kneeling:* A praying position; a position for surrender.

2. *Water up to the knees:* Faith is maturing; spirit of prayers/intercession.

KNEES: Reverence; prayerfulness; submission.

KNIVES: Word of God.

Symbolic Actions

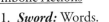

1. *Sword:* Words.

2. *Being stabbed:* Words coming against you; attack from the enemy; accusations.

3. *Being pursued with a knife:* If by a priest/spiritual leader, it may mean the need to read the Word of God; if by an evil person, it is a warning to pray against accusations.

LADDER: A means of change in spiritual position. Means of escape from captivity.

Symbolic Actions

1. *Climbing on a ladder:* May mean go up higher in the Spirit.

2. *Angels on the ladder:* Divine messengers bring blessings from Heaven, and taking prayer requests to Heaven.

LAMB/SHEEP: Jesus. Believer. Gentleness. Blamelessness. Vulnerability. People of God, people with teachable spirit. People who easily follow and obey the Shepherd. People who trust and depend on the Shepherd.

LAME: Shortcomings. A flaw in one's walk with God. Limitation.

1. ***To be lame:*** A situation where one is limited.

LAMP: Source of light. Inward part of man or spirit. Holy Spirit.

1. ***Lamp stand:*** A person who is yielded to God and available to be a channel of light to others.

2. ***Lamp stand without light:*** Potentially capable of giving light, but not actually giving light.

3. ***Lamp stand without oil:*** A potentially gifted person, but no anointing; anointed person without intimate relationship with God.

LAND: Inheritance. Promise given by God.

Symbolic Actions

1. ***Newly cleared land:*** Newly revealed area of God's promise.

2. ***Ripe on the land:*** Fruitful work of the ministry.

3. ***Bare earth or dust:*** Curse, bareness.

4. ***Neglected, unwanted land:*** Neglected promise or inheritance.

LAUGH: Rejoicing. Joy or sarcasm.

Symbolic Actions

1. ***People laughing at you:*** Pray against time of ridicule.

2. ***Laughing loudly:*** God filling the dreamer's mouth with laughter.

LAUGHING: Outburst of excitement or joy.

LAVA: Enemy.

LAWYER: Jesus Christ. The accuser of brethren. Pertaining to legalism. Mediator.

LEAD (METAL): Heavy burden; heavy thing.

LEAVEN: Sin that spreads to others. False belief system. Symbol of rapid, penetrating power.

LEAVES: Trees with healthy leaves are planted by the rivers of life. Healing of the nation.

Symbolic Actions

1. ***Dry leaves:*** Pressures of life.

LEFT: That which is of the Spirit. That which is not natural with man. God manifested through the flesh of man.

Who has gone into heaven and is at God's right hand—with angels, authorities and powers in submission to Him (1 Peter 3:22).

LEGS: Means of support. Spiritual strength to walk in life.

Symbolic Actions

1. ***Female legs:*** Power of enticement.

2. ***One leg in:*** Indecision, wanting the best of both worlds; greed; not firm.

LEOPARD: Powerful, either good or bad. Permanent. Unchanging character.

L

LEMON: Something gone sour; bitter doctrine. Hard to accept teaching.

LEVIATHAN: Ancestral spirit of demonic nature; difficult to eliminate—only God can deal with it.

LIBRARY: A place of knowledge. Schooling. Wisdom.

Symbolic Actions

1. *Finding something in a library:* That which will be available through knowledge.

2. *Going to a library:* Coming to a season of knowledge or inquisitiveness.

3. *Not finding the required book;* not correctly positioned to obtain the required knowledge.

LICE: Concerted attempt to smear you. Accusation, shame.

Symbolic Actions

1. *Lice on the head of a person:* May mean the person is a pathological liar or someone who should not to be trusted.

LIFTING HANDS: Total surrender. Giving worship to God.

LIGHT: Illumination on the established truth. No longer hidden; to show forth.

Symbolic Actions

1. *Dim light:* Showing the need for the fullness of the knowledge of the Word.

2. *Absence of light:* Lack of understanding, absence of God.

3. *Small lamp or flashlight:* Walking in partial grounding of the Word, or pocket of wisdom.

LIGHTNING: God's voice; the Lord interrupting an activity to get man's attention. Something happening very quickly. God's power and mystery. Divine weapon. God's finger of judgment.

Your thunder was heard in the whirlwind, Your lightning lit up the world; the earth trembled and quaked (Psalm 77:18).

He will prepare His deadly weapons and shoot His flaming arrows (Psalm 7:13).

He fills His hands with lightning and commands it to strike its mark (Job 36:32).

LIMOUSINE: Call of God. Pride or exhibitionism. High calling of God, which could give rise to pride. Watch against tendency to be proud.

LION: Conquering nature of Jesus (majority of the time). A powerful spirit, good or bad.

Symbolic Actions

1. *Head of a lion without a body:* Jesus Christ.

2. *Baby lions:* Christians.

LIPS: Word of God. Enticement. Means of testifying. Offering. Speak falsehood/accusation.

LIVING ROOM: Part of your personality that is opened to others to see.

Symbolic Actions

1. ***Stains on the wall:*** Indicate issues that need to be rectified in the life of the dreamer.

2. ***Re-painting the wall:*** Rebuilding public image.

LOST (DIRECTION): Indicating inner confusions or indecision in the dreamer.

MACHINES: Power and might of the Spirit. That which is powered by supernatural force.

MAGGOT: Filthiness or the lust of the flesh. Corruption.

1. ***Presence of maggot:*** Indicates signs of decay, moral fault, or social corruptions.

MAN (UNKNOWN): A spiritual messenger, either God's messenger or evil. Jesus.

MANNA: God's miraculous provision. Coming directly from God. Glory of God. Bread of life. Provision of God that is miraculous; something to survive on. Emergency package to survive on and something that offers not much choice or quality. Something that tests commitment to God.

MAP: Word of God. Instruction. Direction, the logo word. May be given inwardly as rhema word.

MARBLE: Beauty. Majesty of God. Something strong and beautiful.

MARK: Something that distinguishes. Symbol. To set apart. Mark of God or devil.

MARRIAGE: Going deeper into things of God (intimacy). A covenant process. Actual marriage. Jesus Christ's union with the Church.

Symbolic Actions

1. ***Getting married:*** May indicate going higher with Jesus Christ.

2. ***Soiled marriage clothes:*** Issues in the life of the person, need to be taken care of or issues hindering the ability to intimate with Jesus.

3. ***Issues arising during marriage:*** Hindrances that may come against one's effort to go higher with Jesus.

MEAT: Something meant for the spiritually mature. Strong doctrine.

Symbolic Actions

1. ***Chewing meat:*** Season of understanding; deep things of God.

2. ***Hard to chew meat:*** Doctrine that may be difficult for the person to understand.

I gave you milk, not solid food, for you were not yet ready for it. Indeed, you are still not ready (1 Corinthians 3:2).

But solid food is for the mature, who by constant use have trained themselves to distinguish good from evil (Hebrews 5:14).

MERCY SEAT: Indicating the mercy of God. Kingship of the Lord. The throne of God. God's love.

MICE: Something that eats up valuables secretly. Devourer. Spirit of timidity or fear. Evil that can multiple rapidly.

L

M

MICROPHONE: Amplification of the Word of God. Preaching anointing. The prophetic ministry. Ability to influence many people.

Symbolic Actions

1. *Using a microphone:* Supernatural ability to reach/influence other people.

2. *Using a faulty microphone:* Not having the anointing or influence to impart the message.

MICROSCOPE: Need to look more carefully. Obtaining clearer vision. To magnify something to get more details or scritiny.

Symbolic Actions

1. *The presence of a microscope:* Dreamer is being scrutinized or scrutiny is imminent.

2. *Using a microscope:* Being concerned about details, in the process of verification.

MICROWAVE OVEN: Lack of patience. Looking for easy option. Quick acting process, need for alteration. Desiring or engaging in quick acting process. May be caution to avoid lack of patience, or indicating the need for acceleration.

MIDDLE/JUNIOR HIGH: Medium level equipping by God. Post-elementary or foundational level in Christianity, ready for discipleship. An intermediate stage of the situation.

MILK: Good nourishment. Elementary teaching.

MIRROR: Something that enables you to look more closely. Reflecting on something. Word of God revealing the need for change. Self-consciousness; vanity.

Symbolic Actions

1. *Clear mirror:* The Word of God, bringing clarity to something.

2. *Darkly stained mirror:* Poor perception; spiritual mysteries; prophetic utterance not yet fully understood.

3. *Image in the mirror not what is expected:* Disparity between reality and perception.

MISCARRIAGE: To lose something at the preparatory stage, whether good or bad. Plans aborted.

Symbolic Actions

1. *To dream of experiencing a miscarriage:* Pray against termination of some plan, usually something good, which is expected.

2. *Premature delivery:* Often may indicate supernatural intervention; may mean divine acceleration; may be presumptuous situation running ahead of the scheduled time.

MONEY: God's favor. Spiritual and natural wealth. Spiritual authority, power. Man's strength. Greed.

Symbolic Actions

1. *Getting money:* Increase in favor; may be literal.

M

2. ***Short of money:*** A season of lack of money.

3. ***Bundles of money:*** A season of abundance of money/favor.

4. ***International currency:*** Favor or privilege from that country.

MOON: Indicating the rulership. To reign in the night seasons. Light of God at dark season of life. Something bright in darkness.

Symbolic Actions

1. ***Moon to blood:*** The church being prosecuted.

2. ***Moon in dream:*** Dawn of light in otherwise dark season; light in darkness; Lordship of God in the night or difficult season.

God made two great lights—the greater light to govern the day and the lesser light to govern the night. He also made the stars (Genesis 1:16).

MORNING: The beginning of something. Light of God after dark season of life. Sins being revealed. Rejoicing, prayer time, time to lay a good foundation.

Symbolic Actions

1. ***Morning in a dream:*** Solution coming to the problem, or the beginning of God's intervention; approaching a pleasant season.

MOTH: Insect that dwells in dark places. Causes loss by deceitfulness. Corruption and deterioration.

Symbolic Actions

1. ***Moth in dream:*** That which destroys earthly valuables; some-

thing eating up the substance of the matter.

Do not lay up for yourselves treasures on earth, where moth and rust destroy and where thieves break in and steal; but lay up for yourself treasures in heaven, where, neither moth, nor rust destroys and where thieves do not break in and steal (Matthew 6:19-20).

MOTHER: The Church. Jerusalem. Actual person. Spiritual mother. Carer/teacher.

Symbolic Actions

1. ***Mother in a dream:*** The church or fellowship giving the dreamer spiritual nourishment.

MOTHER-IN-LAW: A church that is not the dreamer's church. Actual person. False teacher.

MOTOR: Spirit-powered personal ministry.

Symbolic Actions

1. ***Engine and Battery:*** The source of power and of the anointing.

2. ***Motorcycle:*** Loner. Show-off pride or exhibitionism.

MOUNTAIN: Great power and strength, whether good or bad. A place of revelation or meeting with God or God's glory. Obstacle, difficulty.

MOUTH: Instrument of witnessing, good or bad. Speaking evil or good words. Something from which come the issues of life. Words coming against you.

MOVING: Change in spiritual and emotional

M

well-being; Changing situation; a change is imminent.

MOVING VAN: A time or period of change, either in the natural or in the spirit.

MUSIC: Praise and worship, good or bad. Flowing in spiritual gift. Teaching. Admonishing. A message—nature of music determines whether its meaning is godly or worldly or demonic.

Symbolic Actions

1. *The type of music:* Indicates season in the dreamer's life associated with that song.

2. *Title or words of the music:* The divine message in the revelation.

MUSTARD SEED: Faith. Value or power of faith. Sowing in faith. Word of God. God's promise.

He replied, "Because you have so little faith. I tell you the truth, if you have faith as small as a mustard seed, you can say to this mountain, 'Move from here to there' and it will move. Nothing will be impossible for you" (Matthew 17:20).

NAILS: Makes something more permanent. The way Jesus dealt with our sins.

Symbolic Actions

1. *To nail something:* Applying security or making the situation more secure.

2. *To bring to conclusion.*

NAME: The identity of something; designate; rank or status. Meaning of the name.

Symbolic Actions

1. *To be called a name different from real name:* May indicate what the dreamer will become; something being conferred in the Spirit on the dreamer or the true identity or dispaity between reality and perception.

NATION: Could represent the characteristics of the nation. The calling related to the nation. The actual nation; what the nation is known for.

Symbolic Actions

1. *America:* Cowboy.

2. *France:* Romance.

3. *Germany:* Hardworking. World War.

4. *Jews:* Business minded.

NECK: Stubborn, strong-willed, the thing that leadership rests on.

1. *Stiff-necked:* Rebellious.

2. *Long neck:* Nosy, inquisitiveness.

NEST: Security that is not real; God's place of rest. Something that harbors great potential. A place of rest. A place of maturity.

NET: To trap, ensnare. The plans of the enemy. To win souls.

Symbolic Actions

1. *To be held back by a net:* Possible ensnaring situation.

2. *Using a net:* Means of reaching lost souls, something that could ensnare others.

NEW: New condition.

NEWSPAPER: Proclamation. Bringing something to the public. Prophetic utterance.

NIGHT: Time of trial or difficulty. Lack of God's lights or understanding. Without involvement of the Spirit.

Symbolic Actions

1. *Night in a dream:* Season of difficulty or trials.

NINE: Fruit of the Spirit or gift of the Spirit; harvest.

NINETEEN: Faith, repentance.

NOISE: Irritation that is intrusive. Sound that draws attention.

1. *Not able to hear because of noise in the place:* That which makes it difficult to hear God properly.

NORTH: Refers to great powers that will come.

NOSE: Discerning spirit. Intruding into people's privacy. Discernment, gossiper.

NOSEBLEED: Strife. Need to strengthen your discerning.

OCEAN: Masses of people.

Symbolic Actions

1. *On the ocean:* Influencing the nations of the world; imparting great number of multitudes.

OIL: The anointing. Prosperity. Holy Spirit. Grace/mercy of God. Medicine. Joy.

Symbolic Actions

1. *Oil on the head:* Impartation of divine power; conferment of divine authority.

2. *Oil on the feet:* Prosperity.

…You anoint my head with oil… (Psalm 23:5).

About Asher he said:"Most blessed of sons is Asher; let him be favored by his brothers, and let him bathe his feet in oil" (Deuteronomy 33:24).

when my path was drenched with cream and the rock poured out for me streams of olive oil (Job 29:6).

OLD: Old ways. That which will give way to the new.

OLD MAN: Pre-Christian self. Spirit of wisdom. Former things that are passing away. What is coming from the past. That which needs to give way for the new.

ONE: New beginning. Unity (divinity). Deity.

ONE HUNDRED: Fullness. Hundredfold reward. The promise.

Isaac planted crops in that land and the same year reaped a hundredfold, because the Lord blessed him (Genesis 26:12).

ONE HUNDRED AND FIFTY: The promise and the Holy Spirit.

ONE HUNDRED AND TWENTY: The beginning of the work of Holy Spirit.

In those days Peter stood up among the believers (a group numbering about a hundred and twenty) (Acts 1:15).

N
O

ORANGE: Warning, danger ahead, caution needed.

OVEN: The heart of the matter. Of high intensity. Fervency. Something of high intensity/fervency that needs proper supervision or control. The required training for maturity.

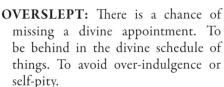

OVERSLEPT: There is a chance of missing a divine appointment. To be behind in the divine schedule of things. To avoid over-indulgence or self-pity.

PAINTING: Creating a new image. Renew or revamp. Renewing the image of something. Revamping one's public relations. To cover up something. To exaggerate something.

PARACHUTING: Bail out, escape and flee. To bail out of danger, with the help of the Holy Spirit.

Symbolic Actions

1. *Faulty parachute:* Presumption.

2. *Parachute difficult to open:* A dangerous complication.

PARENTS: In authority, to nurture, to instruct, pass down, keys to wealth. The source or origin of something. Something inherited from the past generation.

Houses and wealth are inherited from parents... (Proverbs 19:14).

PARK: A place of rest, worship, tranquility. A temporary place. A place of peace.

A place of romance. A place of meditation, exercise, and leisure.

Symbolic Actions

1. *A car park:* Major place for interdenominational gathering; multinational organizations (e.g., United Nations).

PARROT: Something that mimics. Not the original. Beware of imitation, or counterfeit. What is being heard is not the truth.

PATH: The path of life. Personal walk with God. Directions in life. Path is the way to something.

Symbolic Actions

1. *Crooked path:* The way that is full of trouble/difficulties, lack of clarity.

2. *Making the path straight:* To bring correction necessary; to be on the right way; to make more clear.

PEACOCK: Something of pride. Generally, adornment of royal courts.

PEARL: Something of value. Established truth of God. Glory of Heaven.

Symbolic Actions

1. *To find a pearl:* To discover something valuable or truth.

2. *To be given a pearl:* Divine provision of something valuable, such as salvation, blessings, or spiritual gifts.

PEN/PENCIL: Pertaining to writing. Words that are written. To make permanent.

Symbolic Actions

1. *Dream of a pen:* The gift of writing in the dreamer or may be scribe anointing; the gift to bring revelations to the things of God.

PERFUME: Aroma of something. The glory of God. Fragrance of Holy Spirit or anointing.

Symbolic Actions

1. *To buy a perfume:* Increase or a new dimension to one's anointing or acceptance.

2. *Adulterated perfume:* Something interfering with one's anointing, resulting in non-acceptance, adulterated anointing.

PICTURE: Something relating to images. To keep in memory. To honor.

Symbolic Actions

1. *Frames:* Mindset; mentality.
2. *Golden frames:* Divine seal.
3. *Old frame:* Outdated.

PIG: Unclean spirit. Spirit of religion. Caged by mindset. Phony, not trustworthy. Selfish, hypocritical.

Symbolic Actions

1. *A pig in the sitting room:* Allowing the spirit of religion to color how people see the person.

2. *Pigs in a cage:* An evil spirit, selfishness; spirit of religion that is held back from attacking the person.

PILLAR: The main support of something. Spiritual and natural. Foundational truths. What something stands on, the foundation of something. The main support of a ministry.

PINK: Flesh or natural desire. Not showing great passion for the things of God.

PIT: Enticement, trap; a hole on the pathway.

Symbolic Actions

1. *To see a pit on one's path:* Caution—a trap ahead.

2. *To fall in a pit:* To be ensnared or trapped, requires prayer.

PLATTER: Something on which to present things.

1. *To be given something on a platter:* To receive something without much struggle/effort; to receive something without the adequate training.

PLAY: Life competition. Spiritual warfare/contention.

1. *To be involved as a player in a game:* Most often indicates the reflection of the state of play of life.

PLAYING: Reflective of true-life situation. The game of life.

PLOUGH: Preparing the heart to receive the Word of God. Cracking fallow grounds hardened by sin.

POSTAGE STAMP: The seal of authority. Authorization. Empowered.

P

"In the days of the prophet Jeremiah, the people did not take cognizance of this fact and so sometimes in *desperation, they compelled the prophets to tell their dreams whether they had received any or not. To save face, these prophets made up stories even though they did not receive dreams or visions. This is obviously dangerous because unless God gives the revelation, the prophet receives nothing. In a way, therefore, the prophetic person is like a postman and should not feel bad if the mail is scanty because God can sometimes instigate this and the heavenly mail may be few."*

More information about prophets, dreams, and visions is found in my book, *The Watchman.*[4]

POST-MORTEM: Examination of what has happened. Giving testimony.

POT: The vessel or container, e.g., tradition. A person.

PREGNANCY: In the process of reproducing; preparatory stage. The promise of God. The Word of God as seed. Prophetic word.

Symbolic Actions

1. *Labor pains:* Process of birthing something, good or bad. Final stages of trial or preparation; wilderness period.

PREACHER/PASTOR (PRIEST AND PROPHET): A person who represents God. Timely message from God. Spiritual authority.

PRISON: A place where a person is restricted and where human rights are limited. A place of bondage or confinement. Often indicates a place of depression, areas of stronghold bondage.

PRISONER: The lost soul. A period of emotional depression in one's life.

PURPLE: Related to royalty. Kingly anointing or authority.

One of those listening was a woman named Lydia, a dealer in purple cloth from the city of Thyatira, who was a worshiper of God. The Lord opened her heart to respond to Paul's message (Acts 16:14).

PURSE/WALLET: Treasure, heart, personal identity; precious and valuable.

Symbolic Actions

1. *Empty:* Bankrupt.

2. *Stolen purse:* Beware of wrong decision that could lead to loss, something that will take away what is valuable.

3. *Misplaced purse:* Beware of misplaced priorities or wrong decisions/wrong investment.

RABBIT: Evil spirit. Something capable of carnal multiplication.

RADIO: Continuous broadcasting of news, nuisance. Prophetic utterance. Teaching gospel.

Symbolic Actions

1. *Listening to radio broadcast:* Something that is currently imparting the dreamer.

2. ***What is being said on the radio:*** The essence of what is being imparted to the person, good or bad.

3. ***Difficulty in tuning to the right frequency:*** Not being in the frame of mind to receive. Something extraneous interfering with one's ability to hear what is being said in the spirit.

RAFT: Without purpose or direction.

RAGS: Poverty, humility, or lack.

RAILROAD TRACK: Tradition, unchanging habit. Stubborn. Caution, danger.

RAIN: Blessings, God's Word. Outpouring of the Spirit. Hindrance, trial or disappointment.

Symbolic Actions

1. ***Drought:*** Lack of blessing. Absence of the presence of God.

RAINBOW: Sign of God's covenant. Sign of natural agreement.

RAINING: The blessing from God. Testing time or trial.

RAM: Satanic or of the occult.

Symbolic Actions

1. ***Fighting or playing with ram:*** Beware of evil spirit that needs to be warded off or character defect to be curtailed.

RAPE: Violate one's integrity or sanctity. Defile. To treat as a harlot.

Now Dinah, the daughter Leah had borne to Jacob, went out to visit the women of the land. When Shechem, son of Hamor the Hivite, the ruler of that area, saw her, he took her and violated [raped] her (Genesis 34:1-2).

The sons of Jacob came upon the dead bodies and looted the city where their sister had been defiled (Genesis 34:27).

But they replied, "Should he have treated our sister like a prostitute?" (Genesis 34:31)

RAT: Rubbish (sin), left out to eat. A passion that is unclean or something that feeds it.

REAP: Harvest. Reward of effort, good or bad.

REAPING: Reward of labor.

RED: Passion. Blood of Jesus. Strong feeling, danger, anger. Heated emotion. Zeal, enthusiasm.

REED: Weakness: spiritual or natural. Too weak to be relied on; not firm, coward.

REFRIGERATOR: Where "issues" are kept. Heart issues. Motivation. Thoughts. Storing up spiritual food for the right time.

Symbolic Actions

1. ***Stored food:*** Things stored in the heart.

2. ***Spoiled food:*** To harbor a grudge, unclean thoughts or desires.

REFUGE: The place of protection, safety, or security.

REINS: A means of control or to restrain.

RENDING: Sorrow or disagreement. To tear apart as sign of anger. Grief, repentance, sorrow, disagreement.

REST: A state of stillness or inactivity, tranquility. A place where you can receive from God. Laziness.

RESTAURANT: A place of choice regarding the spiritual food you need. A place where the fivefold ministry is taught.

RESTING: Not in activity; lax.

RICE: Sustenance. Poor sustenance. Earthly. Lacking flavor.

RIGHT: Natural inclination, authority, or power. What you are naturally able to do.

RIGHT TURN: Natural change.

RING: Never-ending, unchanging, uninterrupted. Unity of purpose in a place. Covenant relationship. Relating to God's authority.

Symbolic Actions

1. *Wedding ring:* Symbol of our covenant with God. Marriage between man and woman.

2. *Engagement ring:* Promise. Sign of commitment.

3. *Rings worn as jewelry:* Vanity, worldliness.

RIVER: Movement of God. Flow of the Spirit. River as an obstacle. Trial.

Symbolic Actions

1. *Deep:* Deep things of God.

2. *Muddy:* Operating in mixtures, flesh and spirit.

3. *Dangerous currents:* Difficulty in moving in the flow of the Spirit. Danger ahead.

4. *Dried up:* Lack of the presence of God, traditions or legalism. Empty of spiritual power.

ROACHES: Unclean. Something that can cause and thrive on sin.

ROBE: The true covering from God. Righteousness; right standing with God.

ROCK: Jesus Christ; solid foundation. Obstacle. A place of refuge. Stumbling block.

And drank the same spiritual drink; for they drank from the spiritual rock that accompanied them, and that rock was Christ (1 Corinthians 10:4).

He is the Rock, His works are perfect, and all His ways are just. A faithful God who does no wrong, upright and just is He (Deuteronomy 32:4).

ROCKET: A ministry or person with great power or potential for deep things of the Spirit. Capable of quick take-off and great speed.

ROCKING: Reflective.

ROCKING CHAIR: Long standing in nature, intercession, recollection, prayer, relaxation, old age.

ROD: Staff or scepter of authority. To guard. Discipline.

Even though I walk through the valley of the shadow of death, I will fear no evil, for You are with me; Your rod and Your staff, they comfort me (Psalm 23:4).

The rod of correction imparts wisdom, but a child left to himself disgraces his mother (Proverbs 29:15).

ROLLER COASTER: Something that moves up and down. Swings of season or moods. Faith needing more faith.

ROLLER SKATES: Skillful walk with God. Speedy progress. Fast but may be dangerous.

ROOF: Relating to the mind, thinking, meditation. Spiritual rather than the natural. Revelations from above; covering.

ROOT: The origin of something. The source of something. The heart of the matter, the means of sustenance or survival, the motives.

Symbolic Actions

1. *To see the root of something:* The main cause or service of something.

2. *To retain the root or stump:* To retain the ability to survive despite the situation.

A shoot will come up from the stump of Jesse; from his roots a Branch will bear fruit (Isaiah 11:1).

In the morning, as they went along, they saw the fig tree withered from the roots (Mark 11:20).

ROPE/CORD: Something used in binding, either in covenant or in bondage.

Symbolic Actions

1. *To see rope/cord:* Source of covenant or possibly source of bondage.

2. *To be tied with rope:* Limitations, bondage, to render impotent.

ROUND (SHAPE): Never-ending. Favor, love, or mercy.

ROWBOAT: A ministry that intervenes for others. Offering earnest prayers.

ROWING: Working at something, to labor in spirit. Travailing in the spirit. Hard work.

RUG: To cover up something. Protection.

RUNNING: Trying to catch up with something. Hard work. Race.

Symbolic Actions

1. *Running:* Participating in the race of life (the race set before each one of us).

SACRIFICE: To give up something. To lay down one's life for another. Something to cover up or wash away or to give up something.

But King David replied to Araunah, "No, I insist on paying the full price. I will not take for the Lord what is yours, or sacrifice a burnt offering that costs me nothing" (1 Chronicles 21:24).

SALT: Something that adds value. Something that preserves. Something that purifies. To make to last or to make more palatable.

You are the salt of the earth. But if the salt loses its saltiness, how can it be made salty again? It is no longer good for anything, except to be thrown out and trampled by men (Matthew 5:13).

Let your conversation be always full of grace, seasoned with salt, so that you may know how to answer everyone (Colossians 4:6).

SALT WATER: To add flavor. To cleanse.

R
S

SANCTUARY: A sacred place. A place set apart for spiritual offering, sacrifices. A place of immunity or rest. An asylum, a refuge. A sacred place reserved for communion with God, or gods or evil power.

Symbolic Actions

1. *To come to Sanctuary in a dream:* To come to a place of higher relationship with God.

Observe My Sabbaths and have reverence for My sanctuary. I am the Lord (Leviticus 26:2).

On the contrary, it is to be a witness between us and you and the generations that follow, that we will worship the Lord at His sanctuary with our burnt offerings, sacrifices and fellowship offerings. Then in the future your descendants will not be able to say to ours, "You have no share in the Lord" (Joshua 22:27).

SAND: Symbolic of work of flesh. Not suitable for foundation. Numerous. Seeds. Promises.

But you have said, "I will surely make you prosper and will make your descendants like the sand of the sea, which cannot be counted" (Genesis 32:12).

But everyone who hears these words of mine and does not put them into practice is like a foolish man who built his house on sand (Matthew 7:26).

SCEPTER: Staff of authority. Office. Staff of sovereignty.

The scepter will not depart from Judah, nor the ruler's staff from between his feet, until He comes to whom it belongs and the obedience of the nations is His (Genesis 49:10).

Your throne, O God, will last for ever and ever; a scepter of justice will be the scepter of Your kingdom (Psalm 45:6).

SCHOOL: A ministry with teaching anointing.

Symbolic Actions

1. *Classroom:* Training period, a place of teaching.

SCORPION: Highly demonic spirit or any evil spirit. Something that could be poisonous.

SEA: Great multitude of people. Nations of the world. Unsettled, as the mark of sea. Something by which to reach the nations. Great obstacle.

Four great beasts, each different from the others, came up out of the sea (Daniel 7:3).

SEACOAST: Transition phase. Borderland.

SEAL: Confirmation or authenticity or guarantee. Mark of God's approval or belonging. Mark of evil.

SEA OF GLASS: Peaceful and clear. Symbol of revelation. Stillness/transparency.

SEAT: The power base. Rulership. Authority. Coming to rest. A place of mercy.

SEED: Word of God. Promise. Something capable of giving rise to many or greater things, whether good or bad.

SERPENT: Symbol of satan. Kingdom of the world. An accursed thing or cunning.

S

Symbolic Actions

1. **Snake (if hung on a pole, stick, tree):** Emblem of Christ on the cross.

2. **Viper:** Gossip or persecution.

3. **Python:** Spirit of divination.

4. **Rattles:** Evil words against the dreamer.

5. **Fangs:** Dangerous intentions coming against the dreamer.

6. **Cobra:** Vicious verbal attack, capable of spreading far, capable of forming hooded neck and can send off poison from a distance.

7. **Anaconda:** Attacks that will drain the dreamer of spirituality. Kills by squeezing out air (spiritual life) from the victim.

SEVEN: The number of perfection, earthly completion, or finished work. Rest. A time of blessing or holy time. Freedom.

Remember the Sabbath day by keeping it holy. Six days you shall labor and do all your work, but the seventh day is a Sabbath to the Lord your God. On it you shall not do any work, neither you, nor your son or daughter, nor your manservant or maidservant, nor your animals, nor the alien within your gates. For in six days the Lord made the heavens and the earth, the sea, and all that is in them, but He rested on the seventh day. Therefore the Lord blessed the Sabbath day and made it holy (Exodus 20:8-11).

These are the laws you are to set before them: If you buy a Hebrew servant, he is to serve you for six years. But in the seventh year, he shall go free, without paying anything (Exodus 21:1-2).

SEVENTEEN: Spiritual process of maturation. Not yet matured.

This is the account of Jacob. Joseph, a young man of seventeen, was tending the flocks with his brothers, the sons of Bilhah and the sons of Zilpah, his father's wives, and he brought their father a bad report about them (Genesis 37:2).

SEVENTY: Impartation of God's spirit/increase/restoration.

The Lord said to Moses:"Bring Me seventy of Israel's elders who are known to you as leaders and officials among the people. Have them come to the Tent of Meeting, that they may stand there with you. I will come down and speak with you there, and I will take of the Spirit that is on you and put the Spirit on them. They will help you carry the burden of the people so that you will not have to carry it alone (Numbers 11:16-17).

SEVENTY-FIVE: Period for purification and separation. Abraham was seventy-five when he set out from Haran.

So Abram left, as the Lord had told him; and Lot went with him. Abram was seventy-five years old when he set out from Haran (Genesis 12:4).

SEWAGE: Something that carries waste. Good appearance but carrying waste within. Waste could defile flesh.

SEWING: Putting together something. Amendment; union; counseling.

SEXUAL ENCOUNTER: Soulish desires.

Symbolic Actions

1. **With old lover:** May indicate desire for old life.

"The spirit of Jezebel is a high level form of the spirit of witchcraft. This spirit controls by remote manipulation. It is also the power of control from the unseen realm. This spirit is very influential as it is a major ruling power in the kingdom of darkness. The spectrum of activities of this devious spirit ranges from mild cases when the victims are not aware of being used, to deep-rooted evil in people who are basking in the euphoria of this evil spirit's power. Predominantly, females are more commonly involved, but this spirit has no gender preference. The springboard for this evil spirit is sexual exploitation. Jezebel targets spiritual leadership, especially the prophetic and intercessory ministries."

For more about the Jezebel spirit and other spirits coming against the local church, read my book, *The Watchman.*⁵

SHADOW: Not the real thing, reflection of something. The spiritual cover. A place of safety, security. Only partially illuminated. Poor resemblance of. Delusion or imitation. Imperfect or lacking the real substance.

Symbolic Actions

1. *Dark shadows:* Demons.

He who dwells in the shelter of the Most High will rest in the shadow of the Almighty (Psalm 91:1).

SHEPHERD: Jesus Christ, God. Leader, good or bad. Ability to separate goat from sheep. Selfless person. Protector.

Symbolic Actions

1. *Sheep:* Belonging to the Lord. To go astray, wander.

2. *Sheepdog:* To bring together. Instrument used by God for good means of control.

Then he blessed Joseph and said, "May the God before whom my fathers Abraham and Isaac walked, the God who has been my shepherd all my life to this day" (Genesis 48:15).

I am the good shepherd. The good shepherd lays down His life for the sheep (John 10:11).

Wherever I have moved with all the Israelites, did I ever say to any of their rulers whom I commanded to shepherd My people Israel, "Why have you not built Me a house of cedar?" (2 Samuel 7:7).

For you were like sheep going astray, but now you have returned to the Shepherd and Overseer of your souls (1 Peter 2:25).

SHIELD: A protective thing. God's truth. Faith in God. Something trusted to protect based on past experience.

After this, the word of the Lord came to Abram in a vision: "Do not be afraid, Abram. I am your shield, your very great reward" (Genesis 15:1).

In addition to all this, take up the shield of faith, with which you can extinguish all the flaming arrows of the evil one (Ephesians 6:16).

The Lord is my strength and my shield; my heart trusts in Him, and I am helped. My heart leaps for joy and I will give thanks to Him in song (Psalm 28:7).

SHIP: A big ministry capable of influencing large numbers of people.

Symbolic Actions

1. *Battleship:* Built for effective spiritual warfare.

2. *Crashing:* End of the ministry or end of one phase.

3. *Fast:* Operating its great power.

4. *Large:* Large area of influence.

5. *Sinking:* Out of line with the purpose of God, losing spiritual control.

6. *Small:* Small or personal.

7. *On dry ground:* Without the move of the Spirit. Moving more with the work of flesh. A miracle if moving on dry ground.

SHOES: Readiness to spread the gospel. Knowledge of the Word of God.

Symbolic Actions

1. *Boots:* Equipped for spiritual warfare.

2. *Does not fit:* Walking in something you're not called to.

3. *Giving away:* Depending on the context, equipping others.

4. *High heels:* Seduction/ discomfort.

5. *Need of shoes:* Not dwelling on the Word of God. In need of comfort or protection.

6. *New shoes:* Getting new understanding of the Gospel. Fresh mandate from God.

7. *Putting on:* Preparation for a spiritual journey.

8. *Slippers:* Too comfortable or too lax.

9. *Snowshoes:* Faith, walking in the Spirit, supported by faith in the Word of God.

10. *Taking off:* Honoring God, ministering to the Lord.

11. *Taking someone else's shoes off:* To show respect.

12. *Tennis shoes:* Spiritual giftedness. Running the race of life.

And with your feet fitted with the readiness that comes from the gospel of peace (Ephesians 6:15).

SHOPPING CENTER: Ministry that has multi-faceted giftedness within its midst.

Symbolic Actions

1. *Marketplace:* Coming to a place of choices that may lead to not being single-minded. Could also indicate the various methods of the enemy strategies.

SHOULDER: The responsibility; the authority.

Symbolic Actions

1. *Broad shoulders:* Capable of handling much responsibility.

2. *Bare female shoulders:* Enticement.

3. *Drooped shoulders:* Defeated attitude. Overworked; overtired. Burned-out.

SHOVEL: Digging up something. To smear someone.

S

SICKLE: Reaping. Word of God. The harvest.

SIEVE: To separate the impure from the pure. Trial or testing.

For I will give the command, and I will shake the house of Israel among all the nations as grain is shaken in a sieve, and not a pebble will reach the ground (Amos 9:9).

SIFT: Separation by testing.

Simon, Simon, Satan has asked to sift you as wheat (Luke 22:31).

SIGN: A witness of something. A foreshadow. To draw attention to something.

Symbolic Actions

1. *Crossroad/intersection:* A place for decision. Time for change.

2. *Stop sign:* Stop and pray for guidance.

3. *Yield:* A sign of submission.

SIGNATURE: Commitment and ownership or take responsibility for.

SILVER: Symbol of redemption. Understanding, knowledge. Something of valor, worldly knowledge, betrayal. Furnace of affliction.

SINGING: The words of the song = message from God. Rejoicing. Heart overflow.

SISTER: Sister in Jesus Christ. Actual person. Similar qualities in you.

SISTER-IN-LAW: Same as sister. A Christian in another fellowship. A relationship without much depth. Actual person. Person with similar qualities.

SITTING: A place of authority, position in power. Throne of God or seat of satan.

SIX: The number of man. Symbol of satan. Pride in the work of man.

SIX-SIX-SIX: Number of satan. Mark of the beast. Number of human hubris.

This calls for wisdom. If anyone has insight, let him calculate the number of the beast, for it is man's number. His number is 666 (Revelation 13:18).

SIXTEEN: Set free by love. The power of love or salvation. Sixteen characteristics of love mentioned in First Corinthians 13.

SKIING: Stepping out in faith. The power of faith. Smooth riding in God is provision. Making rapid process.

SKINS: The covering of; something closely linked and difficult to separate.

SKY: Above the natural. God's presence. Related to God or high things of the Spirit.

SKYSCRAPER: A ministry or person that has built-up structure to function on multi-level. A church or person with prophetic giftedness. High level of spiritual experience. Revelation.

SLEEPING: Being overtaken. Not being conscious of something. Hidden. Laziness. State of rest; danger. Out of control.

Symbolic Actions

1. *Overslept:* In danger of missing a divine appointment. Prone to laziness.

SMILE: Sign of friendliness. Act of kindness. To agree with.

SMILING: Sign of friendship. Seductive process.

SMOKE: The manifested glory of God. Prayers of saints. Praise; worship. Sign of something. Hindrance.

SNAKE: Backbiting; divination; false accusations; false prophecies. Gossip; long tales; slander. See *Serpent*.

SNARE: A trap. The fear of man. Bring into bondage.

SNOW: Favor of God. Totally pure.

Symbolic Actions

1. ***Dirty snow:*** No longer pure.

He spreads the snow like wool and scatters the frost like ashes (Psalm 147:16).

As the rain and the snow come down from heaven, and do not return to it without watering the earth and making it bud and flourish, so that it yields seed for the sower and bread for the eater (Isaiah 55:10).

As I looked, thrones were set in place, and the Ancient of Days took His seat. His clothing was as white as snow; the hair of His head was white like wool. His throne was flaming with fire, and its wheels were all ablaze (Daniel 7:9).

SOAP: Something that cleans. Forgiveness. Interceding for others.

SOCKS: Reflective of the state of the heart as the fertile ground for the Word of God. Peace. Protection of the feet.

Symbolic Actions

1. ***White socks:*** Heart and walk before God that is unblemished.

2. ***Dirty or torn socks:*** Heart and walk before God that is blemished.

SOLDIER: Spiritual warfare. Call for more prayers fasting/worship. A period of trial or persecution.

SON: A ministry or gifting from God. Actual child has similar traits to you. Child of God.

SOUR: Corrupted. False.

SOUTH: A place of peace. The source of refreshment. The natural inclination.

SOWING: Planning for the future, good or bad. The art of spreading the Word of God.

SPEAKING: Revealing the contents of your heart. Proclamation.

SPEAR: Words, whether good or bad. Word of God. Evil words, curses.

SPIDER: An evil spirit that works by entrapping people. False doctrine.

Symbolic Actions

Spider web: Seen or unseen, but imminent danger.

SPOT: A fault. Contamination.

Symbolic Actions

1. ***Without spot:*** Glorious church.

SPRINKLING: Spiritual change by washing away dirt. Cleansing, purifying, consecrating.

S

SQUARE: Tradition. Mindset. Worldly and blind to the truth.

STADIUM: Tremendous impact.

STAFF: Symbol of authority. Part of authority.

STAIRS: Means of bringing about changes.

Symbolic Actions

1. *Down:* Demotion; backslide; failure.

2. *Guardrail:* Safety; precaution; warning to be careful.

STANDING: Firmness in faith. Committed to the belief. Not finished.

Symbolic Actions

1. *Straight:* No crookedness but in the correct direction.

STARS: Important personality. Great number. Descendant. Supernatural. Jesus Christ.

Symbolic Actions

1. *Falling star:* Apostate church.

STONE: Jesus Christ—chief cornerstone. Hard and sturdy foundation. Word of God. Defiance.

STONING SOMEONE: Involved in malicious accusation of others. Unforgiveness. Act of wickedness.

Dragged him out of the city and began to stone him. Meanwhile, the witnesses laid their clothes at the feet of a young man named Saul (Acts 7:58).

STORM: Trial. Testing period. Satanic attacks.

Symbolic Actions

White storm: God's power, revival.

Before very long, a wind of hurricane force, called the "northeaster", swept down from the island. The ship was caught by the storm and could not head into the wind; so we gave way to it and were driven along (Acts 27:14-15).

STRAW: Worthless.

STRAIGHT: To be fixed in attitude. Going in the right direction.

STUMBLING: To make mistakes, to fail, in error. Lack of the truth.

SUICIDE: Act of self-destruction, foolishness. Sinful behavior. Pride. Lack of hope.

SUITCASE: On the move. Transition. Private walk with God.

SUMMER: Time of harvest. The opportune time. Fruits of the Spirit.

SUN: The light of God. The truth. Glory of God.

SUPPER: The body and blood of Jesus. Marriage supper. God's provision. God's enabling power.

SWEATING: Signs of intense work of the flesh. Much work without Holy Spirit. Difficult and agonizing time.

SWEEPING: Getting rid of sinful things. Cleaning the place from evil. The process of making clean. Repentance. Correcting process.

SWEET: Something gratifying. Reflection in the Word of God. Communion with the Spirit.

SWIMMING: Moving in spiritual gifts. Prophetic utterance.

SWIMMING POOL: Church, place, or provision available for moving in the Spirit.

Symbolic Actions

1. *Dirty or dry:* Corrupt or apostate.

SWING: Moving in ups and downs of life.

SWINGING: Full flow of peace.

Symbolic Actions

1. *High:* Overindulgence. Take unnecessary risks.

SWORD: Word of God. Evil words.

TABLE: A place of agreement or covenant. To iron out issues. Altar. Community, fellowship.

You prepare a table before me in the presence of my enemies. You anoint my head with oil; my cup overflows (Psalm 23:5).

TAIL: The end of something. The least of something. The last time.

TAR: Covering; bitterness.

TARES: Children of darkness. Evil ones. Degenerates. Deceptive, e.g., grains.

TASTING: To experience something, good or bad. Judging something. Try something out.

TEA: A place or time of rest. Revelation or grace of God. Soothing.

TEACHER: Jesus Christ. Holy Spirit. Gift of God.

TEARS: Emotional sowing; mostly distress, but could represent brokenness. Joy.

TEETH: Wisdom, gaining understanding; to work something out.

Symbolic Actions

1. *Baby teeth:* Childish. Without wisdom or knowledge.

2. *Broken teeth:* Inexperienced. Difficulty in coming to understanding.

3. *Brushing teeth:* Gaining wisdom or understanding.

4. *False teeth:* Full of reasoning of this world instead of pure spiritual understanding.

5. *Toothache:* Tribulation coming; heartache.

TELEPHONE: Spiritual communication, good or evil. Godly counsel.

TELESCOPE: Looking or planning for the future. To make a problem appear bigger and closer.

TELEVISION: Visionary revelations or prophetic dreams. Prophetic utterance.

TEMPLE: A place of meeting with God. A place of refuge. God's habitation. Human body.

TEN: Law, government order and obligation. Responsibilities. Pastor. Testing trial.

S
T

TENT: Temporary covering. Flexible.

 TEN THOUSAND: Army of the Lord. Battle readiness.

And he said: "The Lord came from Sinai, and dawned on them from Seir; He shone forth from Mount Paran, and He came with ten thousands of saints; From His right hand came a fiery law for them" (Deuteronomy 33:2 NKJV).

Now Enoch, the seventh from Adam, prophesied about these men also, saying, "Behold, the Lord comes with ten thousands of His saints" (Jude 1:14 NKJV).

TERMITES: Something that can cause hidden destruction.

THIEF: Satan. Deceiver. Secret intruder. Unexpected loss.

THIGH: Strength; flesh. To entice. Oath taken.

THIRTEEN: Rebellion; backsliding.

THIRTY: Beginning of ministry. Mature for God's work. Jesus was thirty when He began His ministry; Joseph was thirty when he became prime minister.

THORNS: Evil disturbance. Curse. Gossip.

THOUSANDS: Maturity approved.

THREE/THIRD: Witness; divine fullness; Godhead. Triumph over sin. Resurrection. Conform.

THREE HUNDRED: Chosen by God. Reserve of the Lord.

The Lord said to Gideon,"With the three hundred men that lapped I will save you and give the Midianites into your hands. Let all the other men go, each to his own place." So Gideon sent the rest of the Israelites to their tents but kept the three hundred, who took over the provisions and trumpets of the others. Now the camp of Midian lay below him in the valley (Judges 7:7-8).

THRONE: A seat of power. A place of authority. God's throne. Evil throne.

At once I was in the Spirit, and there before me was a throne in heaven with someone sitting on it. And the one who sat there had the appearance of jasper and carnelian. A rainbow, resembling an emerald, encircled the throne (Revelation 4:2-3).

THUMB: Apostolic; authority; soul power.

THUNDER: Loud signal from God. God speaking, touching. Warning or blessing.

TIN: Something of low valor. Not original, an imitation.

TITANIC: Big plan that is not going to work out.

TITLE/DEED: Ownership seal. Potential to possess something.

TOILET: A place of repentance.

<u>Symbolic Actions</u>

1. ***To pass feces:*** To get rid of sins or unforgiveness, anger, bitterness, or any ungodly thing or habit.

2. ***Difficulty in locating a toilet:*** Hindrances to repentance within the dreamer or the circumstance.

3. ***Unable to use the toilet because it is dirty:*** Not fully ready to undergo repentance.

4. ***Repeated dreams of toilets:*** This is common with intercessors because they are supposed to

repeatedly repent for the sins of others to ensure they are effective in their ministries.

TONGUE: Powerful. National language. Something that cannot be tamed.

TORCH: Intense light. To examine. Source of light. Word of God. Godly wisdom.

TORNADO: Distressing situation. Great trouble. Spiritual warfare.

TOWER: High spiritual thing. Supernatural experience. Great strength. Pride, e.g., the tower of Babel.

TRACTOR: Groundbreaking ministry. Prepare the mind to receive.

TRAILER: An equipping ministry. A caring service. A ministry that is migrating.

TRAIN: A large ministry that influences a lot of people. Move or send people out. Movement of God.

TREE: Leader, good or bad. Person or organization. Nations or kingdom.

Symbolic Actions

1. *Christmas:* Celebrations.
2. *Evergreen:* Long-lasting, everlasting.
3. *Oak:* Great strength. Durable. Righteousness.
4. *Olive:* Anointed of God. Israel. Church. Anointing oil.
5. *Palm:* A leader who is fruit producing.
6. *Tree stump:* Tenacity or stubbornness. Retaining

hope despite circumstances. Keeping the root in place.

7. *Willow:* Indicating sadness; defeat.

And provide for those who grieve in Zion—to bestow on them a crown of beauty instead of ashes, the oil of gladness instead of mourning, and a garment of praise instead of a spirit of despair. They will be called oaks of righteousness, a planting of the Lord for the display of His splendor (Isaiah 61:3).

These are the visions I saw while lying in my bed: I looked, and there before me stood a tree in the middle of the land. Its height was enormous (Daniel 4:10).

A shoot will come up from the stump of Jesse; from his roots a Branch will bear fruit (Isaiah 11:1).

But let the stump and its roots, bound with iron and bronze, remain in the ground, in the grass of the field. Let him be drenched with the dew of heaven, and let him live with the animals among the plants of the earth (Daniel 4:15).

TROPHY: Victory.

Symbolic Actions

1. *To receive a trophy:* To be honored as the winner.
2. *To raise a trophy:* To celebrate the victory.

TRUCK: A personal ministry that brings provision.

TRUMPET: Voice of the prophet. The second coming of Christ. Proclaiming the good news. Blessing; promise.

To gather the assembly, blow the trumpets, but not with the same signal (Numbers 10:7).

For the Lord Himself will come down from heaven, with a loud command, with the voice of the archangel and with the trumpet call of God, and the dead in Christ will rise first (1 Thessalonians 4:16).

TUNNEL: A passage. A time or place of transition. Troubled or dark seasons of life.

He tunnels through the rock; his eyes see all its treasures (Job 28:10).

TWELVE: Government of God. Divine order. Discipleship. Government by election, theocracy.

TWENTY: Holiness and redemption.

TWENTY-FOUR: Complete order of God. Maturity or perfect government. Elders in the throne room.

Surrounding the throne were twenty-four other thrones, and seated on them were twenty-four elders. They were dressed in white and had crowns of gold on their heads (Revelation 4:4).

TWO: Witnessing; confirmation. Division. Whole in marriage.

TWO HUNDRED: Fullness confirmed. Promise guaranteed.

TWO STORY: Multi-level giftedness. Symbolic of flesh and spirit. Multi-talented church.

UPSTAIRS: Pertaining to the Spirit. Pentecost. Zone of thought; great balance. Spiritual realm.

UPWARD MOTION: Moving onto higher spiritual things.

URINATING: Releasing pressure. Compelling urge or temptation. Repentance.

VAN (MOVING): A time or period of change, either in the natural or in the spirit. To walk.

VAPOR: Something temporary. Presence of God. Evidence of something.

VEIL: To conceal. To conceal glory or sin. To deceive. Blind to the truth. Lack of understanding.

Even to this day when Moses is read, a veil covers their hearts. But whenever anyone turns to the Lord, the veil is taken away (2 Corinthians 3:15-16).

And even if our gospel is veiled, it is veiled to those who are perishing (2 Corinthians 4:3).

VESSEL: People as instrument of use, for good or bad purposes. The Christian believers.

VINE: Jesus Christ. Christian believers.

I had planted you like a choice vine of sound and reliable stock. How then did you turn against Me into a corrupt, wild vine? (Jeremiah 2:21).

I am the true vine, and My Father is the gardener (John 15:1).

VINEYARD: A place planting; harvest. Heavenly Kingdom.

The vineyard of the Lord Almighty is the house of Israel, and the men of Judah are the garden of His delight. And He looked for justice, but saw bloodshed; for righteousness, but heard cries of distress (Isaiah 5:7).

VOICE: Message from God or devil. The Word of God. Godly instruction.

T
U
V

VOLCANO: Something sudden and explosive. Out of control and unstable; unpredictable. Judgment.

VOMIT: Distasteful, unhealthy. Forceful expulsion. Compulsive return. Unpleasant return of ill-gotten things.

So, because you are lukewarm— neither hot nor cold—I am about to spit you out of My mouth (Revelation 3:16).

WALKING: Walking the path of life; life in the Spirit. Progress, living in the Spirit.

Symbolic Actions

1. *Difficulty:* Trials or opposition; evil opposition to destiny.

2. *Unable to walk:* Hindrance to doing what you are called to do.

WALL: Obstacle, barrier, defense, limitation. Great hindrance. Blocking the view of presenting spiritual signs.

WAR: Spiritual warfare.

WASHING: To clean.

WASHBASIN: Means of cleansing. Prayers and intercession.

WASHCLOTH: Something that enhances the cleansing process.

WATCH: Need to be watchful. Time for something. Watch what is about to happen.

WATERMELON: Spirit-ruled soul. Fruitfulness.

WATERS: Move of the Spirit; Holy Spirit. Nations of the world.

Symbolic Actions

1. *Stagnant:* Instability or stale in the things of God.

2. *Muddy or polluted:* Corrupted spiritual moves/sin/false doctrine.

3. *Troubled water:* Troubled mind.

4. *Water fountain:* God's Spirit welling up in man. Salvation.

5. *Water well:* Revival coming.

6. *Healing pool:* Time of refreshing.

WEEDS: Sinful nature or acts.

WEIGHT: Great responsibility, load, or burden.

WELL: Source of livelihood. Salvation. Source of comfort, life, replenishing. To renew.

Jacob's well was there, Jesus, tired as He was from the journey, sat down by the well… (John 4:6).

WHEEL: Pertaining to life cycle. Long-lasting. Continuously.

WHIRLWIND: Powerful move in the Spirit, good or bad.

WHITE: Something that is pure, righteousness. God's glory, light of God. Innocence, blamelessness.

WIFE: Actual person. Someone joined to you in covenant. Spirit of submission. The Church. Israel; what or who you are called to.

WILDERNESS: Hard times. Place of trial/testing. Distant from God. Place of training. Place of provision.

V
W

WIND: Movement of the Spirit, usually good, but may be evil. Disappears quickly. Unstable. Difficult to understand.

WINDOW: Prophetic gifting. Revelation knowledge. Gaining insight.

WINE: Holy Spirit. Counterfeit spirit. Communion. Teaching; blessing.

Then I will send rain on your land in its season, both autumn and spring rains, so that you may gather in your grain, new wine and oil (Deuteronomy 11:14).

No, new wine must be poured into new wineskins (Luke 5:38).

Likewise, teach the older women to be reverent in the way they live, not to be slanderers or addicted to much wine, but to teach what is good (Titus 2:3).

WINE PRESS: True doctrine; spiritual birthplace.

WINESKINS: The human body as a vessel. The Church. Saints.

WINGS: Prophetic. To be under the protection of God.

You yourselves have seen what I did to Egypt, and how I carried you on eagles' wings and brought you to Myself (Exodus 19:4).

Have mercy on me, O God, have mercy on me, for in You my soul takes refuge. I will take refuge in the shadow of Your wings until the disaster has passed (Psalm 57:1).

Each of the four living creatures had six wings and was covered with eyes all around, even under his wings. Day and night they never stop saying: "Holy, holy, holy is the Lord God Almighty, who was, and is, and is to come" (Revelation 4:8).

O Jerusalem, Jerusalem, you who kill the prophets and stone those sent to you, how often I have longed to gather your children together, as a hen gathers her chicks under her wings, but you were not willing! (Luke 13:34)

WINTER: Season of unfruitfulness. Latent period.

Pray that your flight will not take place in winter or on the Sabbath (Matthew 24:20).

Do your best to get here before winter. Eubulus greets you, and so do Pudens, Linus, Claudia and all the brothers (2 Timothy 4:21).

WITCH: Spirit of rebellion. Non-submission. Manipulative person. Spirit of control.

For rebellion is as the sin of witchcraft… (1 Samuel 15:23 NKJV).

WOLF: A tendency to destroy God's work. False minister. Opportunistic person.

WOMAN (UNKNOWN): A messenger from God or satan. An angel or demonic spirit. Seducing spirit.

WOOD: Life. Dependence on flesh. Humanity. Carnal reasoning. Lust.

WORK AREA: The place or time of your service.

WORM: Something that eats from the inside, often secretly. Not obvious on the surface. Disease; filthiness.

WRESTLING: Struggling with something in the Spirit or real life. To battle. Perseverance. To contend with, struggle.

YARD: The opened part of your personality.

<u>Symbolic Actions</u>

1. ***Back of the house:*** Behind or past.

YEAR: Time of blessing or judgment.

YELLOW: Hope; fear; mind.

YOKE: Bondage. Tied to something; usually evil, but sometimes good. Enslaved.

ZION: A place of strength. A place of protection. God's Kingdom.

Here am I, and the children the Lord has given me. We are signs and symbols in Israel from the Lord Almighty, who dwells on Mount Zion (Isaiah 8:18).

Their bloodguilt, which I have not pardoned, I will pardon. The Lord dwells in Zion! (Joel 3:21)

But on Mount Zion will be deliverance; it will be holy, and the house of Jacob will possess its inheritance (Obadiah 1:17).

W
X
Y
Z

PART II

GLEANING FROM BIBLE SYMBOLISM

ANATOMY OF DREAMS IN THE BIBLE

ANATOMY OF THE DREAM OF THE GREAT TREE

Daniel 4:4-28

I, Nebuchadnezzar, was at home in my palace, contented and prosperous. I had a dream that made me afraid. As I was lying in my bed, the images and visions that passed through my mind terrified me. So I commanded that all the wise men of Babylon be brought before me to interpret the dream for me. When the magicians, enchanters, astrologers and diviners came, I told them the dream, but they could not interpret it for me. Finally, Daniel came into my presence and I told him the dream. (He is called Belteshazzar, after the name of my god, and the spirit of the holy gods is in him.) I said, "Belteshazzar, chief of the magicians, I know that the spirit of the holy gods is in you, and no mystery is too difficult for you. Here is my dream; interpret it for me. These are the visions I saw while lying in my bed: I looked, and there before me stood a tree in the middle of the land. Its height was enormous. The tree grew large and strong and its top touched the sky; it was visible to the ends of the earth. Its leaves were beautiful, its fruit abundant, and on it was food for all. Under it the beasts of the field found shelter, and the birds of the air lived in its branches; from it every creature was fed. "In the visions I saw while lying in my bed, I looked, and there before me was a messenger, a holy one, coming down from heaven. He called in a loud voice: 'Cut down the tree and trim off its branches; strip off its leaves and scatter its fruit. Let the animals flee from under it and the birds from its branches. But let the stump and its roots, bound with iron and bronze, remain in the ground, in the grass of the field. "'Let him be drenched with the dew of heaven, and let him live with the animals among the plants of the earth. Let his mind be changed from that of a man and let him be given the mind of an animal, till seven times pass by for him. "'The decision is announced by messengers, the holy ones declare the verdict, so that the living may know that the Most High is sovereign over the kingdoms of men and gives them to anyone he wishes and sets over them the lowliest of men.' "This is the dream that I, King Nebuchadnezzar, had. Now, Belteshazzar, tell me what it means, for none of the wise men in my kingdom can interpret it for me. But you can, because the spirit of the holy gods is in you." Then Daniel (also called Belteshazzar) was greatly perplexed for a time, and his thoughts terrified him. So the king said, "Belteshazzar, do not let the dream or its meaning alarm you." Belteshazzar answered, "My lord, if only the dream applied to your enemies and its meaning to your adversaries! The tree you saw, which grew large and strong, with its top touching the sky, visible to the whole earth, with beautiful leaves and abundant fruit, providing food for all, giving shelter to the beasts of the field, and having nesting places in its branches for the birds of the air—you, O king, are that tree! You have become great and strong; your greatness has grown until it reaches the sky, and your dominion extends to distant parts of the earth. You, O king, saw a messenger, a holy one, coming down from heaven and saying, 'Cut down the tree and destroy it, but leave the stump, bound with iron and bronze, in the grass of the field, while its roots remain in the ground. Let him be drenched with the dew of heaven; let him live like the wild animals, until seven times pass by for him.' "This is the interpretation, O king, and this is the decree the Most High has issued against my lord the king: You will be driven away from people and will live with the wild animals; you will eat grass like cattle and be drenched with the dew of heaven. Seven times will pass by for you until you acknowledge that the Most High is sovereign over the kingdoms of men and gives them to anyone he wishes. The command to leave the stump of the tree with its roots means that your kingdom will be restored to you when you acknowledge that Heaven rules. Therefore, O king, be pleased to accept my advice: Renounce your sins by doing what is right, and your wickedness by being kind to the oppressed. It may be that then your prosperity will continue." All this happened to King Nebuchadnezzar.

Symbol	Meaning & Symbolic Connotation
*"Stood **a tree in the middle of the land**. ...Its height was enormous."*	This is indicative of extensive growth of the kingdom of Babylon. The height of the tree was the sign of the dominion and influence of the kingdom on the world scene.
1. Stood	1. To stand one's ground. To take one's place.
2. A tree	2. A leader, (trees were common symbols of leaders in Asia).
3. The middle of the land	3. A place of effective and coordinated reach or vantage position.
4. Its height was enormous	4. The high degree of influence and power over enormous numbers of people.
*"**The tree grew large and strong** and its top touched the sky";*	The phrase expresses the growth and rise to prominence of the kingdom of Babylon and King Nebuchadnezzar's rulership. The prominence would reach most places of the world just as the sky covers the earth. That the king and his kingdom would have a far-reaching influence on people and nations of the world. The tree also is a symbol of the king himself, wealthy and powerful.

Symbol	Meaning & Symbolic Connotation
*"**The beasts** of the field found shelter, and the **birds of the air, nesting places.**"*	Indicating that the kingdom will be a place where many people groups would reside and find somehow security under the authority of Nebuchadnezzar. The kingdom would also meet the needs the people and provide a place of rest and increase.
1. The beast	1. The beasts in this instance were used as symbols of the people who would be tended to.
2. The field	2. The field indicates the area of influence.
3. Shelter	3. Shelter indicates the provision of a place of safety, a place of comfort/for providing the essentials of life.
4. The birds of the air	4. The birds of the air refer to the catered-to people who will come from limitless borders.
*"**A messenger,** a holy one, coming down from heaven"*	Indicating that the message is the decree of the Most High coming down to the people on earth.
1. Messenger	1. Divine messenger from God
2. Coming down from heaven	2. Emphasizing the source of the message (coming from Heaven).

Symbol	Meaning & Symbolic Connotation
*"**A loud voice:** 'Cut down the tree and trim off its branches; strip off its leaves and scatter its fruit."*	A loud voice indicates sound that will be undeniably loud and would draw compelling attention. Judgment from God that the kingdom would be temporarily taken from Nebuchadnezzar would be loud and clear to all.
1. A loud voice	1. The loud voice = the voice of God signifying marked influence, something that draws attention, or that which must be taken notice of.
2. Its branches	2. Its branches refer to the means of exerting or commanding the influence or of exercising power.
3. Its leaves	3. The leaves indicate the means of provision for the people as leaves provide for plants.
4. Scatter its fruits	4. Scattering its fruits means to destroy the means of producing fruits or the ability to provide for others or by so doing remove his influence on the people. This refers only to Nebuchadnezzar himself as the kingdom maintained its dominion in the temporary absence of Nebuchadnezzar.
*"But let the **stump and its roots,** bound with iron and bronze; remain in the ground"*	This dream, because the roots of the stump remained in the ground, indicates that there remains the capacity for the kingdom to be restored to the king when he acknowledges God as the king of all. Binding by chains of iron and bronze indicates captivity or insanity—the mind of the king would be deranged.
1. The stump	1. The stump indicates what survives after punishment.
2. Its roots	2. Its roots means to retain the capacity for sustenance.
3. Bound by iron and bronze	3. This indicates the mind or mental bondage that the king would experience.
4. Remain in the ground	4. To retain the ability to survive and recover, eventually when the right condition comes.

Symbol	Meaning & Symbolic Connotation
"But let the stump and its roots, bound with iron and bronze… *"'Let him be drenched with the dew of heaven."*	The figure changed from that of the tree to that of an individual ("Let him") who is forcibly bond with the fetters of iron and brass. The purpose of this superimposition is to give hint that *stump* is used only as a symbol of man.
1. Be drenched with dew of heaven	1. To live like an animal, sustained by the dew of heaven.
"Let him live with the animals"	Driven away from his people and live with wild animals, he will eat grass until he acknowledges that God is supreme.
1. Live with the animals	1. To behave and live like an animal for a period as divinely specified.
"Let his mind be changed from that of a man"	The darkness and the bestiality that would dominate the king's mind during the period of bondage or lunacy. The king would have the mind of an animal for a time and a season.
1. His mind was changed	1. To reason like an animal was part of what was ordained in Heaven to happen to him.
"Let him be given the mind of an animal"	To have the mind of animal was occasioned in Heaven.

THE FULFILLMENT

Daniel 4:28-36

> *All this happened to King Nebuchadnezzar. Twelve months later, as the king was walking on the roof of the royal palace of Babylon, he said, "Is not this the great Babylon I have built as the royal residence, by my mighty power and for the glory of my majesty?" The words were still on his lips when a voice came from heaven, "This is what is decreed for you, King Nebuchadnezzar: Your royal authority has been taken from you. You will be driven away from people and will live with the wild animals; you will eat grass like cattle. Seven times will pass by for you until you acknowledge that the Most High is sovereign over the kingdoms of men and gives them to anyone he*

wishes." Immediately what had been said about Nebuchadnezzar was fulfilled. He was driven away from people and ate grass like cattle. His body was drenched with the dew of heaven until his hair grew like the feathers of an eagle and his nails like the claws of a bird.

At the end of that time, I, Nebuchadnezzar, raised my eyes toward heaven, and my sanity was restored. Then I praised the Most High; I honored and glorified Him who lives forever. His dominion is an eternal dominion; His kingdom endures from generation to generation. All the peoples of the earth are regarded as nothing. He does as He pleases with the powers of heaven and the peoples of the earth. No one can hold back His hand or say to Him: "What have you done?" At the same time that my sanity was restored, my honor and splendor were returned to me for the glory of my kingdom. My advisers and nobles sought me out, and I was restored to my throne and became even greater than before.

ANATOMY OF NEBUCHADNEZZAR'S DREAM OF THE LARGE STATUE

Daniel 2:31-41

You looked, O king, and there before you stood a large statue—an enormous, dazzling statue, awesome in appearance. The head of the statue was made of pure gold, its chest and arms of silver, its belly and thighs of bronze, its legs of iron, its feet partly of iron and partly of baked clay. While you were watching, a rock was cut out, but not by human hands. It struck the statue on its feet of iron and clay and smashed them. Then the iron, the clay, the bronze, the silver and the gold were broken to pieces at the same time and became like chaff on a threshing floor in the summer. The wind swept them away without leaving a trace. But the rock that struck the statue became a huge mountain and filled the whole earth. "This was the dream, and now we will interpret it to the king. You, O king, are the king of kings. The God of heaven has given you dominion and power and might and glory; in your hands he has placed mankind and the beasts of the field and the birds of the air. Wherever they live, he has made you ruler over them all. You are that head of gold. "After you, another kingdom will rise, inferior to yours. Next, a third kingdom, one of bronze, will rule over the whole earth. Finally, there will be a fourth kingdom, strong as iron—for iron breaks and smashes everything—and as iron breaks things to pieces, so it will crush and break all the others. Just as you saw that the feet and toes were partly of baked clay and partly of iron, so this will be a divided kingdom; yet it will have some of the strength of iron in it, even as you saw iron mixed with clay.

Dream	Meaning
An enormous, dazzling statue, awesome in appearance.	The size and appearance of this statue was indicative of what Babylon would become. Babylon was the first of the ancient world powers according to this dream. The symbolic use of the various qualities of metals was a representation of the successive government that would arise in the land of Babylon. In this dream God used quality metals, probably because as a king, Nebuchadnezzar amassed precious metals from conquered kingdoms. So as the dreamer, he understood the quality of metals. God knew the superiority of the metals, one over the other, would communicate to the king the comparative superiority of the various kingdoms.
The head of the statue was made of pure gold. Its chest and arms of silver. Its belly and thighs of bronze. Its legs of iron, its feet partly of iron and partly of baked clay.	
	Notice the dreamer was not directly participating in this dream, yet the dream was about him and his kingdom. For interpretation, the Holy Spirit should guide the significance of the dreamer's participatory and observatory roles in the dreams.
	Worshiping of statues was prevalent in Nebuchadnezzar's time hence it played up in his dream. Later in his life he attempted to create this great statue as an idol for worshiping (see Dan. 3).

Dream	Meaning
A rock was cut out, but not by human hands	*This indicates Sovereign intervention* Sometimes in a dream situation, the dreamer may see, perceive, or know things while in the dream that may be beyond the realm of the capacity of the human mind to know. *"A rock cut not with human hands"* connotes knowledge beyond the immediate awareness or environment. Therefore, this insight is essentially word of knowledge.
The wind swept them away without leaving a trace.	*All kingdoms of this world will eventually be wiped away and replaced by the Kingdom of God and Jesus Christ.* The wind here is the symbol of the move of God or the Spirit of God.
But the rock that struck the statue became a huge mountain and filled the whole earth.	*The Kingdom of God shall cover the whole earth* The kingdom of this world will eventually disappear and in its place the Kingdom of God shall stand forever.
You, O king, are the king of kings.	*A head of fine gold was the symbol of Babylon and of the King Nebuchadnezzar himself.* The head of the statue made of gold refers to the Babylonian empire personified by Nebuchadnezzar. This is the operation of the word of knowledge and of the word of wisdom in the giftedness of Daniel, the interpreter.
After you, another kingdom will rise, inferior to yours.	*Silver is considered inferior to gold.* The chest and arms of silver represent the Medo-Persian empire. Medo-Persia would become the second world power after defeating the Babylon. The application of minimal logical deduction, so logically, the second kingdom, represented by silver, shall be inferior to that represented by gold. The mind and intellect should only come into interpretation of dreams after the Holy Spirit prompting.

Dream	Meaning
Next, a third kingdom, one of bronze, will rule over the whole earth	*As bronze is considered inferior to silver*
	The belly and thighs of bronze represent Greece.
	Greece would emerge as the third world power after defeating the Medo-Persia empire. Greece will be inferior to Medo-Persia, even as bronze is considered inferior to silver.
Finally, there will be a fourth kingdom, strong as iron—for iron breaks and smashes everything	Iron is inferior to bronze, but iron is generally known for being strong, so though inferior to bronze, this kingdom will have the strength to conquer other kingdoms.
	The leg of iron and the feet of iron and clay symbolized the **Roman empire.** Rome would defeat Greece and become the fourth world power.
	The strength of this kingdom is played out in this dream dramatization with the symbol of iron.
	Notice that the focus is shifted from the value of the metal to the comparative strength.
	Leg is symbolic of what you stand on and iron represents strength, which also indicates that this kingdom will focus on shear strength, and that would be the basis of its standing.
	The fourth kingdom—generally identified as **Rome**—after a time became divided into two as represented by the **two legs**: the eastern and the western empires. Later still these two became divided into **ten** that formed the confederacy of European nations—just as the two legs of the large statue end in ten toes.

Dream	Meaning
The feet and toes were made partly of baked clay and partly of iron, so this will be a divided kingdom; yet it will have some of the strength of iron in it, even as you saw iron mixed with clay.	The mixture of iron and clay indicate that this kingdom, despite its strength, will lack coherent unity. It will be a divided kingdom The weakness of the fourth strong kingdom is that it lacked unity. Feet often symbolize attitudes of the heart. Clay is the symbol for frailty or weakness of humanity. Put together it means that this kingdom, though strong, will suffer from lack of unity just as clay and iron cannot mix, mainly due to poor attitude of hearts (symbolized by feet) of the emerged leaders.
Daniel 2:34-35 While you were watching, a rock was cut out, but not by human hands. It struck the statue on its feet of iron and clay and smashed them.	In the dream, the gold, the silver, and the bronze were crushed at the same time as the legs of iron and the feet of clay and iron, obscuring the actual sequence of the rise and fall of the successive kingdoms. Therefore in dream interpretation, one should continuously rely on the Holy Spirit for the insight embedded in divine symbolism, as the limit of time does not apply in dreams. Events that may span or transcend decades in actual occurrence, may be portrayed in a few seconds or minutes.

"We can take deliberate actions to enhance the easy flow of divine revelations over a place. By availing ourselves to the open heaven we can experience the clarity of revelations in a place reflecting the openness of the third heaven over the place. Open heaven can also mean other material and immaterial blessings from the third heaven. An opening of the heavens is the bypassing of the hindrances of the second heaven to connect God's abode with the earth."

More information about connecting earth and Heaven is found in my book, *The Justice of God: Victory in Everyday Living.*[6]

VISION OF THE RIVER FROM THE TEMPLE

Ezekiel 47:1-32

The man brought me back to the entrance of the temple, and I saw water coming out from under the threshold of the temple toward the east (for the temple faced east). The water was coming down from under the south side of the temple, south of the altar. He then brought me out through the north gate and led me around the outside to the outer gate facing east, and the water was flowing from the south side.

As the man went eastward with a measuring line in his hand, he measured off a thousand cubits and then led me through water that was ankle-deep. He measured off another thousand cubits and led me through water that was knee-deep. He measured off another thousand and led me through water that was up to the waist. He measured off another thousand, but now it was a river that I could not cross, because the water had risen and was deep enough to swim in—a river that no one could cross. He asked me, "Son of man, do you see this?" Then he led me back to the bank of the river. When I arrived there, I saw a great number of trees on each side of the river. He said to me, "This water flows toward the eastern region and goes down into the Arabah, where it enters the Sea. When it empties into the Sea, the water there becomes fresh. Swarms of living creatures will live wherever the river flows. There will be large numbers of fish, because this water flows there and makes the salt water fresh; so where the river flows everything will live. Fishermen will stand along the shore; from En Gedi to En Eglaim there will be places for spreading nets. The fish will be of many kinds—like the fish of the Great Sea. But the swamps and marshes will not become fresh; they will be left for salt. Fruit trees of all kinds will grow on both banks of the river. Their leaves will not wither, nor will their fruit fail. Every month they will bear, because the water from the sanctuary flows to them. Their fruit will serve for food and their leaves for healing."

This is what the Sovereign Lord says: "These are the boundaries by which you are to divide the land for an inheritance among the twelve tribes of Israel, with two portions for Joseph. You are to divide it equally among them. Because I swore with uplifted hand to give it to your forefathers, this land will become your inheritance.

"This is to be the boundary of the land:

"On the north side it will run from the Great Sea by the Hethlon road past Lebo Hamath to Zedad, Berothah and Sibraim (which lies on the border between Damascus and Hamath), as far as Hazer Hatticon, which is on the border of Hauran. The boundary will extend from the sea to Hazar Enan, along the northern border of Damascus, with the border of Hamath to the north. This will be the north boundary.

"On the east side the boundary will run between Hauran and Damascus, along the Jordan between Gilead and the land of Israel, to the eastern sea and as far as Tamar. This will be the east boundary.

"On the south side it will run from Tamar as far as the waters of Meribah Kadesh, then along the Wadi of Egypt to the Great Sea. This will be the south boundary.

"On the west side, the Great Sea will be the boundary to a point opposite Lebo Hamath. This will be the west boundary.

"You are to distribute this land among yourselves according to the tribes of Israel. You are to allot it as an inheritance for yourselves and for the aliens who have settled among you and who have children. You are to consider them as native-born Israelites; along with you they are to be allotted an inheritance among the tribes of Israel. In whatever tribe the alien settles, there you are to give him his inheritance," declares the Sovereign Lord.

Symbol	Meaning & Symbolic Connotation
The temple	The throne of God.
Water coming out from under the threshold of the temple	Of God/outpouring of the Holy Spirit. Under the sovereignty of the throne of God.
He then brought me out through the north gate And led me round	To be divinely carried along. To be led by the Spirit of God in a specific direction. Through the gate that trouble has come from in the past, shall God Himself move and prevail.
With a measuring line in His hand	The Spirit of God gives to each man, his measure, as He determines such things as faith, gift, and mission.
Then led me through water that was ankle-deep	The Spirit will apportion to us according to our level of faith, God will not give us more than we can cope. "Ankle-deep" therefore often symbolizes the initial level of something, a small or little level of faith, the beginning of faith.
He measured off another thousand cubits	The Spirit allows us to grow in faith and allows measured challenges to confront us according to the level of faith we possess.
Led me through water that was knee-deep.	Thousand cubits represent a certain level of maturity in the spirit. A higher level of faith, high enough to allow us to stand firm in God. Knee-deep often represents bringing the person to a place of prayer.

Symbol	Meaning & Symbolic Connotation
He measured off another thousand and led me through water that was up to the waist.	With a higher level of faith, we become more reliant on God. Up to waist level connotates increase and reproduction, therefore a place where our faith enables us to have spiritual offspring or godly offspring to impact posterity. Our trust in God increases.
He measured off another thousand, but now it was a river that I could not cross, because the water had risen and was deep enough to swim in—a river that no one could cross.	Another level of maturity in our walk with God is attained with obedience and due diligence. The Spirit of God now brings us to great height in faith. At this level we can move freely in the gifts of God. As swimming allows the water to carry the swimmer, so at this level of faith, we become dependant on the Holy Spirit to carry us through. At this level of faith things happen by the Holy Spirit. It is no longer by might nor by power, but by the Spirit.
Then He led me back to the bank of the river. When I arrived there, I saw a great number of trees on each side of the river.	God will now bring us to closer intimacy with Himself and gives us clear direction for the call in our lives. Now people will begin to notice the hand of God in our lives and we begin to gain acceptance with men. Our faith will allow us to bless or to influence others and empower them to greater height.

Symbol	Meaning & Symbolic Connotation
This water flows toward the eastern region and goes down into the Arabah, where it enters the Sea. When it empties into the Sea, the water there becomes fresh.	East represents a place of beginning; whatever level maturity a person may attain, he still requires continuous dependence on the original source, which is God's throne. The refreshing of the Dead Sea: The amazing picture of the renewal of the Dead Sea. The Dead Sea is the lowliest point on earth and symbolically it is reached by God's living water so it can renew any person from any depth! The Dead Sea is the saltiest gathering of water so there is no dirt too much for God to wash away! The Dead Sea is unable to support life until renewed by the living water so there is no barrenness too heavy for God to break! This is therefore symbolic of the immeasurable power of the living water of God to renew, restore, and support life. The impartation of the Spirit on the people and nations who receive the gospel. At this level of faith, our ministry brings life to others, especially to those whose hearts are yielded to God. The Spirit gives life and refreshment. The heart of the people will be made receptive to the gospel by the sovereign moves of the Holy Spirit.
Swarms of living creatures will live wherever the river flows.	The move of the Spirit of God and the gift of the Spirit will bring life to the people wherever the river of life flows.
There will be large numbers of fish, because this water flows there and makes the salt water fresh; so where the river flows everything will live.	New converts will come to God by the impartation of the Holy Spirit. The move of the Spirit will bring newness and softness (goodness) to the human hearts of stone and also turn old human doctrine and tradition into doctrines of God

Symbol	Meaning & Symbolic Connotation
Fishermen will stand along the shore; from En Gedi to En Eglaim there will be places for spreading nets.	Eventually, many people who will yield themselves to the Spirit of God will became instruments of change to many other people.
	There will be opportunities to spread the gospel to all nations of the world before the end of the age.
The fish will be of many kinds—like the fish of the Great Sea.	God does not show favoritism; all people of the nations of the world, all races, all colors. In God there is neither Jew nor Gentile, male or female, slave or master.
But the swamps and marshes will not become fresh; they will be left for salt.	The nations/land that would be imparted by the Spirit of God will experience transformation and refreshment, but others who resist the gospel will not be refreshed by the rejuvenating power of the Holy Spirit.
Fruit trees of all kinds will grow on both banks of the river.	The harvest will be plentiful, yielding fruits at every season.
Their leaves will not wither, nor will their fruit fail. Every month they will bear, because the water from the sanctuary flows to them.	Resources from God will not run dry for those who continually rely on God and trust Him in all their ways. The leaves are symbols of resources and of provision for the plants, so that they will no longer become dry in any season.
Their fruit will serve for food, and their leaves for healing.	The harvest will bring provisions to the people and nations. There will be healing for the afflicted.

SYMBOLS FROM SYMBOLIC ACTIONS IN THE BIBLE

Symbols	Meaning/Enactment

The Spear of God's Victory

Joshua 8:18	Joshua 8:19-20
"...Hold out toward Ai the javelin that is in your hand, for into your hand I will deliver the city...."	*"As soon as he did this, the men in the ambush rose quickly from their position and rushed forward. They entered the city and captured it and quickly set it on fire. The men of Ai looked back and saw the smoke of the city rising against the sky, but they had no chance to escape in any direction, for the Israelites who had been fleeing toward the desert had turned back against their pursuers."*
Hold out toward Ai the javelin	*"For Joshua did not draw back the hand that held out his javelin until he had destroyed all who lived in Ai"* (Josh. 8:26).
	Somehow this enactment activated and set in motion certain spiritual forces from God directed to bring defeat to Ai.

A Mighty Angel Acts Out a Prophecy

Revelation 18:21	This signifies an "act of God," a mighty force, will be raised up to bring judgment to Babylon and that the force with which the stone touched the water reflects the force with which Babylon will be defeated. Therefore the essence of this prophetic action is to reveal the intensity of the force with which Babylon will be destroyed and the finality of that divine action, just as the stone sank down into the sea never to be seen again.
*"Then a mighty angel picked up a **boulder the size of a large millstone** and threw it into the sea, and said: 'With such violence the great city of Babylon will be thrown down, never to be found again.'"*	

The Healing of Water

2 Kings 2:19-22

"...this town is well situated, as you can see, but the water is bad and the land is unproductive.

a new bowl put salt in it

threw the salt into it...'I have healed this water....'"

2 Kings 2:22

"And the water has remained wholesome to this day, according to the word Elisha had spoken"

A symbolic action enacted by the prophet to break the curse on the city, turning barrenness to fruitfulness. And the water has remained wholesome to this day, according to the word Elisha had spoken.

A new bowl = the people need a new and receptive heart of flesh and not the heart of stone

Salt in it = allow God to purify their heart and keep it preserved in its pure state, as salt is a purifying and preserving agent.

Into the spring = allow the people's hearts to be aligned with the move of God to bring freshness.

As the spring reflects the move of God and when purified hearts meet with the move of God, it produces freshness.

Elijah Rebuilt the Altar with 12 Stones

1 Kings 18:30-33

"...he repaired the altar, which was in ruins. **twelve stones,** *one for each of the tribes descended from Jacob, to whom the word of the Lord had come, saying, 'Your name shall be Israel.' With the stones he built an altar in the name of the Lord...and said,* **'fill** *four large jars with water and* **pour it** *on the offering and on the wood.'"*

1 Kings 18:36-39

"At the time of sacrifice, the prophet Elijah stepped forward and prayed: "O Lord, God of Abraham, Isaac and Israel, let it be known today that You are God in Israel and that I am Your servant and have done all these things at Your command. Answer me, O Lord, answer me, so these people will know that You, O Lord, are God, and that You are turning their hearts back again." Then the fire of the Lord fell and burned up the sacrifice, the wood, the stones and the soil, and also licked up the water in the trench. When all the people saw this, they fell prostrate and cried, "The Lord—He is God! The Lord—He is God!"

Symbols	Meaning/Enactment
12 stones	Twelve stones, one for each of the tribes descended from Jacob, to whom the word of the Lord had come, saying, "Your name shall be Israel." A level of unity, predicated on forgiveness and reconciliation that is important before miracles can come from God.
Fill four large jars with water and pour it	Fill four large jars with water and pour it on the offering and on the wood. Statement of faith, because water scarcity. It was also to allow the Spirit of God, symbolized by the water, to take pre-eminence or prevail (the pouring of water on the altar).

Satanic Enactment to Tap Into Counterfeit Power

2 Kings 3:27	2 Kings 3:27b
"Then he took his firstborn son, who was to succeed him as king, and offered him as a sacrifice on the city wall...."	Powers on the supernatural realm can be accessed by legal or illegal ways. Here the evil king tapped into to evil power in the spirit realm, (the power and authority in the evil realm).
	The fury against Israel was great; they withdrew and returned to their own land. These counterfeit laws are anti-God in principles and they are largely self-centred, self-exalting, destructive, and inconsiderate of others. These are the laws that regulate the kingdom of darkness.

Israel Defeated the Amalekites

Exodus 17:8-12

The Amalekites

"I will stand on top of the hill with the staff of God in my hands."...As long as Moses held up his hands, the Israelites were winning, but whenever he lowered his hands, the Amalekites were winning...."

I will stand on top of the hill

The staff of God in my hands

Exodus 17:13-16

"So Joshua overcame the Amalekites army with the sword. Then the Lord said to Moses, 'Write this on a scroll as something to be remembered and make sure that Joshua hears it, because I will completely blot out the memory of Amalek from under heaven.' Moses built an altar and called it The Lord is my Banner. He said, 'For hands were lifted up to the throne of the Lord. The Lord will be at war against the Amalekites from generation to generation.'"

Top of the hill = the place of prayers/ intercession

Staff of God = the anointing and mantle of God on his life

Hands held up = surrender and total submission to God enacted

As long as these conditions were met, Israelites prevailed. When these conditions are not met, the Amalekites gained the upper hand.

Ezekiel 5:1 (Action)

"Now, son of man, take a sharp sword and use it as a barber's razor to shave your head and your beard…"

Ezekiel 5:11-12 (Meaning)

Ezekiel was told to take a sharp sword, cut off his hair and beard, and then divide the hair into three parts—each of which symbolized inhabitants of Jerusalem, killed by different methods:

- Burning
- Striking with the sword
- Scattering to the wind
- (A few strands were laid aside to represent a remnant, some of whom will also be burned with fire)

Shaving the head was an act portraying shame or disgrace in Hebrew culture (see Ezek. 7:18, 2 Sam. 10:4).

It also represented a type of pagan practice.

Shaving the head was a mark of defilement, making a priest like Ezekiel ritually unclean, and so unable to perform his duties in the temple (see Lev. 21:5). This message was telling the people that they were about to be humiliated and defiled and may not be usable to God.

SYMBOLS FROM THE PARABLES IN THE BIBLE

Mysteries = a truth that has not been previously revealed

The parables of Jesus serve two purposes, both for revealing truth to those who are believers and further concealing the truth from those who reject Him or are unbelievers. Positive response is rewarded with further understanding.

THE PARABLE OF TWO EAGLES AND A VINE (EZEKIEL 17)

Symbol	Meaning
Ezekiel 17:1-8	Ezekiel 17:12-16
"The word of the Lord came to me: 'Son of man, set forth an allegory and tell the house of Israel a parable. Say to them, "This is what the Sovereign Lord says: A great eagle with powerful wings, long feathers and full plumage of varied colours came to Lebanon. Taking hold of the top of a cedar, he broke off its topmost shoot and carried it away to a land of merchants, where he planted it in a city of traders. He took some of the seed of your land and put it in fertile soil. He planted it like a willow by abundant water, and it sprouted and became a low, spreading vine. Its branches turned toward him, but its roots remained under it. So it became a vine and produced branches and put out leafy boughs. But there was another great eagle with powerful wings and full plumage. The vine now sent out its roots toward him from the plot where it was planted and stretched out its branches to him for water. It had been planted in good soil by abundant water so that it would produce branches, bear fruit and become a splendid vine."	*"Say to this rebellious house, 'Do you not know what these things mean?' Say to them: 'The king of Babylon went to Jerusalem and carried off her king and her nobles, bringing them back with him to Babylon. Then he took a member of the royal family and made a treaty with him, putting him under oath. He also carried away the leading men of the land, so that the kingdom would be brought low, unable to rise again, surviving only by keeping his treaty. But the king rebelled against him by sending his envoys to Egypt to get horses and a large army. Will he succeed? Will he who does such things escape? Will he break the treaty and yet escape? As surely as I live,' declares the Sovereign Lord, 'he shall die in Babylon, in the land of the king who put him on the throne, whose oath he despised and whose treaty he broke.'"*

Symbol	Meaning
He took some of the seed of your land and put it in fertile soil.	Jerusalem
Another great eagle with powerful wings and full plumage	The king rebelled against the King of Babylon by sending his envoys to Egypt to get horses and a large army. Egypt was a competitive rivalry powerful nation to the Babylonians in the then known world.

ANATOMY OF THE PARABLE OF THE SOWER

Matthew 13:1-23

Seed	Word of God; God's promises (something capable of multiplication); something that could be greatness; offerings, and means of connecting with
Soil	Heart of man; potential for multiplication— either good or bad; or the essence of life
Farmer	Jesus Christ, God, pastor, spiritual leaders
"Seed sown along the path" (Matt. 13:19)	No understanding, ungrounded, shallow or poor understanding; easily taken away by the devil or unprotected
a. Along the path	a. Type of heart
b. Birds came	b. The work of the devil
c. Ate it up	c. Succumb to the wiles of the evil one

"Seeds fell on rocky places" (Matt. 13:20-21)	Receives the Word with joy, but lacks depth and so easily stolen by trouble and persecution of the world; not rooted; poor foundation. To dream of walking on rocky places is symbolic of times of trouble, persecution, and lack of depth in the matter.
a. Rocky places	a. Type of heart that receives the word of God
b. Not much soil	b. Shallow understanding
c. Sprang up quickly	c. Eagerness and joy in receiving the word of God
d. Soil was shallow	d. Not depth because of poor understanding
e. Sun came	e. The challenges of life
f. They withered	f. Succumb or to be overwhelmed the challenges of life
g. No root	g. Lack of solid foundation and therefore not being properly established in the things of God.
"Seeds fell on thorns" (Matt. 13:22).	The Word of God is heard but choked by worries of life or the attraction of worldly riches. Thorns are symbolic of the worries of life, distraction by worldly riches, or by inordinate ambitions.
a. Thorns	a. Worries of life
b. Thorns grew up	b. The increasing challenges of life
c. Choked the plant	c. Worries of life, the desires of the riches of this world create ground not conducive for the Word of God to prosper.
"Seeds on good soil" (Matt. 13:23)	Hears the word, understands and obeys. Therefore becomes fruitful, good state of attitude. Well-prepared for life expectancy, conducive for growth in natural and spiritual things.
a. Good soil	a. Type of heart
b. Produce a crop	b. Productivity
c. 100, 60, or 30 times what was sown	c. Different levels of rewards

THE PARABLE OF THE WEED

Matthew 13:24-30

A man who sowed	The Son of Man, Teacher, Pastor, the teaching of parents/guardians.
Good seed (wheat)	The sons of the Kingdom—people with good hearts.
in his field	The world, life circumstances
While everyone was sleeping	The most vulnerable time, time of least resistance; time of the weakest defences; the weakest link or point.
The weeds (tares)	The sons of the evil one, people who had no God in their lives
His enemy	The devil, those against the work of God
The harvest	The end of the age, the produce of one's labour
The harvesters	Angels, means by which God brings about our reward.
The kingdom of heaven	The good seed in the field.
Why everyone was sleepy	Time of vulnerability.
It's enemy came	The enemy seizes every opportunity at the time of weakness.
Sowed weeds	To sow thoughts or ideas not of God in the lives of God's people.
Went away	Camouflage the deception of the devil
The wheat sprouted and formed ears The weed (tares) also appeared	When the people of the kingdom blossom, the weed also blossomed
• The owner servant	• Servants of God
• Fate of the weed (tares)	• Burnt in Hell
• Fate of the wheat	• Kept in the barns

Matthew 13:36-43

Tares closely resemble wheat but are poisonous to humans. They are indistinguishable from wheat until the final fruit appears. Thereafter, the farmer would weed out tares just before the wheat is harvested.

The parable of the tares teaches that until Jesus Christ returns—both genuine believers and counterfeits will be allowed to coexist. There will be a period or an age in which the good and the evil remain together, but in the end, the two groups shall be separated.

THE PARABLE OF THE MUSTARD SEED

Matthew 13:31-42

A mustard seed is a small seed capable of enormous multiplications.

The parable of the mustard seed teaches that although the kingdom may have small numbers of people at the beginning of age, it will ultimately be large and prosperous. Here the birds of air are not evil.

Note that in this parable, the birds of the air are not symbols of evil as they were in the parable of the sower.

THE PARABLE OF THE YEAST AND BREAD

Matthew 13:33

Though in general, leaven in the Scriptures often represents evil, the leaven in this parable could not possibly mean evil.

This parable is pivoted on the picture of the dynamic character of yeast that once it starts, it is impossible to stop, the picture shows that numerical growth will take place—rather not from the power of an external force but will grow from internal dynamic of the working of Holy Spirit.

In reality, in the world today, the growth of Christendom is doubling each succeeding generation.

THE PARABLE OF THE HIDDEN TREASURE

Matthew 13:44

The parable teaches values and responsibilities.

The ground to this teaching is that the disciples were forced to count cost contrary to their expectation of a great kingdom; but this parable teaches that despite immediate pressures of earthly problems, the immense value of the kingdom far outweighs any sacrifice of inconvenience that one might encounter on earth to possess it. It is each person's responsibility to try to pay the price and possess it.

THE PARABLE OF THE PEARL

Matthew 13:45

The parable teaches that the person finds the pearl not by accident but by diligent search.

Jesus' desire here was to imbue them with a high sense of calling to the Kingdom of God. Though salvation is by faith, ultimately it is a choice that one has to make at an individual level.

THE PARABLE OF THE NET

Matthew 13:47-52

Teaching on the need to lay a large enough net to gather a great number of all kinds of fish without discrimination.

The job of judging or ferreting out the false catch belongs to God at the end of the age; believers are not equipped to do this.

Spread the Word and the gospel to all nations, all races, all people or hearts.

THE PARABLE OF THE WORKERS IN THE VINEYARD

Matthew 20:1-16

This parable teaches about the redemption of time for the righteous who continue to stand in faith to the end.	The Lord/the Kingdom of God

Vineyard owner:

• Early workers	• The Jews to whom belong the ancestry of Jesus, the promises/covenant (see Rom. 3:1-2; 9:4-6).
• Agreed to pay them a denarius for a day	• the promises/covenant
• The other workers (the late comers to the vineyard)	• The Gentiles who will come into some covenant (see Eph. 2:11-13).
• Paid them all the same wages	• Through faith in Jesus Christ, salvation becomes available to all (see Rom. 11:16-17).

THE PARABLE OF THE LOST SHEEP

Matthew 18:10-14

This parable teaches that it is not the wish of God that any should perish but that all would come to the knowledge of Him.

1. A man owns a hundred sheep.

1. Father in Heaven, the Lord owns the earth and the fullness thereof.

2. One of them wanders away.

2. Lost soul, those who fall occasionally, backslider.

3. Look for the one that wandered off.

3. Not willing that any of these little ones should be lost. God's wish that none should perish.

4. He is happier about that one sheep than about the ninety-nine that did not wander off.

4. There is rejoicing in Heaven over a lost soul who is saved. Jesus said He came not for those who are well but those who are sick.

PART III

COMMON BIBLE
AND PROPHETIC TERMS

A

AARON: *Meaning: mountaineer or enlightener or "light bearer."* A man who was mightily used by God; his parents were Amram and Jochebed and were of the tribe of Levi, married Elisheba daughter of the prince of Judah and had four sons—Nadab, Abihu, Eleazar, and Ithamar. He was the older brother of Moses and a junior brother to Miriam and became the spokesman ("mouth") to Moses. He was divinely chosen and consecrated to carry the bloodline for the high priesthood in Israel, and he was a custodian and teacher of God's instructions. He died at the age of 123 years.

Contemporary/Symbolic Connotation:

Priesthood or high priesthood; a spokesperson, or one who is consecrated to perform priestly duties.

The Lord bless you and keep you; the Lord make His face shine upon you and be gracious to you; the Lord turn His face toward you and give you peace (Numbers 6:24-26).

ABBA: *Meaning: Hebrew and Aramaic for "father."*

ABEDNEGO: *Meaning: Hebrew for "servant of Nebo (Babylonian god)."*

This was the name given to Azariah, one of the youths of Jewish nobility in Babylonian captivity. He was probably named after a Babylonian god. He refused to be defiled by non-Jewish food from the royal palace of Nebuchadnezzar, or to worship the statue that King Nebuchadnezzar had erected. For this commitment and trust in God of the Hebrews,

Almighty God rescued him and his friends in a spectacular way.

Contemporary/Symbolic Connotation:

Steadfast in God, a true worshiper of God, guaranteed saving arm of God; divine promotion.

Shadrach, Meshach and Abednego replied to the king, "O Nebuchadnezzar, we do not need to defend ourselves before you in this matter. If we are thrown into the blazing furnace, the God we serve is able to save us from it, and He will rescue us from your hand, O king. But even if He does not, we want you to know, O king, that we will not serve your gods or worship the image of gold you have set up" (Daniel 3:16-18).

ABEL: *Meaning: Hebrew for "breath, vapour, or that which is insubstantial" or vanity.*

The second son of Adam and a symbol of righteousness and true worshiper of God; he became the first shepherd on earth. His sacrifice was considered proper and acceptable to God. His brother Cain murdered him and his blood cries out for vengeance. The blood of Jesus Christ is superior to that of Abel.

Contemporary/Symbolic Connotation:

Righteousness; true worshiper of God, the blood that cries out for vengeance.

ABIATHAR: *Meaning: Hebrew for "father of abundance" or father of plenty or excellent father.*

A high priest in Israel and the son of Ahimelech of the tribe of Levi and of the lineage of Eli; he escaped the slaughter of his family by King Saul and later became David's high priest. Supported David against Absalom but supported Adonijah, and he was finally deposed by King Solomon. He was the last of the lineage of Eli, the fulfillment of the prophecy against Eli's priesthood.

ABIB: *Meaning: the ear of a corn.* It is the first month of the Hebrew calendar and spans mid-March to about mid-April. This month is also called Nisan.

Observe the month of Abib and celebrate the Passover of the Lord your God, because in the month of Abib He brought you out of Egypt by night (Deuteronomy 16:1).

ABIGAIL: *Meaning: Hebrew for "father is rejoicing" or "father of exaltation."*

Key biblical people with this name:

1. Best known was the wife of Nabal, who was portrayed as a wise woman for her swift intervention to save her family from David's anger against her husband's foolish action. She later became one of King David's wives.

2. Mother of Amasa (one of Absalom's commanders).

ABIHU: *Meaning: Hebrew for "father is he" (man) or "God is father."*

He was one of the sons of Aaron. He was consecrated as priest by Moses but was later killed for offering "strange and unauthorized fire" before God.

ABIMELECH: *Meaning: Hebrew for "father is king" or "father of king."*

Key people with this name:

1. A king of Gerar to whom Abraham pretended that Sarah was his sister. He was told in a dream that Sarah was Abraham's wife. He returned Sarah to Abraham with repentance gifts and God healed his household.

2. Another king of Gerar to whom Isaac pretended that Rebekah was his sister. He discovered the truth about Rebekah and returned her to Isaac. Later he made a covenant with Isaac.

3. One of the sons of Gideon. He slaughtered the other sons of Gideon in one day and on one stone. He reigned for three years over Israel, but later God sent an evil spirit between him and his supporters and he died in battle.

ABISHAG: *Meaning: Hebrew for "father errs or wanders" or "father of error."*

A young virgin brought to comfort King David in his old age. David had no intimate relationship with her. Solomon later killed Adonijah for wanting to marry her.

ABNER: *Meaning: Hebrew for "father is a lamp" or "father of light."*

He was the commander of Saul's army. After Saul's death, he was instrumental in making Ish-bosheth king. He later defected to David but was killed by Joab and Abishai.

ABOMINATION: Something that causes great revulsion spiritually; something detestable spiritually. Something

A

that causes intense dislike spiritually and culturally.

ABRAHAM: *Meaning: Hebrew for "father of multitude;" Abram means "high father."*

He was the son of Terah, his original name Abram, and became husband of Sarai. He fathered Ishmael with Hagar and Isaac with Sarah. Abraham had many other children with Keturah. God made a covenant with him through which all families shall be blessed. He was known by many titles; as a prophet of God, the father of Israel, and father of all believers, and a friend of God. He died at the age of 175 years.

Contemporary/Symbolic Connotation:

Carrier of divine blessing, the father of all families on earth; a person who is a friend of God, someone God can trust; faith and obedience.

I will make you into a great nation and I will bless you; I will make your name great, and you will be a blessing. I will bless those who bless you, and whoever curses you I will curse; and all peoples on earth will be blessed through you (Genesis 12:2-3).

And the scripture was fulfilled that says, "Abraham believed God and it was credited to him as righteousness and he was called God's friend" (James 2:23).

ABSALOM: *Meaning: Hebrew for father is peace or "father of peace."*

He was the revengeful son of David. He killed his half brother Amnon for raping his sister Tamar and ran to Geshur. He was banished from the kingdom but was later reconciled with David and returned to the kingdom. However, he rebelled against David and was killed by Joab during the conspiracy.

Contemporary/Symbolic Connotation:

Vindictive, rebellious or cunning person, or the spirit of manipulation, vainglory.

And Absalom would add,"If only I were appointed judge in the land! Then everyone who has a complaint or case could come to me and I would see that he gets justice." Also, whenever anyone approached him to bow down before him, Absalom would reach out his hand, take hold of him and kiss him. Absalom behaved in this way toward all the Israelites who came to the king asking for justice, and so he stole the hearts of the men of Israel (2 Samuel 15:4-6).

ABYSS: The place in the depths of the earth where some demons are imprisoned until their final punishments.

ACACIA: A tree with hard and durable wood.

ACHAN: *Meaning: sorrow or pain, or "troubler."* He is remembered because of his notorious theft of forbidden things from Jericho. This sin caused Israel to be defeated by a small city called Ai. As a consequence he was stoned to death, in a place that came to be known as the "Valley Achor."

Contemporary/Symbolic Connotation:

Reproach, disobedience; dishonesty, wrath of God; the Valley Achor became a place of ostracism and trouble.

Therefore I am now going to allure her; I will lead her into the desert and speak tenderly to her. There I will give her back her vineyards, and will make the Valley of Achor a door of hope. There she will sing as in the days of her youth, as in the day she came up out of Egypt (Hosea 2:14-15).

ACHISH: A King of Gath, before whom David pretended to be insane. He gave David the town of Ziklag. He once trusted David and wanted to take him along to war, but his officials could not trust David.

ACHOR: *Meaning: Hebrew for "disaster" or "trouble."*

Then Joshua, together with all Israel, took Achan son of Zerah, the silver, the robe, the gold wedge, his sons and daughters, his cattle, donkeys and sheep, his tent and all that he had, to the Valley of Achor. Joshua said, "Why have you brought this trouble on us? The Lord will bring trouble on you today." Then all Israel stoned him, and after they had stoned the rest, they burned them. Over Achan they heaped up a large pile of rocks, which remains to this day. Then the Lord turned from his fierce anger. Therefore that place has been called the Valley of Achor ever since (Joshua 7:24-26).

Contemporary/Symbolic Connotation:

Pain; trouble; difficulty.

ADAM: *Meaning: Hebrew for "taken out of the red earth."*

He was the first man made by God. Adam also translates to mean mankind, or generically group of persons. He was gloriously made in the image of God. Though made from the dust of the earth, he became a living being by the breath of God. He followed his will instead of that of the will of God and disobeyed God. Therefore sin, pains, hardship, and death became parts of man's existence on earth. He is remembered for being instrumental to the fall of man, for the pivotal role of Jesus Christ in reversing the fallen nature of humanity; Jesus is regarded as the "second Adam." Adam was the crown of God's creation; and despite the severe consequences of the fall of Adam, it did not remove the place of honor and glory God has for man.

Contemporary/Symbolic Connotation:

The first man made by God; disobedience and the fall of man; preferring personal will to the will of God; Christ was the second Adam. He descended from the first Adam; he was obedient to God's will and became victorious over the devil. Through His blood, death, burial and resurrection man reconciled to God.

ADAR: The twelfth month of the Hebrew calendar. It spans mid-February to about mid-March.

ADONIJAH: *Meaning: Hebrew for "the Lord is Jehovah" or "God is my Lord."*

He was the son of David who attempted to usurp the kingship at the latter part of David's reign. This prompted King David to immediately make Solomon king instead. Later he wanted Abishag, one of David's concubines, as his wife, and for this he was killed at Solomon's command.

ADULLAM: *Meaning: Hebrew for "refuge or retreat" or justice of the people.*

This is the place where David hid his followers in a cave and where his men risked their lives to get water from Bethlehem for David. David considered himself not worthy to drink such water and sacrificed it to God.

Contemporary/Symbolic Connotation:

The place of divine protection and anointing; where champions are made; turning point.

David left Gath and escaped to the cave of Adullam. When his brothers and his father's household heard about it, they went down to him there. All those who were in distress or in debt or discontented gathered around him, and he became their leader. About four hundred men were with him (1 Samuel 22:1-2).

Three of the thirty chiefs came down to David to the rock at the cave of Adullam, while a band of Philistines was encamped in the Valley of Rephaim. At that time David was in the stronghold, and the Philistine garrison was at Bethlehem. David longed for water and said, "Oh, that someone would get me a drink of water from the well near the gate of Bethlehem!" So the Three broke through the Philistine lines, drew water from the well near the gate of Bethlehem and carried it back to David. But he refused to drink it; instead, he poured it out before the Lord. "God forbid that I should do this!" he said. "Should I drink the blood of these men who went at the risk of their lives?" Because they risked their lives to bring it back, David would not drink it. Such were the exploits of the three mighty men (1 Chronicles 11:15-19).

ADULTERY: Sexual unfaithfulness to one's spouse, or unfaithfulness to the things of God.

Contemporary/Symbolic Connotation:

See under Dream Symbols.

AGABUS: *Meaning: Locust (same as Hagab).* He was a prophet in the early church. He predicted a severe worldwide famine that was later fulfilled and involved all of the then-known earth. He also predicted Paul's arrest and torture in Jerusalem, though the Spirit of God compelled Paul to continue his journey to Jerusalem despite his warning (see Acts 23:11).

Contemporary/Symbolic Connotation:

Prophecy or prophet; renown for accurate prophetic words; attested as a prophet.

After we had been there a number of days, a prophet named Agabus came down from Judea. Coming over to us, he took Paul's belt, tied his own hands and feet with it and said, "The Holy Spirit says, 'In this way the Jews of Jerusalem will bind the owner of this belt and will hand him over to the Gentiles!'" When we heard this, we and the people there pleaded with Paul not to go up to Jerusalem. Then Paul answered, "Why are you weeping and breaking my heart? I am ready not only to be bound, but also to die in Jerusalem for the name of the Lord Jesus." When he would not be dissuaded, we gave up and said, "The Lord's will be done" (Acts 21:10-14).

AGAG: *Meaning: Hebrew for "violet" or house of flaming.*

A king of Amalekites who was spared by Saul though God has commanded

Saul to kill all the Amalekites. The prophet Samuel later killed King Agag in accordance with the Lord's command.

But Samuel replied, "Does the Lord delight in burnt offerings and sacrifices as much as in obeying the voice of the Lord? To obey is better than sacrifice, and to heed is better than the fat of rams. For rebellion is like the sin of divination, and arrogance like the evil of idolatry. Because you have rejected the word of the Lord, He has rejected you as king" (1 Samuel 15:22-23).

AGRIPPA: *Meaning: Latin for "pain of childbirth."*

He was a king of Palestine and the grandson of Herod the great. Paul was tried before him. He rejected Paul's invitation to the gospel but did declare Paul innocent. He was a man of intrigues and curried the Jew's favor. He was later summarily judged by God as he was dramatically executed by the angel of the Lord and instantaneously eaten by worms (see Acts 12:20-23).

AGUR: *Meaning: Hebrew for "gatherer."*

He was a man of wisdom and the writer of Proverbs 30.

The sayings of Agur son of Jakeh—an oracle... (Proverbs 30:1).

AHAB: *Meaning: Hebrew for "mother of the father" or uncle.* A king of Israel who became the husband of Jezebel and together they promoted Baal worship in Israel. Ahab coveted Naboth's vineyard and because Naboth refused to sell it to him, he connived with his wife to kill Naboth in order to possess the vineyard. His name became a symbol of wickedness.

Contemporary/Symbolic Connotation:

Wickedness, idol worshiping; covetousness.

Some time later there was an incident involving a vineyard belonging to Naboth the Jezreelite. The vineyard was in Jezreel, close to the palace of Ahab king of Samaria. Ahab said to Naboth, "Let me have your vineyard to use for a vegetable garden, since it is close to my palace. In exchange I will give you a better vineyard or, if you prefer, I will pay you whatever it is worth." But Naboth replied, "The Lord forbid that I should give you the inheritance of my fathers" (1 Kings 21:1-3).

AHAZ: *Meaning: Hebrew for "has grasped."* He was a king of Judah; a son of Jotham.

AHAZIAH: *Meaning: Hebrew for "Jehovah has grasped" or "who God upholds."*

1. A king of Israel who followed after the footsteps of his father King Ahab by worshiping idols. At some point he was noted to have made an alliance with Jehoshaphat and he died while seeking advice from Baal.

2. Another person with this name was a king of Judah. He was an idol worshiper, and at some point during his reign, he made alliance with Joram, king of Israel. While visiting Joram he was killed by Jehu. His son called Joash survived him.

AHIJAH: *Meaning: brother of Jehovah.* He was the prophet who prophesied the breaking up of Israel into two states as judgment upon Solomon's unfaithfulness to God. He gave his prophecy and its dramatization to Jeroboam during the reign of Solomon.

About that time Jeroboam was going out of Jerusalem, and Ahijah the prophet of Shiloh met him on the way, wearing a new cloak. The two of them were alone out in the country, and Ahijah took hold of the new cloak he was wearing and tore it into twelve pieces. Then he said to Jeroboam, "Take ten pieces for yourself, for this is what the Lord, the God of Israel, says: 'See, I am going to tear the kingdom out of Solomon's hand and give you ten tribes. But for the sake of my servant David and the city of Jerusalem, which I have chosen out of all the tribes of Israel, he will have one tribe. I will do this because they have forsaken me and worshiped Ashtoreth the goddess of the Sidonians, Chemosh the god of the Moabites, and Molech the god of the Ammonites, and have not walked in my ways, nor done what is right in my eyes, nor kept my statutes and laws as David, Solomon's father, did" (1 Kings 11:29-33).

AHIMELECH: *Meaning: Hebrew for "brother of a king."*

Key people with this name:

1. A high priest who gave David consecrated bread and Goliath's sword. Doeg saw this and betrayed him. Ahimelech was later killed by Doeg at Saul's command but his son Abiathar escaped to join David.

2. Grandson of Ahimelech who was co-priest with Zadok during David's reign.

3. A warrior in David's army. He was not of the priesthood lineage.

AHITHOPHEL: *Meaning: brother of folly or impiety.* A man trusted as outstanding counselor by David, but he later joined Absalom's conspiracy against David. He advised Absalom but his counsel was frustrated by God and rejected by Absalom. Despite all his wisdom, he later committed suicide.

Contemporary/Symbolic Connotation:

Spirit of wisdom and counsel, a trusted person, betrayal, frustrated or corrupt wisdom.

Now in those days the advice Ahithophel gave was like that of one who inquires of God. That was how both David and Absalom regarded all of Ahithophel's advice (2 Samuel 16:23).

Now David had been told, "Ahithophel is among the conspirators with Absalom." So David prayed, "O Lord, turn Ahithophel's counsel into foolishness" (2 Samuel 15:31).

AI: *Meaning: Hebrew for "ruin" or "heap of ruins."*

The place located in Palestine where Joshua's troops were initially defeated because of Achan's sin and also a place where Abraham once built an altar.

AIJALON: *Meaning: Hebrew for "place of gazelles."*

This is where Joshua prayed to God, *"O sun, stand still over Gibeon, O moon, over the Valley of Aijalon"* (see Josh. 10:12).

Contemporary/Symbolic Connotation:

A place of outstanding miracle.

ALABASTER: A light, creamy, soft stone, from which vases and jars were usually made.

Contemporary/Symbolic Connotation:

The human body; the flesh; that which must go to allow the true anointing to manifest.

ALLEGORY: Using a story form to represent a subject, using people or events portrayed to illustrate deeper meaning or truth or a symbolic representation.

ALMOND: *Meaning: hidden.* A tree of Mediterranean origin. It produced almond seeds. Acts as an indicator of change of season to the farmers.

Contemporary/Symbolic Connotation:

See under Dream Symbols.

ALTAR: A place or platform often elevated where a priest makes an offering or communes with God or the devil. It is a place of sacrifice, prayers, covenant, exchange, and place of spiritual traffic. Angels or demons traffic on the altars.

Contemporary/Symbolic Connotation:

A place of heightened spiritual activities, a place of spiritual exchange; sacred place of worship; a place of prayers; a place of idol worship.

AMALEKITES: They were noted for being a people without the fear of God and they are those who descended from Amalek. Amalek was the son of Eliphaz, the oldest son of Esau.

So Joshua fought the Amalekites as Moses had ordered, and Moses, Aaron and Hur went to the top of the hill. As long as Moses held up his hands, the Israelites were winning, but whenever he lowered his hands, the Amalekites were winning. When Moses' hands grew tired, they took a stone and put it under him and he sat on it. Aaron and Hur held his hands up—one on one side, one on the other—so that his hands remained steady till sunset. So Joshua overcame the Amalekite army with the sword. Then the Lord said to Moses, "Write this on a scroll as something to be remembered and make sure that Joshua hears it, because I will completely blot out the memory of Amalek from under heaven" (Exodus 17:10-14).

AMASA: He was the son of David's sister. He became a commander in Absalom's conspiracy, later came back to David and was offered the place of Joab as David's army chief, then was killed by Joab.

AMAZIAH: *Meaning: Hebrew for "one whom Jehovah strengthens."*

Key people with this name:

1. King of Judah who, after killing those who assassinated his father, raised a strong army and defeated Edom. He worshiped Edom's gods for which a prophet rebuked him. He was defeated by Israel and killed by conspirators.

2. Mentioned in the Book of Amos as a priest who opposed Amos.

AMMONITES: *Meaning: Ammon is Hebrew for "a people" or "of my nation."*

The people who lived in the east of Jordan and a people whose land God asked the Israelites not to trespass upon on their way to the Promised Land. They are descendants of Ammon.

AMNON: The firstborn of David who raped Tamar, his half-sister. Absalom eventually killed him.

AMON: Key people with this name:

1. A king of Judah. His father, King Manasseh, was one of the wicked kings of Judah and he followed after him by promoting evil practices but was later assassinated.

2. Another person with this name was a ruler of city of Samaria at the time of Ahab. He was the person whose care the prophet Micaiah was put while Ahab fought at Ramoth-Gilead.

3. One of Solomon's servants (see Neh. 7:57-59).

4. An Egyptian deity (see Jer. 46:25).

AMORITES: *Meaning: Hebrew for "mountain dwellers."*

They were one of the groups of wicked inhabitants of the Canaanite nations. They were notorious for their sinfulness and they worshiped the god Molech. God waited for their cup of sins to be full before allowing the Israelites to displace them from the Promised Land.

You, however, will go to your fathers in peace and be buried at a good old age. In the fourth generation your descendants will come back here, for the sin of the Amorites has not yet reached its full measure (Genesis 15:15-16).

AMOS: *Meaning: Hebrew for "burden bearer."*

Key people with this name:

1. A prophet of God and the writer of the book in the Bible that bears his name. Amos was a prophet whose message was directed to the northern kingdom of Israel. He was a farmer and shepherd before he received his call and was noted for confronting the prophet Amaziah. The prophet denounced Israel's sin, injustice, corruption and idol worship. He ended his message that some day Israel would be restored by the mercy of God.

Then Amaziah said to Amos, "Get out, you seer! Go back to the land of Judah. Earn your bread there and do your prophesying there. Don't prophesy anymore at Bethel, because this is the king's sanctuary and the temple of the kingdom." Amos answered Amaziah, "I was neither a prophet nor a prophet's son, but I was a shepherd, and I also took care of sycamore-fig trees. But the Lord took me from tending the flock and said to me, 'Go, prophesy to My people Israel'" (Amos 7:12-15).

2. Another Amos, mentioned in Luke 3:25, as an ancestor of Jesus.

ANAK: *Meaning: Hebrew for "long-necked."*

A tribe of people of extraordinary size, they were a tribe of giants.

ANAKIM: Those belonging to Anak and a race of people of extraordinary size; inhabitants of mountainous region of Canaan. Their size frightened ten of the twelve Hebrew spies to the Promised Land (see Num. 13:28-33).

ANANIAS: *Meaning: Greek for "Jehovah has been gracious" or "God is gracious."*

Key people with this name:

1. The husband of Sapphira. Together with his wife, they kept back part of their money of the sales of their property while pretending to others that it was the full money from the sales. They died for lying to God.

2. Another person with this name was a disciple of Christ in Damascus who was asked by God to pray and commission Paul. He initially hesitated because of the story of Paul's persecution of the followers of Jesus, but he was later convinced and prayed for him.

3. A man with this name was a high priest during the time of Paul's arrest.

ANCESTRAL DEITY: The god of the ancestor.

ANCESTRAL SPIRIT: The spirit or influence originating from grandparent or parent tradition.

ANCESTRY: The lineage from which one is descended. An ancestor is a grandparent or the forebearer, or the original type of a later thing.

ANCESTRY WORSHIP: The paying of allegiance or worship to the god of one's grandparent.

ANDREW: *Meaning: Greek for "manly" or "courageous."*

He was a man with evangelistic gifting and the brother of Simon Peter. He was originally a fisherman who became a disciple of John the Baptist, and later a disciple of Jesus. Notably he introduced Peter to Jesus, introduced little boy to Jesus, and also introduced the Greeks to Jesus.

ANGEL: *Meaning: messenger or ministering spirit.* They are spirits created by God. They were created early in creation. They are not to be worshiped and they are asexual and do not marry or die. There are numerous angels in the service of God and His saints. While all angels were created good, some have acquired an evil nature.

Contemporary/Symbolic Connotation:

Help; divine miraculous intervention; superhuman activities; divine rescue.

ANNA: *Meaning: Greek for "grace."*

She was a woman of outstanding commitment and faith. She was a prophetess from the tribe of Asher. Though she lost her husband only after seven years of marriage, she did not remarry but remained in the temple fasting and praying until she was eighty four years old and witnessed to others about baby Jesus as the salvation of Israel.

Contemporary/Symbolic Connotation:

Commitment; prayerful person; intercessor; salvation of God's people.

There was also a prophetess, Anna, the daughter of Phanuel, of the tribe of Asher. She was very old; she had lived with her husband seven years after

A

her marriage, and then was a widow until she was eighty-four. She never left the temple but worshiped night and day, fasting and praying. Coming up to them at that very moment, she gave thanks to God and spoke about the child to all who were looking forward to the redemption of Jerusalem (Luke 2:36-38).

ANNAS: Meaning: Greek for "merciful" or "gracious."

A high priest at the time of John the Baptist and became the father-in-law of Caiaphas, who also was at one time a high priest. Jesus was on trial before him and he was the one who sent Jesus to Caiaphas. Peter and John also stood trial before him.

ANOINTING: The powerful expression of the Spirit of God or the process of pouring oil on the servant of God; often an outward manifestation of an inward grace from God.

Contemporary/Symbolic Connotation:

See under Dream Symbols.

ANTICHRIST: Technically he is the one who opposes Christ. He was symbolized in the Bible by:

- Daniel's little horn; the king who exalts himself
- The abomination of desolation
- The man of lawlessness; the beast
- He will be destroyed at Christ's return.

ANTIOCH: *Meaning: the city after Antiochus.* The capital of Syria and where the first Gentile church was located; Barnabas and Paul once ministered in this city and it was where the disciples were first

called Christians. Agabus prophesied at Antioch. Also where Peter and Paul once had conflict. The saints in Antioch looked to the leaders in Jerusalem and once sent delegates to council in Jerusalem to resolve a conflict. The Antioch church was a missionary church and was the church that sent out Paul and Barnabas.

In the church at Antioch there were prophets and teachers: Barnabas, Simeon called Niger, Lucius of Cyrene, Manaen (who had been brought up with Herod the tetrarch) and Saul. While they were worshiping the Lord and fasting, the Holy Spirit said, "Set apart for me Barnabas and Saul for the work to which I have called them." So after they had fasted and prayed, they placed their hands on them and sent them off (Acts 13:1-3).

And when he found him, he brought him to Antioch. So for a whole year Barnabas and Saul met with the church and taught great numbers of people. The disciples were called Christians first at Antioch (Acts 11:26).

ANTS: A group of insects which are small, can be extremely numerous and widespread. They live in colonies and are noted for their industriousness and instinctive wisdom.

Contemporary/Symbolic Connotation:

See under Dream Symbols.

APOCALYPSE: A prophetic disclosure or revelation. An event characterized by violent destruction; revelation pertaining to the end of the world; predictions full of doom.

APOLLOS: *Meaning: belonging to Apollo.* Jewish Christian from Alexandria who spoke eloquently and had remarkable knowledge of Hebrew Scriptures. He was only aware of the baptism of John the Baptist until he was instructed by Aquila and Priscilla about the ministry of Jesus Christ and the work of the Holy Spirit.

What, after all, is Apollos? And what is Paul? Only servants, through whom you came to believe—as the Lord has assigned to each his task. I planted the seed, Apollos watered it, but God made it grow (1 Corinthians 3:5-6).

APOSTASY: Falling away from the truth.

APOSTLE: *Meaning: Greek for "messenger, envoy, ambassador."*

Someone sent out on an official commission for God. Paul was an apostle and he was called by the risen Christ as an apostle to the Gentiles.

APPARITIONS: Spiritual happening that is perceptible to the natural eyes.

APPRENTICE: Someone who by agreement serves another or works for another person and who in turn receives instruction.

APTITUDE: A natural skill; the quickness in learning and understanding.

AQUILA: *Meaning: Greek/Latin for "eagle."*

He was a professional tentmaker and the husband of Priscilla. Together as a couple they cared for Paul and opened their home to him and his ministry. Subsequently she and her husband made missionary journeys with Paul. He was one of those who instructed

Apollos and was considered a fellow worker by Paul.

ARCHANGEL: A chief angel or angel of high ranking. Angel Michael is mentioned as archangel in the Bible. Gabriel and lucifer were supposed to be of the rank archangels.

ARIEL: *Meaning: Hebrew for "lion of God" or "altar hearth."*

Woe to you, Ariel, Ariel, the city where David settled! Add year to year and let your cycle of festivals go on. Yet I will besiege Ariel; she will mourn and lament, she will be to me like altar hearth (Isaiah 29:1-2).

The destruction and the bloodshed in Jerusalem would make the city appear like an altar where a sacrifice of blood has just been made.

ARK OF THE COVENANT: *Meaning: the chest of covenant.* The Ark of the Covenant of God was made of acacia wood and was overlaid with gold. It had gold rings for poles for its transportation and in its lid it had the mercy seat. Its contents were particularly symbolic of Israel's history and faith: a pot of manna; Aaron's rod that had budded; the Ten Commandments. It was Israel's most sacred possession.

Contemporary/Symbolic Connotation:

- God's presence among His people
- The power of God
- Mercy seat and sprinkled blood symbolized forgiveness of sin

ARM: The limb from shoulder to the hand; a weapon; something used to fortify.

A

Contemporary/Symbolic Connotation:
See under Dream Symbols.

ARMAGEDDON: The final battle between the forces of evil and good.

Contemporary/Symbolic Connotation:
May be used loosely to refer to any great conflict with widespread destruction.

ARROW: Literally a thin shaft shot from a bow. Anything with a pointed end.

Contemporary/Symbolic Connotation:
See under Dream Symbols.

ARTAXERXES: *Meaning: Hebrew, probably a title for several Persian kings.*
He was a Persian king who permitted Ezra and his group to return to the Promised Land. He also employed Nehemiah as cupbearer and though at one time he also issued order to stop rebuilding Jerusalem, he is notably remembered as the one who sent Nehemiah to rebuild walls of Jerusalem and appointed him as governor.

ARTEMIS: The virgin goddess of hunting, also identified by the Romans as Diana. The Ephesians' Artemis was a fertility goddess worshiped at Ephesus. The temple of Artemis is ranked as one of the Seven Wonders of the World.

ASA: *Meaning: Hebrew for "healer."*
He was a king of Judah who was a godly reformer and removed his evil grandmother as queen. However, later in his life he used the silver and gold from the house of God to secure alliance with Ben-hadad. He became enraged when Prophet Hanani

rebuked him on this. In his later years, he became diseased on his feet, though it was severe, he did not seek God's help.

In the thirty-ninth year of his reign Asa was afflicted with a disease in his feet. Though his disease was severe, even in his illness he did not seek help from the Lord, but only from the physicians (2 Chronicles 16:12).

ASAHEL: *Meaning: Hebrew for "whom God made."*
He was one of David's warriors. He was one of David's twelve commanders and unwittingly pursued Abner during one of the conflicts between Israel and Judah. Abner had to kill him when he refused to turn back from the pursuit. Later Joab avenged his death by killing Abner.

ASAPH: *Meaning: collector.*
Key people with this name:
1. The father of Hezekiah's recorder.
2. A Levite musician who was also called a seer; his descendants were singers who wrote many psalms.

ASCENSION: The return of Jesus to Heaven, it occurred forty days after the resurrection.

ASHER: *Meaning: Hebrew for "happy."*
Key people with this name:
1. One of the sons of Jacob, he fathered five sons.

And Leah named him Asher (meaning "happy") for she said, "What a joy is mine! The other women will think of me blessed indeed" (Genesis 30:13 TLB).

About Asher he said: "Most blessed of sons is Asher; let him be favored by his brothers, and let him bathe his feet in oil. The bolts of your gates will be iron and bronze, and your strength will equal your days" (Deuteronomy 33:24-25).

2. Also refers to a tribe that descended from Asher. They were blessed by Moses but failed to support Deborah in Israel at a time of crisis. Anna was from the tribe of Asher. Asher was one of the tribes of the 144,000 in the Book of Revelation.

ASHERAH: A goddess of the Phoenicians and Syrians, often represented by a sacred pole or occult pillar; a Canaanite goddess of fertility. Wife of the Phoenicians and Syrians god, sometimes also regarded as the wife of Baal. The Israelites during time of Judges also worshiped Asherah.

ASHES: Residue from burnt material and symbolic of mourning, humiliation, or repentance.

ASHTORETH: This was the name of a goddess of the Canaanites who was considered to be the wife of Baal. Ashtoreth was the goddess of the moon, sexuality, and fertility. The worship of Ashtoreth dates back to antiquity, probably even to the days of Abraham. Her worship involved sex orgies in high places devoted to Baal worship, places that were often served by male and female prostitutes.

ASIA: Represented by present-day Turkey. These people opposed Stephen and incited riot against Paul in Jerusalem.

ASSIGNMENT: The act of assigning a task or responsibility, or a divine burden to carry out some duty by a person or group of people. A position or a duty divinely assigned to a person or an angel.

ASSYRIANS: They were descendants of Cush and capital city is Nineveh. Assyria was originally the land between the upper Tigris and Zab rivers.

ATHALIAH: The only woman who ever reigned as a king in Judah. She was the wicked daughter of Ahab who became wife of Jehoram and mother of Ahaziah. She made herself queen by killing Ahaziah's sons, and she ruled for six years. She was killed when Joash, son of Ahaziah was made king.

Contemporary/Symbolic Connotation:

Wickedness; inordinate ambition.

ATHEISM: The disbelief in or denial of the existence of God, or the doctrine of non-existence of God.

ATONEMENT: *Meaning: Greek for "reparation."*

This is the process of reconciling sinners to God or the bringing together into harmony those who have separated as enemies.

ATONEMENT, THE DAY OF: Important Israel holy day, when the high priest offers sacrifices for the sins of the people of Israel (see Lev. 16). Usually held in the seventh month of the Hebrew calendar.

AUGUSTUS: Venerable. Emperor of Rome and during his reign Christ was born (see Luke 2).

AXE: A tool with an iron head and a sharpened edge for cutting; anything capable of acting drastically to reduce or cut off something. A weapon of war such as a battle-axe, or men as battle-axes of God. A means of forceful determination, or making a decision on an issue.

AZARIAH: *Meaning: Jehovah has helped, or whom Jehovah has helped.* There were many people with this name; also the original name of Abednego.

BAAL: *Meaning: Hebrew for "possessor or husband, or master."*

The chief god of the Phoenicians and the Canaanites. In the days when judges ruled Israel, the apostate of Israel sometimes worshiped Baal.

No sooner had Gideon died than the Israelites again prostituted themselves to the Baals. They set up Baal-Berith as their god and did not remember the Lord their God, who had rescued them from the hands of all their enemies on every side (Judges 8:33-34).

BAAL-BERITH: *Meaning: the lord of covenant.* Worshiped it as El-Berith, meaning god of the covenant at the central shrine in Shechem.

BAAL OF PEOR: *Meaning: the lord of opening.* A form of Baal worshiped at Mount Peor by both Moabites and Midianites.

BAAL PERAZIM: The master of the breaking through.

BAAL PROPHETS: Those who predict the future by drawing inspiration from Baal.

BAAL WORSHIP: The worship of Baal; or put broadly in derogatory terms; the worship of a fake god.

BAAL-HAMON: *Meaning: the lord of multitude.*

BAAL-HERMON: *Meaning: the lord of Hermon.*

BAAL-TAMAR: *Meaning: the lord of palm trees.*

BAAL-ZEPHON: *Meaning: the lord of winter; the master of the north.*

BAALZEGBUB OR BEELZEBUB: Owner of flies and was used to refer to Baal who was worshiped by the Philistines at Ekron; name for any false god or a derogatory name for false gods by the ancient Jews.

BAASHA: Boldness or wickedness. He was a king of Israel.

BABEL: *Meaning: Hebrew for "the gate of God" or confusion.*

This was the name of one of the cities that was built after the flood of Noah's time. This is where God confused the language of all the earth, so Babel may literally mean confusion. This was the place where an attempt was made to build a tower with the top reaching to the sky for the celebration of the achievements of the builders.

Contemporary/Symbolic Connotation:

The place of confusion; vainglory, self-exaltation.

BABY: Early form of life or young child.

Contemporary/Symbolic Connotation:

See under Dream Symbols.

BABYLON: *Meaning: Hebrew probably derived from Babel—"the gate of God"; Greek for Babel.*

This was the name later name given to the city of Babel; a city renounced and located along Euphrates River.

BABYLONIAN CAPTIVITY: The period of seventy years that the Israelites were held in slavery in Babylon.

BABYLONIAN RELIGION: The religion of the people of Babylon.

BACA: *Meaning: weeping.*

Contemporary/Symbolic Connotation:

A place sorrow, a place of preparation or of equipping.

BALAAM: *Meaning: Hebrew for "one who devours, a devourer" or "the Lord of the people."* He was considered a pagan prophet but sometimes also operated in divination and was easily swaged by financial rewards. He lived in Mesopotamia and was the son of Beor. He was asked by Balak to curse Israelites. He was later killed by Israelites.

Contemporary/Symbolic Connotation:

False prophet or prophecy, personal gain above God's desire, material motivation, or gain.

Then Balaam uttered his oracle: "Balak brought me from Aram, the king of Moab from the eastern mountains. 'Come,' he said, 'curse Jacob for me; come, denounce Israel.' How can I curse those whom God has not

cursed? How can I denounce those whom the Lord has not denounced?" (Numbers 23:7-8)

Woe to them! They have taken the way of Cain; they have rushed for profit into Balaam's error; they have been destroyed in Korah's rebellion (Jude 1:11).

BALAK: *Meaning: Hebrew for "devastator" or "destruction."*

He was a king of Moab, during the time of the Jews' exodus from Egypt, who hired Balaam to pronounce a curse on Israelites.

BALM: The name of a resin used as an ointment for the treatment of wounds. Symbolic of the healing power of God.

Is there no balm in Gilead? Is there no physician there? Why then is there no healing for the wound of My people? (Jeremiah 8:22)

Babylon will suddenly fall and be broken. Wail over her! Get balm for her pain; perhaps she can be healed (Jeremiah 51:8).

Contemporary/Symbolic Connotation:

See under Dream Symbols.

BANNER: Typically a piece of cloth either hung overhead or carried between poles bearing a message or slogan. Banners were used to designate different families, or to rally troops. Symbolically refers to something that unifies or brings people together under one purpose or goal.

Contemporary/Symbolic Connotation:

- The Lord as our Banner
- Jesus Christ as a banner for all nations
- The banner of love

BAPTISM: A Christian sacrament symbolic of spiritual regeneration, renewal or rebirth; transformation. It was typified in the Old Testament: in the story of the flood; in the rite of circumcision; in the crossing of the Red Sea.

- **Baptism of John the Baptist**

Paul said, "John's baptism was a baptism of repentance. He told the people to believe in the one coming after him, that is, in Jesus." On hearing this, they were baptized into the name of the Lord Jesus. When Paul placed his hands on them, the Holy Spirit came on them, and they spoke in tongues and prophesied (Acts 19:4-6).

His baptism symbolized repentance, his baptism meant to reveal Jesus, his baptism looked ahead to Spirit baptism, and he baptized Jesus.

- **Baptism of Moses**

For I do not want you to be ignorant of the fact, brothers, that our forefathers were all under the cloud and that they all passed through the sea. They were all baptized into Moses in the cloud and in the sea. They all ate the same spiritual food and drank the same spiritual drink; for they drank from the spiritual rock that accompanied them, and that rock was Christ (1 Corinthians 10:1-4).

- **Baptism of Jesus Christ**

On hearing this, they were baptized into the name of the Lord Jesus (Acts 19:5).

- **Baptism of the Spirit**

When Paul placed his hands on them, the Holy Spirit came on them, and they spoke in tongues and prophesied (Acts 19:6).

BAPTISM OF THE HOLY SPIRIT: To be transformed by the power of the Holy Spirit, and the common manifestation of baptism of the Holy Spirit is speaking in tongues. Jesus was baptized with the Holy Spirit. Water baptism is linked with Spirit baptism but they are separate as the Bible says, "born of water and the Spirit." Believers are baptized into one body, washing of rebirth, and renewal by Spirit.

Contemporary/Symbolic Connotation:

Renewal, rebirth or transformation by God.

BAR-JESUS: *Meaning: Greek for "son of Jesus."*

BARABBAS: *Meaning: Greek for "the son of the father."*

He was a prisoner at the time of the trial and crucifixion of Jesus, and he was introduced in the Bible as the object of God's grace and mercy. He committed murder and insurrection but was released free in place of Jesus. A testimony of the fact that when we were yet sinners, Jesus died for us.

Contemporary/Symbolic Connotation:

Unmerited favor; the depth of Jesus' suffering; death on the cross; redemption from punishment.

BARAK: *Meaning: Hebrew for "lightning" or "thunderbolt."*

Fought with Deborah against Sisera. He was considered an example of faith in the Book of Hebrews.

Barak said to her, "If you go with me, I will go; but if you don't go with me, I won't go." "Very well," Deborah said,

"I will go with you. But because of the way you are going about this, the honor will not be yours, for the Lord will hand Sisera over to a woman." So Deborah went with Barak to Kedesh, where he summoned Zebulun and Naphtali. Ten thousand men followed him, and Deborah also went with him (Judges 4:8-10).

And what more shall I say? I do not have time to tell about Gideon, Barak, Samson, Jephthah, David, Samuel and the prophets, who through faith conquered kingdoms, administered justice, and gained what was promised; who shut the mouths of lions, quenched the fury of the flames, and escaped the edge of the sword; whose weakness was turned to strength; and who became powerful in battle and routed foreign armies. Women received back their dead, raised to life again (Hebrews 11:32-35).

BARNABAS: *Meaning: Greek for "son of exhortation" or "son of comfort."*

He was introduced as a man full of the Holy Spirit and faith; sold property and brought proceeds to the church; considered a prophet, teacher and apostle. He was also known as the son of encouragement.

For instance, there was Joseph (the one the apostle nicknamed "Barny the Preacher"). He was of the tribe of Levi, from the Island of Cyrus (Acts 4:36 TLB).

Joseph, a Levite from Cyprus, whom the apostles called Barnabas (which means Son of Encouragement) (Acts 4:36).

Contemporary/Symbolic Connotation:

Encourager, preacher; selfless service; considerate person.

BARREN: Not productive of offspring.

Contemporary/Symbolic Connotation:

- Not bearing fruits
- Giving no results or gains
- Infertile or sterile land
- Devoid or lacking in usefulness

BARTHOLOMEW: *Meaning: Greek for "son of Tolmai."*

One of the disciples of Jesus and was among those who later became an apostle.

BARUCH: *Meaning: Hebrew for "blessed."*

He was a secretary and friend of the prophet Jeremiah and son of Neriah. He was among those forced to go to Egypt. At a critical time in his life, he received comforting message from Jeremiah.

"Should you then seek great things for your self? Seek them not. For I will bring disaster on all people," declares the Lord, "but wherever you go, I will let you escape with your life" (Jeremiah 45:5).

BARZILLAI: *Meaning: Hebrew for "made of iron" or "son of iron."*

He was a man from Gilead who helped David, but he was too old to go with David when he returned to Jerusalem after Absalom's rebellion. Barzillai asked his son to go with David instead. David showed favor to his son as a reward for his goodness.

BATHSHEBA: *Meaning: Hebrew for "daughter of Sheba" or "daughter of an oath."*

B

This was the name of the wife of Uriah who committed adultery with David. The son of her adulterous relationship with David died, but she later became the mother of King Solomon.

BEERSHEBA: *Meaning: Hebrew for "a place of well of seven (the seventh well)" or "well of the oath."*

The place that Hagar fled to when she ran from Sarah. It was the place where Abraham made a treaty with Abimelech and lived for a while. It was also the place that Isaac made a treaty with Abimelech (possibly another person with the same name.) Therefore, the place is also known as the city of covenant. This city is situated in the southern most land of Israel.

BELIAL: *Meaning: wickedness, good for nothing, or worthless.*

BELL: A metallic instrument meant to produce sound as signal for timing, or the means of drawing attention to the need to change.

Contemporary/Symbolic Connotation:

See under Dream Symbols.

BELLY: The part of the human body between the ribcage and the pelvis.

Contemporary/Symbolic Connotation:

See under Dream Symbols.

BELSHAZZAR: *Meaning: Hebrew for "may Bel protect the king" or "may Bel protect."*

A king of Babylon who gave a huge sacrilegious feast with golden cups from the temple of God, but gave glory to other gods instead. He

suffered swift judgment from God. He saw handwriting on the wall and was killed by the Medes the night that he saw the writing on the wall.

BELT: Technically a band worn around the waist to support the clothing.

Contemporary/Symbolic Connotation:

- May refer to an armor
- A sign of preparedness (the belt of preparation)
- Also may refer to a defined geographical region

BELTESHAZZAR: *Meaning: Hebrew for "may she (goddess) Bel protect king's life" or "may Bel protect his life."*

This was the name given to the prophet Daniel by Nebuchadnezzar's steward.

BEN: *Meaning : Hebrew for "son."*

BEN-HADAD: *Meaning: son of noise or son of god (Hadad).* This is a common name among the people of Damascus. There were three kings of Damascus with this name:

1. One who made treaty with Asa and fought against Israelite cities.

2. Another king of Damascus who fought against Ahab but was defeated by Ahab. He later besieged Samaria but the siege was miraculously lifted; Hazael killed him.

3. Another king of Damascus who was the son of Hazael; defeated by Jeboash three times and the prophet Amos also prophesied against him.

BENJAMIN: *Meaning: son of my right hand.* He was the youngest of the twelve sons of Jacob and the younger brother of Joseph, second son of Rachel. The mother had given him another name—Ben-Oni (meaning "the son of my sorrow")—but his father called him Benjamin (meaning "son of the right hand"). He was greatly favored by his father Jacob.

Then they moved on from Bethel. While they were still some distance from Ephrath, Rachel began to give birth and had great difficulty. And as she was having great difficulty in childbirth, the midwife said to her, "Don't be afraid, for you have another son." As she breathed her last—for she was dying—she named her son Ben-Oni But his father named him Benjamin. So Rachel died and was buried on the way to Ephrath (that is, Bethlehem). Over her tomb Jacob set up a pillar, and to this day that pillar marks Rachel's tomb (Genesis 35:16-20).

BETH: *Meaning: house.*

BETHANY: *Meaning: Greek for "the place (house) of unripe figs" or "house of dates."*

A town on the Mount of Olives less than two miles from Jerusalem. Bethany was the hometown of Mary, Martha, and Lazarus. Jesus stayed there after triumphal entry, where Mary anointed Jesus.

BETHEL: *Meaning: Hebrew for "the house of God."*

Originally called Luz, it is situated close to Ai on the border between Ephraim and Benjamin. This is where Jacob anointed a pillar after the dream of a ladder from earth to Heaven. It is a place of historical importance to the Israelites. Also later known as El-Bethel (the God of the house of God).

Contemporary/Symbolic Connotation:

A place of divine encounters; open heaven; the house of God; a place of vow; a place of covenant.

BETHLEHEM: *Meaning: Hebrew for "the house of bread."*

Originally called Ephrath; known as "the town of David," a city given to Judah. Jacob buried Rachel on way to Ephrath. Ephrath means Bethlehem (see Gen. 48:7). This is the place that was the home of Elimelech and Naomi and the place where Ruth married Boaz.

Contemporary/Symbolic Connotation:

The birthplace of Jesus; the house of abundance, where God meets one's desires.

As I was returning from Paddan, to my sorrow Rachel died in the land of Canaan while we were still on the way, a little distance from Ephrath. So I buried her there beside the road to Ephrath" (that is, Bethlehem) (Genesis 48:7).

BETHSAIDA: *Meaning: Greek for "house of fishing."*

This was a town in Galilee where three of the disciples of Jesus came from, where five thousand were fed, and where Jesus healed a blind man. Jesus denounced Bethsaida for unbelief.

BEULAH: *Meaning: married.*

B

BEZALEL: *Meaning: in the shadow of God.* Craftsman filled with God's Spirit in wisdom to supervise the building of the tabernacle that God showed Moses to build. One of the sons of Hur of the tribe of Judah.

Contemporary/Symbolic Connotation: Gifted by God; anointed for skillful job; divinely chosen.

Then the Lord said to Moses, "See, I have chosen Bezalel son of Uri, the son of Hur, of the tribe of Judah, and I have filled him with the Spirit of God, with skill, ability and knowledge in all kinds of crafts (Exodus 31:1-3).

BILDAD: One of Job's friends whose original intentions were noble and good and who tried to comfort Job. He made three speeches during his visit to Job and soon ran into presumption and accused Job of sinfulness. He later offered sacrifices to God after Job's restoration.

BILHAH: *Meaning: Hebrew for "foolish."* She was a concubine of Jacob who was the servant of Rachel. She became the mother of Dan and Naphtali. Reuben defiled his father's bed by sleeping with her.

BLACK MAGIC: *Meaning: magic inspired by satanic power.* Power maintained in league with the devil.

BLASPHEMY: Bringing reproach against God, such as speaking against God.

BLIND SPOT: Any part of an issue that a person cannot directly observe with his natural rationalization. Also refers to an area where perception is weak or a subject about which one is markedly ignorant or prejudiced.

BLOOD: A symbol of life, which could also symbolize danger because of its color.

Contemporary/Symbolic Connotation:
- Abel's blood meant his life
- Eating blood means eating life
- Shedding blood means taking a life
- Being innocent of blood means not being responsible for spiritual death

BOAZ: *Meaning: Hebrew for "strength" or "swift."*
A kinsman redeemer to Ruth who acted kindly to Ruth and later married her. He was a Bethlehemite and was recorded as an ancestor of David and Jesus.

Contemporary/Symbolic Connotation: Kinsman redeemer, a type of Jesus.

BODY: The human body is the tangible and material aspect of man's existence and the means by which man can interact with this fallen world. Made by God from the dust of the earth. The Church is also regarded as the Body of Christ. Christ as the head of His Body; Christ as the Savior of His Body.

Contemporary/Symbolic Connotation: Flesh; the Church of God; perishable thing; opposed to the Spirit.

BORN AGAIN: To accept Jesus Christ Lord and Savior, to be born of the Spirit and water.

Contemporary/Symbolic Connotation:

- Unless a man is born again of spirit and water, he can not enter the Kingdom of God.
- Spiritual rebirth is by the power of Jesus.
- We all need to be born again because we are dead in sin.

BREAD: A means of sustenance or livelihood. Bread in Old Testament is used in fellowship offerings and was used in Aaron's ordination; the bread of the Presence was placed in tabernacle. David was once given this bread as food when he was hungry.

Contemporary/Symbolic Connotation:

See under Dream Symbols.

BRONZE: Metal made of copper and tin, with or without the traces of other metals.

BRONZE AGE: The period between the Stone Age and the Iron Age.

BRONZE SNAKE: The image of a snake made of bronze that Moses made in the wilderness that brought healing to those who looked up to it.

Contemporary/Symbolic Connotation:

A symbol of Jesus Christ (see Num. 21:4-9).

BROTHERS AND SISTERS: Literally people with the same parents as in common use of brother and sister.

Contemporary/Symbolic Connotation:

See under Dream Symbols.

BUL: The eighth month of the Hebrew calendar, it spans mid-October to about mid-November.

BURDEN OF PROPHECY: A weight of divine urge to prophesy.

BURNT OFFERING: A special form of sacrifice in which all the parts of the animal are completely burnt on the altar.

CAESAREA: Apostle Philip's home and headquarters for his preaching, and also where Cornelius was stationed. It was a Roman capital of Palestine.

CAIAPHAS: He was a high priest at the time of John the Baptist, and son-in-law of Annas. He also spoke prophetically about Jesus. Jesus, Peter, and John were tried before him.

CAIN: *Meaning: possession, or something produced, or a spear.* The firstborn son of Adam and also was the first farmer on earth. He offered an unsatisfactory offering. He murdered his brother Abel because he became jealous of him when Abel's sacrifice was more acceptable to God. He was cursed and became a wanderer.

Contemporary/Symbolic Connotation:

Unsatisfactory offering; sacrifice not accepted by God; self-pity; jealousy; murderer; wanderer; vengeance; accursed person.

CALAMUS: A sweet-smelling plant.

CALEB: *Meaning: Hebrew for "faithful."*

He was one of the chosen spies of Canaan and together with Joshua gave a positive report and pleaded with Israelites to have faith and not to disobey

God. For his faith and trust in God, he was allowed to enter Canaan and allotted the city of Hebron. He was the son of Jephunneh and came from the tribe of Judah.

Contemporary/Symbolic Connotation: The spirit of excellence, faith in God, boldness.

Now the men of Judah approached Joshua at Gilgal, and Caleb son of Jephunneh the Kenizzite said to him, "You know what the Lord said to Moses the man of God at Kadesh Barnea about you and me. I was forty years old when Moses the servant of the Lord sent me from Kadesh Barnea to explore the land. And I brought him back a report according to my convictions, but my brothers who went up with me made the hearts of the people melt with fear. I, however, followed the Lord my God wholeheartedly. So on that day Moses swore to me, 'The land on which your feet have walked will be your inheritance and that of your children forever, because you have followed the Lord my God wholeheartedly.' Now then, just as the Lord promised, He has kept me alive for forty-five years since the time He said this to Moses, while Israel moved about in the desert. So here I am today, eighty-five years old! I am still as strong today as the day Moses sent me out; I'm just as vigorous to go out to battle now as I was then. Now give me this hill country that the Lord promised me that day. You yourself heard then that the Anakites were there and their cities were large and fortified, but, the Lord helping me, I will drive them out just as he said (Joshua 14:6-12).

CALF: A young cow or bull.

CALL, CALLING: God's summoning us to Himself; the specific endowment to carry out an assignment. The process of fulfilling burden placed in our heart by God to get the job done.

CANAAN: *Meaning: Hebrew for "merchants" or "lowland."*

This was the name of the land of Palestine before the Jews occupied it.

CAPTURING YOUR DREAM: The process of remembering your dreams.

CARRY-OVER: A thought pattern carried over into or from the natural or supernatural realm.

CASSIA: A spice made from the bark of a cassia tree.

CASTING LOTS: The process of throwing a group of nearly identical objects to determine or make a choice.

CATTLE: Capable of multiple functions and serves a variety of purposes in the lives of people in biblical days.

Contemporary/Symbolic Connotation:

- Provides meat, milk, cheese and calf
- Used extensively in sacrificial offerings
- Served as means of exchange in trading
- Used as a form of agricultural mechanization such as ploughing/harvesting
- Used for threshing
- Means of measuring wealth

For every animal of the forest is mine, and the cattle on a thousand hills (Psalm 50:10).

CAVE: A hollow or an opening on the surface of a hill or a cliff.

Contemporary/Symbolic Connotation:

See under Dream Symbols.

CELESTIAL BEINGS: Beings native of the heavens, the invisible supernatural realm.

CHAFF: The husks of grain after separation from the seed.

Contemporary/Symbolic Connotation:

- Trivial matter

- Something worthless

- Something that can be easily blown away by the wind

- Something that needs to be separated from the real substance

May those who seek my life be disgraced and put to shame; may those who plot my ruin be turned back in dismay. May they be like chaff before the wind, with the angel of the Lord driving them away (Psalm 35:4-5).

CHALDEANS: Ancient Semitic people ruled by the Babylonians. Babylon was the capital of Chaldea.

CHANT: A repetitive rhythmic intonation of words for invocation of some spiritual power or miracles.

CHARIOT: *Meaning: Hebrew for "mount and ride."*

This was an ancient form of transport, consisting of a two-wheeled vehicle drawn by horses. It was powerful in the olden days and was used for wars and by royalty for pleasure.

CHARISMA: A personal charm, or an exceptional ability to attract and influence others.

CHEMOSH: A god of the Moab that requires child sacrifice as worship.

CHERUB: A class of angelic beings.

CHERUBIM: Celestial beings associated with God's holiness and glory, and the storm wind upon which God travels (see Ps. 18:10).

CHOSEN: The selected one, the preferred one.

CHRIST: The Anointed One; the Messiah; the Savior; the title of Jesus.

CIRCUMCISION: The cutting off of the foreskin. Spiritually indicates the removal of fleshy actions or attitudes. Circumcision in the Old Testament was done at eight days as a sign of the covenant and a sign of Abraham's faith. Heart circumcision must accompany physical circumcision.

Contemporary/Symbolic Connotation:

See under Dream Symbols.

A man is not a Jew if he is only outwardly, nor is circumcision merely outward and physical. No, a man is a Jew if he is one inwardly; and circumcision is circumcision of the heart, by the Spirit, not by the written code. Such a man's praise is not from men, but from God (Romans 2:28-29).

CLOAK: Literally an outer garment, but often connotes anything that covers what one is wearing.

C

Contemporary/Symbolic Connotation:

Spiritually refers to the mantle or the anointing on the person.

CLOSED VISION: A vision perceived by the spiritual eyes while the natural eyes are closed.

CLOUD: A visible mass in the air of steam, or smoke, or dust.

Contemporary/Symbolic Connotation:

See under Dream Symbols.

COMMISSIONED: An act of giving authority to a person to carry out a particular duty or role. To be qualified and authorized by God to carry out certain functions.

COMMUNION: Sharing of thoughts, feelings, and close rapport in a spiritual atmosphere.

COMPASSION: Deep feeling of concern for suffering of other people.

CONCEPTUALIZATION: The process of forming concepts, theories, or ideas.

CONCUBINE: A servant woman who, although not a wife, had sexual relations with her master. Legally, she has specific rights and her master should be referred to as her husband.

CONFIRMATION: The process of ascertaining a dream's true interpretation. A dream's correct interpretation is that which reveals the true message of the dream or the reason for which the dream was sent.

CONSCIENCE: The innate ability to know right from wrong. For instance, our conscience becomes cleansed through Christ and inspires us to love others. It also inspires us to obey God's law and maintain a clear conscience. Conscience can be defiled so it needs to be washed by the blood of Jesus Christ to be reliable.

This testimony is true. Therefore, rebuke them sharply, so that they will be sound in the faith and will pay no attention to Jewish myths or to the commands of those who reject the truth. To the pure, all things are pure, but to those who are corrupted and do not believe, nothing is pure. In fact, both their minds and consciences are corrupted. They claim to know God, but by their actions they deny Him. They are detestable, disobedient and unfit for doing anything good (Titus 1:13-16).

How much more, then, will the blood of Christ, who through the eternal Spirit offered himself unblemished to God, cleanse our consciences from acts that lead to death, so that we may serve the living God!"(Hebrews 9:14)

CORNELIUS: *Meaning: Greek for "made of a horn" or Latin for "sunbeam."*

He was a God-fearing Roman centurion who had a vision from God to send for Peter. Peter preached to him and he received the Holy Spirit and was baptized in the Holy Spirit.

Contemporary/Symbolic Connotation:

God-fearing person; selfless service; reward of righteousness; God's approval.

Then Peter began to speak: "I now realize how true it is that God does not show favoritism, but accept men from every nation who fear Him and do what is right"(Acts 10:34-35).

COUNCIL: The name of the highest religious court of the ancient Jews. It usually consisted of seventy Jewish leaders and was headed by the high priest.

COUNSELOR: One who gives advice and direction for life. The prophet Isaiah referred to Jesus as wonderful counselor

For to us a child is born, to us a Son is given, and the government will be on His shoulders. And He will be called Wonderful Counselor, Mighty God, Everlasting Father, Prince of Peace (Isaiah 9:6).

COURAGE: The ability to face danger without fear; boldness based on faith or reasoning; the spirit that enables one to overcome fear.

COVENANT: An agreement established between two parties. Most covenants are between two unequal partners, one compensating for the other. There are essential elements in a covenant, including: promises, stipulations, oaths, responsibilities, witnesses, and implied threats to ensure conformity.

COVETING: The sinful desire for what belongs to someone else, greed. To wish excessively for something, crave culpably.

CROSS: The cross was the means by which Jesus' death paid for the redemption of human sins. The death on the cross was a cursed one. It was planned by God and carried out by human hands, but it showed above all the submission and obedience of Jesus to God the Father. He died for us while we were yet sinners.

CROWN: A head covering worn on the head as a symbol of victory, honor, power, sovereignty, or position. The reward in Heaven for the righteous; priests; kings, queens, and Christ wore crowns. God crowns humans with glory and honor.

CULT: A system of religious worship and rituals of ungodly nature. An exclusive group of persons sharing the belief of other esoteric interest or obsessive devotion of person, principle, ideal.

CURSE, CURSING: Invisible spiritual package targeted to bring specific limitation on a person or object. Curse is a consequence of sin (the result of sin). There will be no curses in Heaven. There will be a time when there will be no curse on the new earth when the old one passes away.

CYRENE: *Meaning: wall.* A Libyan city in North Africa.

CYRUS: *Meaning: Greek for "copper" or "womb," or Persian for "sun."*

This was the name of one of the kings of Persia. He allowed Israel to return from exile and commanded rebuilding of the temple in Jerusalem. He was also called the shepherd of the Lord and a Gentile king that the Bible called "anointed of the Lord."

This is what the Lord says to His anointed, to Cyrus, whose right hand I take hold of to subdue nations before him and to strip kings of their armor, to open doors before him so that gates will not be shut (Isaiah 45:1).

DAGON: *Meaning: Hebrew for "fish."*

141

A chief god of the ancient Philistines represented by half-man and half-fish.

DAMASCUS: Capital city of Syria. The Syrians were descendants of Shem. Eliezer, the servant of Abram, was from Damascus.

DAN: *Meaning: justice.* One of the twelve sons of Jacob, and his mother was Bilbab. He is the ancestor of the tribe of Dan.

Rachel named him Dan, meaning Justice, for she said, "God has given me justice and heard my plea and given me a son" (Genesis 30:6 TLB).

DANCING: Rhythmic movements usually to music, or to leap and skip excitedly. To perform a particular set of prescribed movements. Dancing could be used to praise and worship God, to express human elation or used as in inappropriate pagan worship.

Contemporary/Symbolic Connotation:

See under Dream Symbols.

DANIEL: *Meaning: Hebrew for "God is my judge" or the judgment of God.*

He was one of the Hebrew exiles to Babylon. He was educated in Babylonia and his name changed to Belteshazzar. He refused non-Jewish food and interpreted dreams of Nebuchadnezzar, as well as interpreted handwriting on the wall. He also survived the lion's den and had notable dreams and visions.

Contemporary/Symbolic Connotation:

Prophecy; adept in understanding of dreams and visions; outstanding wisdom; able to solve difficult problems.

But Daniel resolved not to defile himself with the royal food and wine, and he asked the chief official for permission not to defile himself this way. Now God had caused the official to show favor and sympathy to Daniel, but the official told Daniel, "I am afraid of my lord the king, who has assigned your food and drink. Why should he see you looking worse than the other young men your age? The king would then have my head because of you." Daniel then said to the guard whom the chief official had appointed over Daniel, Hananiah, Mishael and Azariah, Please test your servants for ten days: Give us nothing but vegetables to eat and water to drink. Then compare our appearance with that of the young men who eat the royal food, and treat your servants in accordance with what you see." So he agreed to this and tested them for ten days (Daniel 1:8-14).

The queen, hearing the voices of the king and his nobles, came into the banquet hall."O king, live forever!"she said. "Don't be alarmed! Don't look so pale! There is a man in your kingdom who has the spirit of the holy gods in him. In the time of your father he was found to have insight and intelligence and wisdom like that of the gods. King Nebuchadnezzar your father—your father the king, I say—appointed him chief of the magicians, enchanters, astrologers and diviners. This man Daniel, whom the king called Belteshazzar, was found to have a keen mind and knowledge and understanding, and also the ability to interpret dreams, explain riddles and solve difficult problems. Call for Daniel, and he will tell you what the writing means"(Daniel 5:10-12).

DARIUS: *Meaning: Hebrew for "inquiring," or Persian for "prosperous."*

Key people with this name:

1. King of the Medes who conquered Babylon.

2. A later king of Persia, who asked for the rebuilding of temple to stop, but later allowed rebuilding of temple to continue.

DARK SPEECH: Speech with concealed meaning, such as parable illustration.

My servant Moses is not so, who is faithful in all mine house. With him will I speak mouth to mouth, even apparently, and not in dark speeches; and the similitude of the Lord shall he behold; wherefore then were ye not afraid to speak against my servant Moses (Numbers 12:7-8 KJV).

Contemporary/Symbolic Connotation:

See under Dream Symbols.

DARKNESS: Created by God and it originally covered the earth. God separated it from light and called it night. Comes when the sun sets. God can see things in the dark. God is the Father of lights.

Contemporary/Symbolic Connotation:

Ignorance, sin or evil, sinful deeds, the way of the wicked and the absence of God's light.

DAVID: *Meaning: Hebrew for "beloved."*

One of the sons of Jesse and was the youngest in the family. He became one of the greatest kings of Israel. God promised his throne will reign forever; Jesus Christ is regarded as the son of David. Had many wives,

including Michal, daughter of Saul; Abigail, widow of Nabal; Bathsheba, widow of Uriah. David was a shepherd, a warrior, a musician, a psalmist, a prophet, and a king.

Contemporary/Symbolic Connotation:

A great king, a man after God's heart; psalmist and priest; a man of faith and repentance.

The Lord is my shepherd, I shall not be in want. He makes me lie down in green pastures, He leads me beside quiet waters, He restores my soul. He guides me in paths of righteousness for His name's sake (Psalm 23:1-3).

When the prophet Nathan came to David after David had committed adultery with Bathsheba: *"Have mercy on me, O God, according to Your unfailing love; according to Your great compassion blot out my transgressions. Wash away all my iniquity and cleanse me from my sin. For I know my transgressions, and my sin is always before me"* (Psalm 51:1-3).

DAY: Day is the period of light after the night. Light was called "day" by God. Day and night are divided into twelve hours each.

Contemporary/Symbolic Connotation:

See under Dream Symbols.

DAY BREAK: The beginning of the day, or the dawn.

DAY OF THE LORD: A term commonly used to refer to the beginning of the Second Coming of our Lord Jesus Christ and will include the final judgment. And therefore may also refer to the consummation of God's Kingdom and victory over satan.

DEACON: Greek for "servant." A layperson who assists the leader or pastor in various capacities.

DEATH: *Meaning: the termination of life, or the state being dead.*

Contemporary/Symbolic Connotation:

See under Dream Symbols.

Physical death: Common meaning of physical death in revelation is dying to flesh or dying to some carnal desires, becoming Christ-like.

Spiritual death: separation from God came as a result of sin and is part of the sinful human nature. Everyone who does not have Christ is spiritually dead and regarded as a friend of this world. Through faith in Christ and by repenting and turning to God one can over come spiritual death.

Eternal death: Irreversible and permanent separation from God. It also means eternal punishment.

DEBORAH: *Meaning: Hebrew for "honeybee."*

Key people with this name:

1. Rebecca's nurse.
2. The name of a woman who rose to fame at a time when men were afraid to go to war. She was a prophetess, she judged Israel, and fought Sisera's army with Barak. As a judge, she held a recognized position or office and rendered decisions on people's inquiries. Her role in the battle against Sisera was not defined in the Bible. Probably as a prophetess and a judge. Her presence was a sign

of God's approval and therefore encouraged the soldiers.

Barak said to her, "If you go with me, I will go; but if you don't go with me, I won't go." "Very well," Deborah said, "I will go with you. But because of the way you are going about this, the honor will not be yours, for the Lord will hand Sisera over to a woman." So Deborah went with Barak to Kedesh (Judges 4:8-9).

DEBT: An obligation to render something to somebody. What is owed to another person.

Contemporary/Symbolic Connotation:

What is owned to the world as a result of God's calling on one's life.

But if I say, "I will not mention Him or speak any more in His name," His word is in my heart like a fire, a fire shut up in my bones. I am weary of holding it in; indeed, I cannot (Jeremiah 20:9).

DECAPOLIS: *Meaning: Greek for "ten cities."*

DEFILE: To corrupt or contaminate spiritually.

DELILAH: *Meaning: Hebrew for "the dainty one" or "the delicate one."*

A woman, presented to us in the Bible as the object of Samson's love. She lured Samson into disobeying God. Samson gave her the secret of his anointing. She betrayed Samson and sold him out for money (see Judg. 16:5).

DELUSION: A false perception that something that does not exist exists, or a false belief.

DEMAS: *Meaning: Greek for "popular" or "ruler of the people."*

He was the person whom Paul described as a faithful helper during his imprisonment in Rome.

DEMETRIUS: *Meaning: Greek for "belonging to Demeter" or "lover of the earth."*

Silversmith in Ephesus who incited a riot against Paul and was concerned about the financial loss that resulted following the evangelistic outreach to the people.

Contemporary/Symbolic Connotation:

A symbol of those who oppose the Gospel of God.

DEMON: An invisible wicked spirit with superhuman powers. The first to become a demon was satan. Their purpose is to turn people against God. Evil spirit that can afflict humans.

DEMONIC DREAM: Dream dominated by demonic activities.

DESERT: A sparsely settled and uncultivated land. Prophetically it refers to a place of barrenness, hardship, and training. A place of preparations for the ministry.

DESTINY: The ultimate final outcome of a person or a country or something.

DEVIL: Slanderer. A descriptive name for satan because he is the slanderer or accuser of brethren.

DIALOGUING DREAMS: Set of dreams on the same subject, separated by an interlude in which the dreamer wakes up and intercedes on the issue.

DINAH: *Meaning: vindicated.* She was the daughter of Jacob who while sight-seeing was raped by Shechem, a prince near where Jacob had camped. Simeon and Levi avenged this sin by destroying the city. Jacob later denounced their action.

DISCIPLE: *Meaning of disciple: a learner.* A disciple is a person who follows and subscribes to the teachings and doctrines of another person especially that of great teachers or leaders.

Followers and those trained by Jesus. They follow the lifestyle outlined by Jesus.

The twelve chosen followers of Jesus and believers in Jesus are disciples of Christ.

DISCIPLINE: Training expected to produce a particular character or pattern of behavior.

God's discipline can be either by instruction and warning or by adversity and affliction.

Church discipline can be done through preaching the Word, or it can be done through direct measures, such as rebuking sinners publicly or having nothing to do with sinners.

DISPENSATION: A period of God administration or management of the earth according to His prescribed rules for the period. This also refers to a distinct phase of God's arrangement of history to fulfill the plan of salvation.

DIVINATION: Refers to using objects to determine spiritual information about people's fortunes and misfortunes, such

D

as card reading or using ungodly means to attain godly knowledge. Divination also means the attempt to discover messages from God or the gods by examining such things as marked stones, or obtaining or the attempt to obtain secret knowledge of the future by reading and interpreting certain signs called omens.

DIVINE: That which belongs to God or pertains to Him.

DIVINE CODE: A system of symbols, letters, numbers, or words that conceal the meaning of a message that requires secrecy by God.

DIVINE INSIGHTS: An in-depth revelation from God.

DIVINE MESSENGER: One who brings a message from God.

DIVINE PREMIUMS ON A DREAM: The measure of God-given motivation to seek a dream's meaning.

DIVINE SIGHT: An open vision where natural surroundings blend into the scene, so one cannot tell if it is real or spiritual.

DIVORCE: The breaking of the marital bond. Physical divorce is divorce not part of God's original plan. Spiritual divorce is the result of sin and idolatry; the break of an intimate bond/association.

DOCTRINE: The teachings concerning faith and life. Principles let down to govern the conduct of a group. Could be pure, impure, or corrupted. Different types of doctrines are mentioned in the Bible: Doctrine of Man, Doctrine of God, and Doctrine of Satan.

DOEG: *Meaning: Hebrew for "anxious or in fright."*

An Edomite and Saul's head shepherd who betrayed priest of Nob by reporting to Saul that he saw the priest of Nob give David Goliath's sword. At the order of Saul he killed the priest of Nob. David wrote a psalm about the incident.

Contemporary/Symbolic Connotation:

Deceptive person. A person, who backbites, gossips, or tells tales.

DORCAS: *Meaning: Greek for "gazelle" or "filled with grace."*

She was a woman of outstanding love and kindness toward others. The Bible describes her as always doing good and helping others. She was a disciple of Christ in Joppa, and when she died apostle Peter raised her to life at the people's request. The only woman in the Bible mentioned as having the word *disciple* applied to her (though all Christians are disciples).

Contemporary/Symbolic Connotation:

The reward of goodness; selfless service.

In Joppa there was a disciple named Tabitha (which when translated, is Dorcas), who was always doing good and helping the poor (Acts 9:36).

DOUBT: A questioning of one's faith. It is not uncommon, but should not get rooted in one's life. It should be overcome as soon as it is detected.

Contemporary/Symbolic Connotation:

Instability or lack of firmness, lack of commitment to a purpose; too unstable like the waves of the sea or indecision that may disqualify one from receiving from God.

DRAGON: *Meaning: Greek for "serpent-like devourer" or "terrifying monster."*

A name for satan; a terrifying serpent-like monster; satan is the dragon cast out of Heaven to earth.

Contemporary/Symbolic Connotation:

See under Dream Symbols.

DREAM: A pictorial revelation received in the spirit when one is sleeping. True dreams are Holy Spirit-inspired.

DREAM CLUSTERING: Dreams on related subjects received by different people, either within the same geographic location or in the same field of interest. Usually this pertains to a divine message for the group.

DREAM ESSENCE: The quality of a dream's main message that gives it substance.

DREAM INTERPRETATION: The study of understanding symbols and elements in dreams for the purpose of understanding the essence of the dream.

DREAM LIFE: The pattern and extent to which the dreamer can receive revelation in dream form.

DREAM MESSAGE: The essential message of a dream.

DREAM PHRASES: Statements of truth in a dream that are either profound or have relevance to a dreamer's life situation.

DREAM PROMISE: A promise revealed in a dream.

DUNAMIS: This is a Greek term that describes dynamic power that generates and manifests the miracle-working powers of God.

DUST: Fine particles such as earth. Dust could symbolize the fact that human beings were created from the dust of the ground and will return to dust. Dust could also mean a state of confusion or a debased or despised condition or something of no worth or a picture of human frailty; a picture of multiplicity.

Contemporary/Symbolic Connotation:

See under Dream Symbols.

EAR: Organ of hearing.

Contemporary/Symbolic Connotation:

See under Dream Symbols.

EARTH: Earth is part of God's creation, the tangible part of the universe. God laid its foundations upon "the waters." God created the earth and called forth plants from it, and He holds the earth in its place by His word. He uses the earth as His footstool, and He will ultimately judge the earth. The present earth is the place for man's delegated authority and will pass away be replaced by new earth.

Contemporary/Symbolic Connotation:

Big and made by God; owned by God but the authority to rule it delegated to man; what will pass away; God's footstool.

EARTHQUAKE: A powerful shaking, originating from deep waters beneath the earth's surface; symbolic of something capable of major changes and transformation. May represent events and circumstances that are capable of shaking the foundation of something and resulting in its total destruction or transformation or deterioration.

Contemporary/Symbolic Connotation:

See under Dream Symbols.

EAST: Literally refers to the direction of sunrise. East could mean the origin and the beginning of human race. Chief entrance to Solomon's temple was on the east. Herod's temple eastern gate was called beautiful. In Ezekiel's vision, he saw the glory leave and return to the temple by the east gate.

Contemporary/Symbolic Connotation:

See under Dream Symbols.

ECCLESIA: The called out; the Church of Christ.

EDEN: *Meaning: pleasantness.* Generally refers to the region in which God planted a garden for the first man and woman. The Garden of God where Adam and Eve lived immediately after their creation; the original intended home of the first human beings.

Contemporary/Symbolic Connotation:

Paradise; pleasant place.

EDOM: *Meaning: red.* Was the name given to Esau, Jacob's twin brother. It applies to him because he despised his

birthright by selling it to his brother for "red stew."

EDOMITES: The people who descended from Esau (Edom). They lived in hill country, also called Mount Seir. They refused passage to Israelites in desert; Israelites passed around their country. Sometime later, Solomon intermarried with them.

Contemporary/Symbolic Connotation:

- Unfaithfulness
- Insecurity
- Brotherly jealousy

EGYPT: *Meaning: Coptic land.* Egypt is also known as the land of Ham. Abram went to Egypt during famine. For the Jews, it was a land of slavery. Joseph was sold as a slave into Egypt, and when he later became Prime Minister of Egypt, his brothers and father joined him in Egypt. Some generation after the death of Joseph, the Jews became slaves and were in Egypt for 430 years.

Contemporary/Symbolic Connotation:

A place of limitations; a place of idolatry; a place of hardship; it could also mean a place of preservation, because it was the place that the child Jesus was preserved from Herod.

ELDER: A seasoned and experienced person; a title for an elevated position because of one's proven experience in life that is commendable and acceptable.

Contemporary/Symbolic Connotation:

A person who can impart godly wisdom to other people; a senior person; proven and acceptable experience.

ELEAZAR: *Meaning: Hebrew for "God has helped" or "whom God helped" or the help of God.* He was one of the sons of Aaron who became high priest after Aaron. He was the high priest when Moses took census and helped Joshua in dividing up Canaan.

Contemporary/Symbolic Connotation:

A carrier of divine inheritance, special gifting/anointing. A continuation of family gifting.

Now these are the areas the Israelites received as an inheritance in the land of Canaan, which Eleazar the priest, Joshua son of Nun and the heads of the tribal clans of Israel allotted to them (Joshua 14:1).

ELECTION: The choice of a person for a specific purpose. God's elect means to be chosen by God. God's sovereign choice.

ELEMENTS IN DREAMS: Objects or persons in a dream or vision.

ELI: *Meaning: Hebrew for "ascended or gone up" or "height" or "my God" or uplifted.*

He was a Jewish high priest and a judge in Israel; descendant of Ithamar, son of Aaron. He lived in Shiloh. He blessed Hannah and Samuel. He could not restrain his children from evil, though God had warned him of dire consequences. At a certain time, a prophet spoke against him. God eventually cursed his family priesthood.

Contemporary/Symbolic Connotation:

Priesthood; cursed blessing; rebellious children; Eli's family became a family whose blessing was cursed (see Mal. 3:2).

Therefore the Lord, the God of Israel, declares: "I promised that your house and your father's house would minister before Me forever." But now the Lord declares: "Far be it from Me! Those who honor Me I will honor, but those who despise Me will be disdained. The time is coming when I will cut short your strength and the strength of your father's house, so that there will not be an old man in your family line and you will see distress in My dwelling. Although good will be done to Israel, in your family line there will never be an old man. Every one of you that I do not cut off from My altar will be spared only to blind your eyes with tears and to grieve your heart, and all your descendants will die in the prime of life" (1 Samuel 2:30-33).

ELIHU: *Meaning: Hebrew for "He is my God."*

He was one of the friends of Job who came to comfort him at the time severe affliction. He was the youngest friend of Job who became angry with Job and his friends and went on to give a lengthy speech.

ELIJAH: *Meaning: Hebrew for "Jehovah is God" or "God is God" or "the Lord is my God."* He was a great prophet of God who performed many outstanding miracles. He had great prophetic power and anointing. He confronted the wicked leadership of his days.

Contemporary/Symbolic Connotation:

Moving in the power and spirit of Elijah. He suddenly came on the scene from the wilderness to prophesy drought in Israel. Among the many remarkable things he did are: raising the widow's dead son; challenging Baal's prophets to a contest; praying for fire from heaven to consume his enemies; and killing the prophets of Baal. He was taken to Heaven without experiencing physical death.

ELIMELECH: *Meaning: Hebrew for "my God is king."*

He fled to Moab during famine, but he and his two sons died in Moab. His wife Naomi later returned to Bethlehem.

Contemporary/Symbolic Connotation:

He who flees from the place of destiny due to temporary hardship.

ELIPHAZ: *Meaning: Hebrew for "God is fine gold" or "to whom God is strength."*

Key people with this name were:

- The firstborn son of Esau, born of a Canaanite woman.

- One of Job's friends who tried to comfort him. He was the first to speak, and he was probably oldest and most influential of Job's friends.

ELISHA: *Meaning: Hebrew for "God is salvation" or "to whom God is salvation or God will save me."*

He was a great prophet with miracle-working power of God, and he was anointed by Elijah as successor. He inherited a double portion of Elijah's mantle, and demonstrated faith, commitment, and loyalty to his calling and to God.

Contemporary/Symbolic Connotation:

Prophet; loyal and committed servant; double portion inheritance; miracle worker. The notable actions in his ministry include: the miraculous increase of the widow's oil, the raising of Shunammite's son, the healing of Naaman's leprosy, causing the axehead to float on water, and prophesying the dramatic end to the siege on Samaria by the Syrians. His bones raised an unknown dead man to life.

ELIZABETH: *Meaning: Greek for "God is my oath."*

The wife of Zachariah. She was barren, but the barrenness was broken by divine intervention. She was a relative of the Virgin Mary, and she gave birth to John the Baptist.

Contemporary/Symbolic Connotation:

Fruitfulness; rescue from barrenness.

At that time Mary got ready and hurried to a town in the hill country of Judea, where she entered Zechariah's home and greeted Elizabeth. When Elizabeth heard Mary's greeting, the baby leaped in her womb, and Elizabeth was filled with the Holy Spirit. In a loud voice she exclaimed: "Blessed are you among women, and blessed is the child you will bear! But why am I so favored, that the mother of my Lord should come to me? As soon as the sound of your greeting reached my ears, the baby in my womb leaped for joy. Blessed is she who has believed that what the Lord has said to her will be accomplished!" (Luke 1:39-45)

ELKANAH: *Meaning: Hebrew for "God has possessed" or "whom God possessed" or "God is jealous."*

He was a worshiper of God who had two wives, Hannah and Peninnah. Every year he worshiped at Shiloh. He was father of the prophet Samuel, by wife Hannah.

EMMAUS: The place of warm springs.

EMOTIONAL BACKLASH: A strong and adverse reaction to an occurrence, which may be delayed and is often construed as a threat or danger.

ENOCH: *Meaning: Hebrew for "God consecrated" or "who is experienced."*

Key people with this name were:

• The eldest son of Cain, for whom the first city was named.

• A descendant of Seth who walked with God and was taken by God to Heaven without dying. The writer of the Book of Hebrews regards him as an example of faith.

Contemporary/Symbolic Connotation:

Symbolizes one of highest and purest forms of righteousness and holy living.

ENOSH: *Meaning: Hebrew for "mortal" or man.*

Son of Seth and grandson of Adam.

ENVY: Intense feeling of ill will or malice.

Contemporary/Symbolic Connotation:

Evil in the sight of God.

EPHESUS: *Meaning: desirable.*

EPHOD: A vestment worn by a Jewish priest, especially when in consultation, to determine the will of God.

EPHRAIM: *Meaning: Hebrew for "double fruit" or "fruitful in the land of affliction."*

Key people with this name were:

• Second son of Joseph. His name means "to be fruitful in the land of affliction." He was blessed ahead of Manasseh, who was his senior brother by Jacob.

• Tribe that descended from Ephraim.

EPISTLE: *Meaning: sending to.*

ERA: A period in history or time typified by some special feature.

ESAU: *Meaning: Hebrew for "hairy."*

The firstborn of Isaac, twin with Jacob, and was also called Edom. He became a hunter and sold his birthright to Jacob. Later, Jacob stole his blessing. He married pagan women but was later reconciled with Jacob. His descendents are called Edomites, meaning red. Jacob chosen over him by God's election. His descendants were later to be obliterated.

Contemporary/Symbolic Connotation:

One who despises the things of God; more concerned about natural things than spiritual things.

ESTHER: *Meaning: Persian for "star" or "who is like a star."*

She was a woman of extraordinary courage and faith. She was the daughter of Abigail and cousin of Mordecai. Also, she was a woman of great beauty. Chosen queen by Ahasuerus/Xerxes. At the risk of her life, she approached the king's palace to plead for the salvation of the Jewish people.

Contemporary/Symbolic Connotation:

Faith; extraordinary courage; salvation.

Go, gather together all the Jews who are in Susa, and fast for me. Do not eat or drink for three days, night or day. I and my maids will fast as you do. When this is done, I will go to the king, even though it is against the law. And if I perish, I perish (Esther 4:16).

ETERNAL: Continuing forever without beginning or end. The eternal God does not change; His love, righteousness and faithfulness endure forever. His purpose for mankind and power are eternal.

ETERNITY: Infinite time, the timelessness of life after death.

EUNICE: *Meaning: Greek for "joyous."* She was the mother of Timothy.

Contemporary/Symbolic Connotation:

Faith; good mother.

EUNUCH: A man who cannot have normal sexual relations, either by deliberate operation or by natural process. Eunuchs were used as officials in the courts of ancient kings.

EUPHRATES: *Meaning: Hebrew for "to break forth."*

One of the rivers of Eden; located in present day Iraq.

EVANGELIST: Publisher of glad tidings.

EVE: *Meaning: Hebrew for "life" or "mother of life."*

Made in God's image; made from Adam's rib. She became Adam's wife, and, unfortunately, she unwittingly entered into conversation with the serpent or the devil. As a consequence, she was persuaded by the deception of the devil to eat from the forbidden fruit and also give the fruit to Adam. Together, they tried to hide from God, and she blamed the serpent for her sin. God cursed her for this disobedience. Eve and Adam were both banished from Eden. She became the mother of Cain, Abel, and Seth, she is also regarded as the mother of all men.

Contemporary/Symbolic Connotation:

Motherhood.

EXPERIENTIAL KNOWLEDGE: The imbibed nature or attributes or knowledge of God, as derived from direct experience of His presence.

EXTRA-BIBLICAL EXPERIENCE: Experience without Bible precedence or example, justifying subsequent similar cases.

EYE: Instrument of sight. The human eye is the means by which human beings gain sight or insight.

Contemporary/Symbolic Connotation:

See under Dream Symbols.

EZEKIEL: *Meaning: Hebrew for "God strengthens" or "whom God has made strong."*

A priest who was carried into exile by the Babylonians. In exile, he received his call to be a prophet. He carried out many prophetic acts, including the following: lying on one side for more than a year, packing his belongings as if going into exile, and not mourning when his wife died. He is one of the major prophets of the Bible.

EZRA: *Meaning: Hebrew for "help."*

He was a priest and historian and a teacher of the law. He led a group of exiles back to Jerusalem.

Nehemiah said, "Go and enjoy choice food and sweet drinks, and send some to those who have nothing prepared. This day is sacred to our Lord. Do not grieve, for the joy of the Lord is your strength" (Nehemiah 8:10).

FAITH: Belief in a God or His doctrine. The basic elements of faith are trust in God, commitment to Christ, and the knowledge of God and of Jesus Christ.

FAITHFULNESS: Remaining steadfast to one's commitments.

FALLING AWAY: Falling away from the faith, backsliding, apostasy.

FALSE DREAM: A dream not sent by God; a made-up story or delusion of the person's mind.

FAMILY: *Meaning: house.* Family could mean a parent and the children alone, or a group of people who are related; class of animals; the unit of human race.

Contemporary/Symbolic Connotation:

See under Dream Symbols.

FASTING: Voluntarily depriving oneself of food or voluntary affliction of the flesh.

FATE: The ultimate end/outcome of something.

FATHER: The male parent, the first ancestor, or the oldest person. This is a title given to God and also used to describe some people in the Bible. God as Father of Jesus Christ; God as Father of His chosen people; God as Father of believers in Jesus.

Contemporary/Symbolic Connotation:

See under Dream Symbols.

FEAR: One's apprehension in a frightening situation.

FEAST: An elaborate meal prepared for some special occasion, a periodic religious celebration. A feast can be in honor of God, devil, or a person.

FELIX: *Meaning: Greek for "happy" or "Latin for "fortunate."*

A governor of Judea. He sought personal interview with Paul and had him imprisoned to please the Jews. Later, he was replaced by Festus.

FELLOWSHIP: A sharing together of common interests and goals between a group of people. The condition of being together, sharing similar interests and experiences, that leads to mutual concern and trust among Christians.

FESTUS: *Meaning: Greek for "joyful."*

He succeeded Felix as governor. He also convened court to deal with Paul's case, but Paul appealed to Caesar before him.

FIRE: Literally refers to rapid reactions that release heat and light.

Contemporary/Symbolic Connotation:

The consuming fire of His presence just as God:

- Appeared in fire to Moses in the burning bush
- Appeared to Israel in the pillar of fire
- The fire of God's wrath to judge sinners on earth and to punish eternally in hell with fire.

FIRST FRUITS: A portion of the produce of the land that represents the first offering to the Lord, in acknowledgement that all products of the land come from God and in thanksgiving for its goodness.

FLESH: Body and soul, not ruled by the Spirit of God. Paul used the term "flesh" to denote the entire fallen human being; the sinful body and the soul as afflicted by sin. Flesh is diametrically opposed to the Spirit and they are pitted against one another. The unbeliever can live only in the flesh (as the Spirit is not regenerated), but the believer can live in either by the Spirit (and not gratify the desires of the flesh) or live in the flesh.

So I say, live by the Spirit, and you will not gratify the desires of the sinful nature. For the sinful nature desires what is contrary to the Spirit, and the Spirit what is contrary to the sinful nature. They are in conflict with each other, so that you do not do what you want. But if you are led by the Spirit, you are not under law (Galatians 5:16-18).

Contemporary/Symbolic Connotation:

Carnality; the sinful nature of man; the human body.

FOLLY: Lack of good sense, understanding or foresight. Folly begins with a denial of God and it is opposite of wisdom.

FOOT: End part of the leg. Symbolically refers to something that one stands on.

Contemporary/Symbolic Connotation:
See under Dream Symbols.

FORETELLING: Ability to forecast what will take place in the future—could be by means of divination or an act of predictive prophecy.

FORGIVENESS: The act of overlooking or pardon for human sins and shortcomings.

FORNICATION: Sex outside of marriage, sexual intercourse with a person to whom one is not married.

FORTH TELLING: Telling forth the will or mind of God on an issue.

FORTUNE TELLING: The act of predicting the economic or financial future of a person.

FOX: A small, alert wild animal of the dog family.

Contemporary/Symbolic Connotation:
- A sly, crafty person
- A deceptive or cunning person
- A seductive female

FRANKINCENSE: A sap of a certain tree that gives a pleasant smell when burnt.

FREEDOM: Being liberated from bondage.

FRIENDSHIP: A relationship with a person who one trusts or likes.

Contemporary/Symbolic Connotation:
See under Dream Symbols.

FROG: Represents unclean spirit from the mouth of the dragon. Often symbolic of perverse spirit that may manifest as sexual immorality.

Contemporary/Symbolic Connotation:
See under Dream Symbols.

GABRIEL: *Meaning: Greek for "man of God" or "to be devoted to God."*

An archangel who interpreted Daniel's visions, and announced birth of John the Baptist and birth of Jesus to Mary.

GAD: *Meaning: Hebrew for "fortune" or "a troop."*

He was one of the twelve sons of Jacob. His mother was Zilpah, and his name means "my luck has turned" (see Gen. 30:11 TLB).

Another person with this name was a prophet and a seer of David who also recorded the events of David's reign.

GALATIA: *Meaning: "Lord of Galli" or "Gaile" or "purity."* A Roman province that occupied central portion of what is now known as Asia minor.

GALILEE: *Meaning: Greek for "the ring" or "circuit."*

The mountainous region belonging to the tribe of Naphtali; also the name of a key city of Kedesh.

GAMALIEL: *Meaning: the reward of God, or the reward or benefits of God.*

Contemporary/Symbolic Connotation:
Renowned scholar, respected person; knowledgeable.

GAMBLING: Stealing, stewardship. Betting on an outcome. A game of chance with money or other valuables.

GATH: *Meaning: Hebrew for "wine press."*
Situated in the plain of Philistia, Gath is one of five great Philistine cities. The birthplace of many giants (including Goliath and his brothers.) Occupied by the Anakim at the time the Israelites crossed over into the Promised Land. It was in Gath that David pretended to be insane. King David conquered it, but it was Rehoboam that fortified it. Later, Hazael king of Syria conquered from Joash, but Uzziah captured it back.
A champion named Goliath, who was from Gath, came out of the Philistine camp. He was over nine feet tall (1 Samuel 17:4).

GAZA: *Meaning: Hebrew for "strong" or "a place that is fortified."* Same as Azzah.
Canaanite city, and one of the Philistine cities that was assigned to tribe of Judah, present region of great conflict between the Hamas and the Israelites.

GEDALIAH: *Meaning: whom God has made great.* The name of a governor of Judah who was appointed by Nebuchadnezza after the destruction of Jerusalem. He became the guardian of Jeremiah, but a man called Ishmael assassinated him.

GEHAZI: *Meaning: Hebrew for "valley of vision."*

The name of covetous servant of Elisha who, against Elisha's advice, sought reward from Naaman. For this lustful act, he was inflicted with leprosy.

Contemporary/Symbolic Connotation:

Covetousness; the desire for material things; leprosy.

GETHSEMANE: *Meaning: oil press.*

Contemporary/Symbolic Connotation:

The Garden of Jesus' agony and betrayal.

GIBEON: *Meaning: Hebrew for "pertaining to a hill."*

This was a city of the Hivites. The inhabitants are called the Gibeonites. They tricked Joshua into making a treaty with them because they were afraid of being conquered by the Israelites. Joshua made treaty with the Gibeonites without consulting God. Gibeon was later given to the tribe of Benjamin. During the reign of King David, the tabernacle was moved to Gibeon. The tabernacle remained there until time of King Solomon, and this is where King Solomon sacrificed early in his reign and where God appeared to him in a dream.

"This bread of ours was warm when we packed it at home on the day we left to come to you. But now see how dry and moldy it is. And these wineskins that we filled were new, but see how cracked they are. And our clothes and sandals are worn out by the very long journey." The men of Israel sampled

their provisions but did not inquire of the Lord Then Joshua made a treaty of peace with them to let them live, and the leaders of the assembly ratified it by oath. Three days after they made the treaty with the Gibeonites, the Israelites heard that they were neighbors, living near them (Joshua 9:12-16).

GIDEON: *Meaning: Hebrew for "hewer" or "feller" or "one who cuts down" or "tree cutter."*

He was the son of Joash, also called Jerubbaal. The angel called him a mighty man of valor, though he was pressing wheat in a wine press for the fear of being discovered by the Midianites. He needed assurance through throwing out a fleece to raise and lead the army of Israel to war. Later, God asked him to reduce the army's size to three hundred, and with that he was able to obtain victory over the Midianites.

Contemporary/Symbolic Connotation:

Man of valor; deliverer.

When the angel of the Lord appeared to Gideon, he said, "The Lord is with you, mighty warrior" (Judges 6:12).

GIFTS OF THE SPIRIT: The special bestowment of divine abilities to carry out things by the Holy Spirit. Such abilities include: speaking in tongues; interpreting tongues; prophecy; serving; being an apostle; contributing to others; exercising leadership; showing mercy; encouraging others.

The acts of the sinful nature are obvious: sexual immorality, impurity and debauchery; idolatry and witchcraft; hatred, discord, jealousy, fits of rage, selfish ambition, dissensions, factions and envy; drunkenness, orgies, and the like. I warn you, as I did before, that those who live like this will not inherit the kingdom of God. But the fruit of the Spirit is love, joy, peace, patience, kindness, goodness, faithfulness, gentleness and self-control. Against such things there is no law (Galatians 5:19-23).

GIHOD: *Meaning: Hebrew for "burst forth."*

This was the name of one of the four rivers in Eden and also the name of a notable spring in Jerusalem.

GILEAD: *Meaning: Hebrew for "rugged" or "the hill of witnesses" or "of testimony."*

Region east of Jordan river.

This was the allotment for the tribe of Manasseh as Joseph's firstborn, that is, for Makir, Manasseh's firstborn. Makir was the ancestor of the Gileadites, who had received Gilead and Bashan because the Makirites were great soldiers (Joshua 17:1).

GILGAL: *Meaning: Hebrew for "circle of stones."*

The first camp of the Israelites after they have crossed the Jordan River.

GLORY: The grandeur and majesty of God. Glory belongs to God. The glory of God was revealed in diverse ways, and in Jesus Christ.

GOLDEN CALF: An object of worship, usually with fertility rites and orgies.

Contemporary/Symbolic Connotation:

Idol worshiping.

GOLIATH: A Philistine giant who hailed from Gath and taunted the Israelite army. He became a reproach to the entire state of Israel and caused great disaffection among the Israel troops at the battle Ellah. David defeated and killed him at this battle.

Contemporary/Symbolic Connotation:

Giant; boastfulness; trust in idols; great obstacle; that which God will defeat.

GOSHEN: *Meaning: mold of earth.* The land of the Israelites inhabited during the days of their sojourn in Egypt. A land that was only suitable for grazing and not for farming. Hence it was given to Jacob's family when they came to Egypt because they were shepherds. Later in their history, Goshen became a place of physical and economic blessings, and of divine protection when God sent plagues upon Egypt.

Contemporary/Symbolic Connotation:

A place of divine protection and provision, favor of God; economy watched over by God.

GOSPEL: The good news of salvation for humanity through Jesus Christ. First revealed to Adam and Eve, then revealed to Abraham and to Israel through prophets.

GOVERNMENT: The rule of humans by other humans.

GRACE: God's free and undeserved favor.

GREAT TRIBULATION: A time of intense distress; the end of the world.

GUILT: The condition of one who breaks the law, the awful stain from breaking the law.

HABAKKUK: *Meaning: Hebrew for "embrace."*

He was one of the minor prophets in the Bible. He was a man of Judah and the son of Naarah. Habakkuk prophesized in the last days of Judah and predicted the impending doom and Babylonian captivity.

HADES: The Greek name used in the New Testament to refer to the world of the dead.

HAGAR: *Meaning: Hebrew for "emigration or flight" or "a fugitive."*

She was the mother of Ishmael, son of Abraham. She was an Egyptian servant of Sarai who later conceived a child for Abraham. When she became pregnant, she became prideful and was driven away by Sarah, but God asked her to return to Sarah. She was driven away again after the birth of Isaac for mocking the seed of promise.

Contemporary/Symbolic Connotation:

Work of the flesh; not of the promise, servant girl.

For it is written that Abraham had two sons, one by the slave woman and the other by the free woman. His son by the slave woman was born in the ordinary way; but his son by the free woman was born as the result of a promise. These things may be taken figuratively, for the women represent two covenants. One covenant is from Mount Sinai and bears children who are to be slaves: This is Hagar. Now Hagar stands for Mount Sinai in Arabia and corresponds to the present city of Jerusalem, because she is in slavery with her children (Galatians 4:22-25).

HAGGAI: *Meaning: Hebrew for "festal" or "festive."*

He was a prophet in Israel after the Babylonian captivity. He prophesied and encouraged the people to rebuild the temple of God. He did this by warning them of the dangers of selfishness.

HAM: *Meaning: Hebrew for "hot."*

The son Noah who laughed at his father's nakedness, and for this his son Canaan was cursed.

He said,"Cursed be Canaan! The lowest of slaves will he be to his brothers." He also said, "Blessed be the Lord, the God of Shem! May Canaan be the slave of Shem. May God extend the territory of Japheth; may Japheth live in the tents of Shem, and may Canaan be his slave"(Genesis 9:25-27).

HAMAN: *Meaning: Hebrew for "well disposed."*

An Agragite descendent and was originally honored by Ahasuerus/Xerxes. He became angry with Mordecai because he would not bow down. As a result, Haman plotted to execute Jews and built gallows to hang Mordecai, but was forced to honor Mordecai and later hanged at his own gallows.

Contemporary/Symbolic Connotation:

Wickedness; hater of the Jews; evil planner; nemesis.

Afterward Mordecai returned to the king's gate. But Haman rushed home, with his head covered in grief, and told Zeresh his wife and all his friends everything that had happened to him. His advisers and his wife Zeresh said to him, "Since Mordecai, before whom your downfall has started, is of Jewish origin, you cannot stand against him — you will surely come to ruin!" (Esther 6:12-13)

HANANI: *Meaning: Hebrew for "God has shown mercy."*

He was a seer in the days of King David.

HAND: The human hand is the means by which we carry out service or work.

The right hand is symbolically associated with: place of honor; position of power; used to confirm an agreement. Laying on of hands is used for ordaining priests or leaders; also, can transfer guilt, confer healing, or transfer the anointing of the Holy Spirit.

Contemporary/Symbolic Connotation:

See under Dream Symbols.

HANNAH: *Meaning: Hebrew for "gracious or merciful."*

She was one of the wives of Elkanah who was barren because God had shut up her womb. When she prayed to have a child, God granted her request. She gave birth to Samuel who she dedicated to the Lord's work. God blessed her with other children.

HARAN: *Meaning: Hebrew for "mountaineer."*

Key people and places with this name were:

1. The father of Lot who died in Ur.

While his father Terah was still alive Haran died in Ur of the Chaldeans... (Genesis 11:28).

2. A city in Mesopotamia, to which Terah, Abram, and Lot emigrated.

Terah took his son Abram, his grandson Lot, son of Haran, and his daughter-in-law Sarai, to go to Canaan. And when they came to Haran, they settled there (Genesis 11:31).

Abraham sent his servant to Haran to find a wife for Isaac. Jacob fled to Haran when Esau vowed to kill him. Jacob lived and married Rachael and Leah in Haran. He lived with his uncle Laban for twenty years.

HARVEST: The season of gathering in ripened crops, the yield of a particular crop.

Symbolically the reward or product of any labor or action, or to achieve something.

As long as the earth endures, seedtime and harvest, cold and heat, summer and winter, day and night will never cease (Genesis 8:22).

Contemporary/Symbolic Connotation:

See under Dream Symbols.

HAZAEL: *Meaning: Hebrew for "God behold."*

A servant of King Ben-hadad of Syria and was anointed by Elijah to be king over Syria. He later murdered Ben-hadad to become king of Syria. In his lifetime, he fought against Israel and Judah and conquered part of Israel. His son Ben-hadad succeeded him.

HEART: The center of the human being; wellspring of all life; essence of something.

H

HEART CONNECTION THROUGH DREAMS: The intent or outworking of the dreamer's heart as revealed by the dream.

HEAVEN: Part of God's creation as a part of the universe. God placed sun, moon, and stars in the heavens. The third heaven is the place where God dwells, where His throne is located, where Christ is seated at the right of God, and where those who died in Christ dwell.

"The term heavenly places is a descriptive term that refers to the invisible realm of the heavens and technically would include the second and the third heaven and other invisible realms of hell."

More information about heavenly places is found in my book, *The Justice of God: Victory in Everyday Living.*[7]

HEBRON: *Meaning: Hebrew for "league or confederacy" or "alliance" or "city of four" or "a company."*

This was the place where Abraham and Sarah were buried. The city of Hebron was formerly called Kiriath-arba and was later allotted to Caleb. King David ruled from Hebron for seven years, and he was also anointed king over all Israel at Hebron. Hebron was also the place where Absalom was crowned king.

(Hebron used to be called Kiriath Arba after Arba, who was the greatest man among the Anakites.) Then the land had rest from war (Joshua 14:15).

HELL: A place of eternal punishment.

Contemporary/Symbolic Connotation:

A place for:

- Fallen angels
- The devil and his angels
- The beast and the false prophet
- Those who worship the beast
- The wicked
- Those who reject the Gospel

Hell is also the place of:

- Condemnation
- The place of torment
- The place of weeping and the grinding of teeth
- The place of eternal punishment
- Everlasting ruin
- A place of permanent separation from God
- The place of the second death

HERESY: A fundamental error in doctrine or religion.

HERMON: *Meaning: lofty or sacred mountain.* Called different names by different groups; was called "Sirion" by the Sidonians and "Senir" by the Amorites.

This was the highest mountain in the Syrian region, located in the northern border of Israel. Mountain well-nourished by Heaven; the Psalmist described as "the dew of Hermon" (Ps. 133:3).

HEROD: Key people with this name were:

1. The notorious king of Judea at the time Jesus was born. He is

also known as Herod the Great. When he learned of Jesus' birth, he ordered babies in Bethlehem to be killed, but Jesus and His family had escaped to Egypt to spare Jesus' life.

2. The Tetrarch of Galilee, called Herod Antipas who reigned during the ministry of John the Baptist. He married his brother's wife and, because John the Baptist denounced him, Herod later beheaded him. Jesus referred to him as a fox.

3. Herod Agrippa reigned in the days of the early church—the church of the Book of Acts. He persecuted the early church and had James killed. When he saw that the death of James pleased the Jews, he arrested Peter, but Peter was miraculously rescued when the church prayed for him. It is recorded that Herod Agrippa died a miserable death.

HERODIAS: The name of the woman who became the wife of Herod Antipas. She was previously married to Herod's brother. She hated John the Baptist for rebuking Herod over marrying her. Later, once the opportunity came her way, she told her daughter to ask for the head of John the Baptist on a platter.

HEZEKIAH: *Meaning: Hebrew for "Jehovah has strengthened."*

A king and reformer in Judah; he carried out the purification of the temple, restored proper sacrifices, and celebrated the Passover for two weeks. He cleansed land of idols, organized priests and Levites. He was known for seeking the face of the Lord for help against Assyria, and for this he witnessed the destruction of Sennacherib. He later had fatal illness and was healed by God when he prayed facing the wall.

HIGH PRIEST: The head priest in Jewish religion and the head of Jewish religious council. One of his main assignments included entering the Most Holy Place in the temple on the Day of Atonement and offering a sacrifice for himself and for the sins of the people of Israel.

HILKIAH: *Meaning: Hebrew for "the portion of Jehovah."*

High priest at the time of Josiah. During his priesthood, the book of law was found and was authenticated by Huldah. He became administrator of the temple. Together with Josiah the temple was cleansed.

HIRAM: *Meaning: Hebrew for "my brother is exalted" or "noble."*

A king of Tyre who is recorded to have assisted David in building his palace. Later, he contributed to the building of the magnificent temple during the reign of King Solomon. He was noted to have engaged in extensive trade across the sea. King Solomon once gave him a town that he did not like.

HITTITES: *Meaning: Hebrew for "belonging to."*

The Hittites were one of the seven Canaan nations who inhabited the Promised Land before the Israelites took possession of it.

HOLINESS: Being set apart from sin; purity. God is holy and He is called the Holy One.

HOPE: Certainty in the present, and firm expectation for the future. Hope is a basic ingredient for faith. Together with faith, hope forms the basis of trust in God.

HOPHINI: *Meaning: Egyptian for "tadpole."*

One of the corrupt sons of Eli. He did not heed his father's advice. Together with his brother Phinehas, the Ark of God was taken to war where they both died, and the enemies captured the Ark.

HOREB: *Meaning: Hebrew for "desert" or "drought."*

This was known as the mountain of God. The mountain where Moses received his commission, the place Moses experienced the burning bush, the place Moses received the law, and where he brought out water from the rock. The place where the prophet Elijah fled to when in fear he ran from Jezebel.

HORSE: A symbol of a powerful force, used in war and transport.

- Horses of fire that carried Elijah to Heaven
- God's angels using horses and chariots
- God's power symbolized by horses
- The returning Lord riding a white horse

Contemporary/Symbolic Connotation:

See under Dream Symbols.

HOSEA: *Meaning: Hebrew for "salvation" or "deliverance."*

He was one of the minor prophets, the writer of the Book of the Bible that bears his name. Hosea was a prophet to Israel prior to its fall in 722 B.C. His unhappy marriage life was symbolic of his nation's relationship with God. His ministering was centered on the unfailing love of God and waywardness of Israel as nation. God asked him to marry the woman Gomer, a prostitute. His wife became a symbol of Israel's unfaithfulness to God. The more Hosea loved her, the more she betrayed him. Nevertheless, he became reconciled with his wife, as Israel will be reconciled to God because of God's love and mercy.

HOSHEA: *Meaning: Hebrew for "salvation" or "help" or "deliverance."*

Key people with this name were:

1. Joshua, the servant of Moses, who eventually led the Israelites into the Promised Land. Joshua's original name was Hoshea.

2. Last king of Israel, he murdered Pekah to get the throne, but later he was captured and deported by Assyria.

HOSPITALITY: Welcoming and generous behavior toward others. The act of being hospitable.

HULDAH: *Meaning: Hebrew for "weasel."* She was a prophetess in the day of Josiah, king of Israel, who was once visited by Hilkiah.

HUMAN REASONING: Reasoning at human level, which is usually independent of divine input.

HUMILITY: Lowliness or freedom from pride or opposite of pride. Humility involves a childlike attitude, repentance, submission before God, seeking God's face in prayer, fasting, following God's laws, working for justice and mercy.

HUR: *Meaning 'her'*
Key people with this name were:

1. A chief magistrate of the Israelites who, with Aaron, supported Moses' hand during a symbolic submission prayer to God in a battle against Amalek.
2. The grandfather of Bezalel—the chief workman in the tabernacle (see Exod. 31:2).
3. One of the Midianite's kings.
4. The father of Rephaiah who helped Nehemiah build the wall (see Neh. 3:9).

HUSHAI: *Meaning: hasting.* A loyal friend of David who helped to outwit Absalom, and frustrated Absalom's revolt by giving poor advice.

HYPOCRISY: Open display of religion without genuine commitment.

HYSSOP: A small, bushy plant used in religious ceremonies to sprinkle liquids.

ICHABOD: *Meaning: the glory has departed.* This was the name given by Phinehas' wife to her son. He was born after the death of Phinehas and the capture of the Ark of God by the enemies.

IDOLATRY: To worship false gods.

ILLUSION: Usually a perverted representation of the real thing, erroneous concept or delusion, conjuring trick. Something that is capable of causing erroneous perception.

IMAGE CENTER: Part of the imagination that handles imagery, pictures, dreams and visions (memory).

IMAGE OF GOD: Something that represents or symbolizes God; mental picture of God; exact likeness of God, and man as bearer of God's image.

IMPARTATION: To bestow anointing upon a person by transference.

INBUILT DIVINE DRIVE IN DREAMS: Divine motivation to seek the meaning of a dream.

INCENSE: The burning of fragrant substance as a pleasant aroma to the Lord God. Incense is detestable if insincere and desirable if incense is used as symbol of prayer.

INHERITANCE: The act of receiving possessions from ancestors or parents. Transference from one generation to a later generation.

INNER DREAM: A dream within a dream.

INNER WITNESS: A verification of truth that arises from within the

H
I

dreamer's spirit. An inner flash of confirmation of something.

INTEGRITY: Honesty in life and adherence to moral principles. Examples of those who showed integrity are Job and David.

INTERACTIVE DREAM: A dream encounter that includes exchange between the dreamer and God.

INTERCESSION: The prayer of one person for another.

INTERPRETATION: The process of deciphering symbols within a dream, and simplifying the meaning of a parable illustration to bring understanding.

ISAAC: *Meaning: Hebrew for "laughs."*

He was regarded as the son of the promise, the seed of the promise (see Rom. 9:6-8). Abraham was prepared to offer him as a sacrifice to God, but God was only testing Abraham, and instead God provided Abraham with a ram for sacrifice. Isaac inherited the Abrahamic Covenant, and he was the father of Esau and Jacob.

Contemporary/Symbolic Connotation:

Son of the promise, or covenant; heir.

ISAIAH: *Meaning: Hebrew for "salvation of Jehovah."*

He was one of the major prophets in the Bible. He was often associated with kings and leaders, and he was sometimes referred to as palace prophet. He gave one of the most accurate and numerous prophecies in the Bible. He prophesied concerning

Jesus, Hezekiah, and the fall of Sennecherib. His ministry lasted about sixty years and spanned the reigns of four kings.

The vision concerning Judah and Jerusalem that Isaiah son of Amoz saw during the reigns of Uzziah, Jotham, Ahaz and Hezekiah, kings of Judah (Isaiah 1:1).

ISCARIOT: *Meaning: Hebrew for a man from Kerioth.*

He was a disciple of Jesus who later betrayed Him. The Bible says he helped himself to the money because he was in charge of the accounts. He was also known as the son of perdition.

ISH-BOSHETH: *Meaning: Hebrew for "man of shame."*

He was the son of Saul who became king after the death of Saul and Jonathan. Jonathan was the rightful heir to the throne, but he died with his father. He reigned for only two years because following his disagreement with his army commander Abner over Saul's concubine, Abner defected to David. Later, Abner was killed by Joab, who was then killed by two of David's supporters.

ISHMAEL: *Meaning: Hebrew for "God bears" or" whom God hears."*

He was the first son of Abraham by the Egyptian maid, Hagar. The son of the slave woman or son of the flesh, he was also blessed by Abraham.

Contemporary/Symbolic Connotation:

Work of the flesh.

ISRAEL: *Meaning: Hebrew for "he strives with God and man and prevails."*

This was the name given to Jacob by God, and means one who has struggled with God and man and has overcome (see Gen. 32:28). The name of the Jewish nation, the descendants of Jacob; the sons of Jacob became the sons of Israel and the Patriarchs of the Israel. The twelve sons of Israel became the twelve tribes; the nation of the people of God. Each son became a tribe; together became known as Israelites; called the house of Israel and the prince of God, a soldier of God or one who prevails with God.

Contemporary/Symbolic Connotation:

Priests of God; the Jewish nation; chosen by God.

ISSACHAR: *Meaning: wages.*

She named him Issachar [meaning wages] for she said God has repaid me for giving my slave girl to my husband (Genesis 30:18 TLB).

ITHAMAR: *Meaning: island of palms.* This was the name of one of the sons of Aaron. He served as a priest during lifetime of Aaron as the high priest. He later founded one of the Levitical families.

JABEZ: *Meaning: Hebrew for "pain."*

The head of a family who the Bible described as more honorable than his brother, but his name means "to bring grief." His mother named him Jabez because of the pains in giving birth to him. He made an honest appeal to God for blessing and God answered him.

Contemporary/Symbolic Connotation:

The power of blessing; prayerful person; honorable person; answered prayers.

JACOB: *Meaning: Hebrew for "supplanter."*

The twin (junior) brother of Esau. He struggled with his brother Esau in the womb of their mother Rebekah and grabbed his brother's heel during their birth. So he was called "supplanter." He later bought the right of the first son from his brother Esau and stole his blessing of the first son. He married Leah and Rachel, and their maids. He fathered twelve sons and one daughter.

Contemporary/Symbolic Connotation:

Trickster; supplanter; manipulation; favored by God.

JAEL: *Meaning: Hebrew for "wild goat" or "mountain climber."*

Jael was reputed to have killed Sisera, a Canaanite army commander by luring him to sleep and pegging his head to the ground. She received praise from the people, Israel, and Deborah.

JAIR: *Meaning: Hebrew for "He enlightens."*

One of the many judges of the Israelites in the days before a kingdom of Israel was instituted. He led Israel for twenty years.

JAIRUS: *Meaning: God enlightens (same as Jair).* He was a synagogue ruler and a man of faith, whose daughter was raised from the dead by Jesus.

Contemporary/Symbolic Connotation:
Man of faith; respected person.

JAMES: Same as Jacob. Key people with this name were:

1. One of the sons of Zebedee who became the disciple of Jesus. A fisherman before he was called to follow Jesus. With his brother John, he sought the top place in Jesus' kingdom. One of the selected who observed the transfiguration and accompanied Jesus to Gethsemane.

2. The name of another disciple of Jesus. Son of Alphaeus who became an apostle and was martyred by Herod.

3. The name of a brother of Jesus, born by Joseph and Mary, and a brother of Jude. Initially, he did not believe in Jesus as the Messiah, but after he witnessed the risen Christ, he kept the company of believers and experienced the Pentecost. Eventually, he became the head of the early church in Jerusalem.

JAPHETH: *Meaning: Hebrew for "may he grant ample space."*

He was one of the sons of Noah. With his brother Shem, covered their father's nakedness with a garment while refusing to look upon Noah's nakedness. For this, Noah blessed him.

JEALOUSY: An emotion expressing possessiveness; related to zeal. Sins that it leads to: envy, discontent, quarrelling, verbal abuse, intense anger, persecution. God is jealous of His people; sin arouses Him to jealousy.

JEHOAHAZ: *Meaning: Hebrew for "Jehovah has grasped or taken hold" or "whom God holds fast."*

Key people with this name were:

1. A son of Jehu. One of the evil kings of Israel. He followed after the evil of Jeroboam, son of Nebat. The Bible says he sought the favor of the Lord and God listened to him. The King Aram reduced his army to fifty horsemen, ten chariots, and ten thousand foot soldiers.

2. Another king with this name was the king of Judah, son of Josiah. He reigned for only three months. Neco, the Pharaoh of Egypt, carried him into Egypt. He died in Egypt.

JEHOASH: *Meaning: Hebrew for "Jehovah supports" or "who God supports."*

Key people with this name were:

1. A king of Judah (also known as Joash).

2. A king of Israel, son of Jehoahaz, who paid homage to Elisha who was then suffering from the illness from which Elisha died. He cried to Elisha and called him "the chariot and horsemen of Israel" (see 2 Kings 13:14). Through a prophetic act, Elisha prophesied that he would only defeat the Arameans three times. He later defeated the Arameans

three times and also Ameziah, king of Judah.

JEHOIACHIN/JECONIAH/ CONIAH: *Meaning: Hebrew for "Jehovah establishes" or "Jehovah has grasped or taken hold."*

A king of Judah, son of Jehoiakim, who was deported to Babylon. He reigned in Jerusalem for three months before the deportation. He did evil in the eyes of the Lord. He was a king of Judah who was cursed by God (see Jer. 22:28-30). He was later freed from prison in Babylon.

JEHOIADA: *Meaning: Hebrew for "Jehovah knows."*

He was a priest during notorious Athaliah's reign. He hid Joash for six years in the temple, arranged for crowning Joash as king. He helped to rid the land of idols, but Joash later became ungrateful to his family.

JEHOIAKIM/ELIAKIM: *Meaning: Hebrew for "Jehovah sets up."*

He was one of the evil kings of Judah, who was installed by Pharaoh Neco following the deportation of king Jehoahaz. He had conflict with Nebuchadnezzar. He killed the prophet Uriah; burned scroll of Jeremiah's prophecies.

JEHORAM/JORAM: *Meaning: Hebrew for "Jehovah is exalted."*

Key people with this name were:

1. Son of Jehoshaphat, king of Judah who warred against Edom and prophesied against by Elijah,

he also warred against the Philistines.

2. A king of Israel.

3. Son of Ahab. He allied with Jehoshaphat against Moab. During a war with Hazael was wounded, but was eventually killed by Jehu.

JEHOSHAPHAT: *Meaning: Hebrew for "Jehovah is judge" or "whom God judges."*

He was the son of Asa and was a king of Judah. He strengthened the kingdom of Judah during his reign. He formed many alliances, joined with Joram of Israel against Moab. On one occasion, he was miraculously delivered from Moab and Ammon when he fought in alliance with the wicked king of Israel. He was a man of prayers. However, he was punished for alliance with the evil king of Israel.

JEHU: *Meaning: Hebrew for "Jehovah is He" or "God is."*

Key people with this name were:

1. The name of a prophet who once spoke against Baasha.

2. King of Israel who Elijah was told to anoint him king. He was anointed by servant of Elisha and appointed to obliterate house of Ahab, killed Joram and Ahaziah, killed Jezebel, killed relatives of Ahab, and killed ministers of Baal.

JEPHTHAH: *Meaning: Hebrew for "opener."*

He was one of the judges who judged Israel. He was from Gilead. First

J

driven from the family because his mother was a prostitute, but later called to lead Israel in the time of war, and he delivered Israel from Ammon. Also remembered because he made a rash vow concerning his daughter.

JEREMIAH: *Meaning: Hebrew for "Jehovah founds" or "exalted one whom God has appointed."*

A prophet in Judah, one of the major prophets in the Bible. God called him at a young age (see Jer. 1:4-10). He had intimate relationship with God throughout the time of his ministry. He prophesied things the people of Judah did not want to hear. As a result, his life was threatened many times. Often known as the weeping prophet, he disliked the role he had to play.

JERICHO: *Meaning: Greek for "moon city" or a place of fragrance.*

This was a city of great prominence in Bible days. Also called the "city of palm trees." It is located near the Jordan River. The Israelite the spies visited it and where Rabab also lived. It was the first city to be taken by Israelites in the Promised Land and so called "the city of first fruits." Joshua pronounced a curse on it, but eventually Elisha prayed for it.

JEROBOAM: *Meaning: Hebrew for "the people contend" or "the people become numerous."* Key people with this name were:

1. He was an official of King Solomon and when Ahijah prophesied he would be king. He later

fled to Egypt. He led rebellion against Rehoboam and became first king of the northern kingdom. He instituted idolatry and was judged for idolatry. He became a symbol of wickedness in the history of Israel.

2. The name of another king of Israel, Son of Jehoash, king of Israel who was denounced by Amos.

JERUBBAAL: Another name for Gideon.

JERUSALEM: *Meaning: a place of peace.* This is a city of great historical and spiritual significance. A city captured by David, who made it his headquarters. The temple was built in Jerusalem, and after David, it became the capital of southern region. It was destructed by Babylonians and was also the main center of activities in the post-exile period. The city was chosen by God, but it was ironically the city where Jesus was crucified. Also called: the city of David; the city of the great King; the city of God; the city of the Lord; the city of righteousness; the city of truth; Zion; the holy city.

Contemporary/Symbolic Connotation:

See under Dream Symbols.

JESSE: *Meaning: gift.* He was the son of Boaz and Ruth, the Moabite. He became the father of David. The prophet Samuel visited him to anoint David as king of Israel. He had eight sons.

JETHRO: *Meaning: Hebrew for "excellence."*

This was the name of the priest of Midian who became Moses' father-in-law. His other name was Reuel. He was rich and owned flocks of sheep. He advised Moses to appoint judges for Israel.

JEW: *Meaning: "an Israelite."* Naturally refers to the people of God, descent of Abraham. Spiritual Jews—those who have accepted Jesus Christ as their Messiah (Lord and Savior).

JEZEBEL: *Meaning: Hebrew for "un-exalted" or "un-husbanded" or who is not married.*

This is the name of the wicked wife of Ahab, king of Israel. She was daughter of the priest of Baal. Together they promoted Baal worship. She killed prophets of the Lord and opposed Elijah. She had Naboth killed. Her death was prophesied, and Jehu killed her.

Contemporary/Symbolic Connotation:

Symbol of wickedness, Baal worship, spirit of witchcraft.

JOAB: *Meaning: Hebrew for "is father" or "God is father."*

He was a commander of David's army. He defeated Ish-bosheth and his army. He killed Abner, and his notable actions include: captured the city of Jerusalem, defeated Ammon, put Uriah in front line of battle, devised plan to reconcile David and Absalom, killed Absalom, and rebuked David's grief over Absalom's death. He was a man of violence but loyal to David. He supported Adoni-jah over Solomon. He was killed on Solomon's orders.

JOASH: The name of a king of Judah. He was sheltered from Athaliah and proclaimed king by Jehoiada at seven years of age. He repaired the temple, but later gave temple objects to king of Aram. Later in his life, he led the people into idolatry and became unfaithful to the family of Jehoiada.

JOB: *Meaning: "persecuted" or "one who is persecuted" or "afflicted."* He was a man of outstanding righteousness who was very wealthy and hailed from the East. His righteousness was tested by personal tragedies. His three friends tried to comfort him, but he cursed the day of his birth and gave rebuttals to his friends. He repented and prayed for his friends. He was made twice as prosperous as he was previously. He is considered an example of righteousness and of perseverance.

JOCHEBED: *Meaning: Hebrew for "Jehovah is glory."*

She was a woman of great courage who defiled the Egyptian law and kept Moses alive. After some time, she hid Moses among the reeds. Pharaoh's daughter discovered him and asked her to take care of her son Moses. She was married to Anram of the tribe of Levi.

JOEL: *Meaning: Jehovah his God.* He was one of the minor prophets, son of Pethuel. He lived in the days when natural disasters were common in Israel and illustrated his prophecies with allegory of the different types of locust. But

J

his message of hope included the warning that the people should repent and return to their faith in God. He emphasized that God will one day reign over everything.

JOHN: *Meaning: Hebrew for "Jehovah has been gracious" or "the gift of God."*

Key people with this name were:

1. John the Baptist, who was the voice sent from God to announce the coming of Jesus Christ. His father was Zachariah and Elizabeth his mother. He ministered in the wilderness, ate locust and wild honey. He preached the baptism of repentance. He baptized Jesus, but later expressed doubts about Jesus. He was arrested and beheaded by Herod. He was a type of prophet Elijah, therefore fulfilled prophecy about Elijah.

2. Another person with this name was a disciple of Jesus, son of Zebedee and brother of James. He was originally a fisherman, he was uneducated and wanted hostile Samaritans killed, but Jesus rebuked and corrected him. He observed the transfiguration of Jesus and sought top place in Jesus' kingdom. Known as a lover of Jesus Christ. He received the Book of Revelation as a visionary experience at the Island of Patmos.

JONAH: *Meaning: Hebrew for "dove."*

Jonah was a prophet who was asked by God to preach repentance to the Assyrians to receive salvation, but he fled from God. God caused a storm during his flight and the prophet had to be thrown overboard. He was swallowed by a big fish and vomited on the shore after three days in the belly of the fish. He was called a second time to preach to Nineveh—this time he obeyed and the people repented. God desires good and salvation for all men.

Contemporary/Symbolic Connotation:

The story of his life considered a sign of resurrection.

JONATHAN: *Meaning: Hebrew for "Jehovah has given" or "the gift of God."*

He was a trained warrior and the eldest son of King Saul. He once attacked an outpost of the Philistines and secured victory for Israel, but unknowingly ate honey, which was forbidden by his father, Saul. He was to be killed for this, but the people rescued him. He became David's best friend. He was killed in battle on the same day as Saul.

Contemporary/Symbolic Connotation:

Faithful friend; selfless service; truthfulness sacrifice; commitment.

JORDAN: *Meaning: descendant or following down.* This is a river of great historical and spiritual significance, flowing from the Sea of Galilee to the Dead Sea. Jordan is noted for many outstanding events, including:

- Here is where Israelites crossed into the Promised Land.

- Elijah and Elisha miraculously divided and crossed the river.

- Naaman, a general from Syria, was cured by washing in the Jordan.
- By the hands of the prophet Elisha, an axe-head floated in the Jordan.
- John the Baptist baptized Jesus in the Jordan.

JOSEPH: *Meaning: Hebrew for "may God add" or "increase" or "He shall increase."*

Key people with this name were:

1. One of the sons of Jacob, his mother's name was Rachael. His name means "may he add." He was favored by Jacob and hated by his brothers. Because of his prophetic dreams and divine promises, his brother sold him to Midianites. He interpreted dreams for Pharaoh and was appointed ruler in Egypt.

And she named him Joseph (meaning "may I also have another for she said, may Jehovah give me another son) (Genesis 30:24 TLB).

2. Another person with this name was Joseph, the earthly father of Jesus. When he discovered that Mary was pregnant and not by him, he considered not marrying Mary, but was visited by angel and told in a dream to marry her. He later went to Bethlehem during census where Jesus was born, and he gave the name "Jesus" to Mary's son. He circumcised Jesus and presented him to the temple. He took Mary and Jesus to Egypt when Jesus' life was in danger. He returned and settled in Nazareth.

3. The third person with this name was a man who was a secret disciple of Jesus. He was a rich man from Arimathea and a member of the Sanhedrin. He had not consented to Jesus' crucifixion. With Nicodemus, they prepared Jesus' body and buried him in his own tomb.

Contemporary/Symbolic Connotation:

Dreamer; forgiveness; favor; interpreter of dreams.

"Dialoguing with God in dreams often takes the form of a series of dreams in which the dreamer awakens between dreams and intercedes in response to the preceding dream. God then replies to the dreamer's response with another dream and so continues the discussion. Actually this phenomenon is common, but most people miss out on it because they regard them as repeat dreams. I believe that Joseph's (of the coat of many colors) dreams were a pair of dialoguing dreams in which God used the second dream to correct the restricted perspectives of Joseph's view of the promised rulership (see Gen. 37:1-11). Joseph was not just going to lord it over his brothers, but his rulership would cover the then known world, hence the moon and the sun in the second dream. In the Book of Genesis, the moon and the sun are rulers. The Bible says 'the sun to rule the day and the moon to rule the night.'"

More information about dialoguing with God is found in my book, *Dreams and Visions Volume 2*.[8]

J

JOSHUA: *Meaning: Hebrew for "Jehovah is salvation."*

Key people with this name were:

1. Son of Nun, whose name was actually changed from Hoshea. He was a servant of Moses who fought the Amalekites. He accompanied Moses on Mount Sinai and was sent out as one of the spies to Canaan. He encouraged Israelites to enter Canaan, and he was allowed to enter land and was appointed as Moses' successor.

2. Another person with this name was a high priest during time of Zerubbabel. He rebuilt altar of the Lord and helped rebuild the temple. He was featured in Zechariah's vision of Joshua's trial in Heaven.

JOSIAH: *Meaning: Hebrew for "Jehovah supports."*

He was a boy-king of Judah, the son of Amon; king of Judah. He began his reign when he was eight years old. He purged the land of idolatry and repaired the temple. The book of law was discovered during his time. He renewed the covenant and celebrated the Passover. Pharaoh Neco killed him in a war he could have avoided.

JOTHAM: *Meaning: Hebrew for "Jehovah is perfect."*

Key people with this name were:

1. Youngest son of Gideon who spoke to Shechemites against Abimelech after Abimelech had murdered all his brothers—then he ran away to Beer.

2. Another person with this name was the son of Uzziah, king of Judah. He reigned while his father Uzziah suffered from leprosy. He repaired the temple and the walls of Jericho.

JUDAH: *Meaning: Hebrew "for praise."*

Key people with this name were:

1. One of the sons of Jacob whose name means praise. His mother's name was Leah.

Once again she became pregnant and had a son and named him Judah (meaning Praise), for she said, "Now I will praise Jehovah" (Genesis 29:35 TLB).

He married a woman from Adullam. He spoke against killing their brother Joseph. He unknowingly had illicit sex with Tamar, his daughter-in-law and fathered Perez and Zerah during that affair. He also fathered five other sons.

1. Tribe of Judah; descendants of Judah, the lineage of Jesus Christ.

JUDAS: *Meaning: Hebrew for "praise."* Greek form of Judah.

Key people with this name were:

1. The name of the disciple who betrayed Jesus. He was the treasurer of the ministry, but he pilfered money. He criticized many for wastefulness. He was identified as the betrayer in the upper room and eventually betrayed Jesus with a kiss, but later committed suicide and died a horrible death. Jesus said he was doomed to de-

struction. Matthias replaced him by casting of lots.

2. Another disciple of Jesus, son of James; probably also called Thaddaeus; one of the apostles.

3. Brother of Jesus and James who was also called Jude.

4. A Christian prophet who was also called Barsabbas.

JUDE: *Meaning: an abbreviation for Judah (praise).* An apostle of Jesus Christ, also called Judas, a brother of Jesus and James.

JUDEA: Region west of River Jordan, in whose town (Bethlehem) Jesus was born. King Herod, Pilate, and Herod Agrippa governed it.

JUSTICE: Fairness in the treatment of others.

JUSTIFICATION: Being declared right with God or acceptance by God.

KADESH OR KADESH BARNEA: A place located in the northeastern region of Sinai. This is the place where Moses sent out twelve spies to the Canaan, and ten of the spies returned to give bad reports. In Kadesh, also, the people refused to go up and take possession of the land and so rebelled against God. It was at Kadesh that Korah led a rebellion of elites against Moses. The place where Moses in anger struck the rock, instead of speaking to it as God has commanded him. The waters of the place was called Meribah Kadesh meaning "strife at Kadesh."

KETURAH: *Meaning: Hebrew for "make sacrificial smoke."*

The wife of Abraham after Sarah; also called Abraham's concubine; mother of six sons.

KINDNESS: A hospitable, friendly attitude toward others.

KINGDOM: The rule of humans or God over others. The Kingdom of God is present in Jesus. "The Kingdom of God is within you;" it comes through Jesus' death and resurrection.

KORAH: *Meaning: Hebrew for "baldness" and "bald."*

One of those who rebelled against Moses, leading a group of elites in the rebellion. He is a descendant of Levi. In judgment, the ground opened and swallowed him and the other rebels. His descendants became temple gatekeepers and also temple musicians. The sons of Korah wrote various psalms.

LABAN: *Meaning: Hebrew for "white."*

The name of the brother of Rebekah and father of Leah and Rachel. He deceived and manipulated Jacob into marrying Leah, though Jacob's love was with Rachel. He made Jacob mark extra years to marry his true love Rachel.

LAMB: *Meaning: Greek for "God has helped."*

Contemporary/Symbolic Connotation:

The lamb is a symbol of extraordinary joy or innocence, peace-loving mis-

J
K
L

sionaries, the age of peace, obedience to commandments of God.

LAZARUS: *Meaning: Greek for Eleazar, "whom God helps."*

Key people with this name were:

1. Poor man in Jesus' parable.

2. Brother of Mary and Martha; became sick and died and was raised from the dead by Jesus. His resurrection caused a stir. Jesus said to His disciples that it was good for them the miracle of Lazarus' resurrection took place.

Contemporary/Symbolic Connotation:

Resurrection; restoration.

LEAH: *Meaning: cow/wild cow.* This was the name of the older daughter of Laban who became the first wife of Jacob, but she was not loved by Jacob. She bore six sons and one daughter.

LEBANON: *Meaning: white mountains.* The name of the region, north of the Promised Land. It consists of mountains and valleys, including Mount Hermon.

Contemporary/Symbolic Connotation:

The majesty and truthfulness of God.

LEGS/FEET: The imagery of legs and feet portrays strength and beauty.

LEVI: *Meaning: adherence or joined, or to be associated or joined.* Key people with this name were:

1. The son of Jacob by Leah, whose name means "companion." Leah thought because she has had Levi that it would earn Jacob's love.

His company described as that of violence by Jacob, because with Simeon he avenged rape of sister Dinah.

2. The people that descended from Levi—notable among them are Moses and Aaron.

LION: The lion is a symbol of majesty and fierceness, and of meanness when hungry.

The lion as a symbol of evil means of enemies attacking God's people. The devil is like a roaring lion looking for whom to devour.

Contemporary/Symbolic Connotation:

The lion as a symbol of God represents Christ, the triumphant ruler. Lions also represent the bravery and boldness of believers. The righteous are as bold as a lion.

LORD'S SUPPER: The sacramental meal of God's people. It was instituted the night before Jesus was betrayed. He commanded His disciples to commemorate the ordinance as often as possible in this remembrance.

LOT: *Meaning: Hebrew for "envelop" or "covered" or a means of determining the will of God on an issue.*

Key people with this name were:

1. This is the name of the nephew of Abram who went with Abram to Canaan. He chose to live in Sodom. When he ran into problems, he was rescued from four kings by Abraham and rescued from Sodom by the Angels. However, his wife was killed

while fleeing Sodom because she disobeyed the instructions given by the angel. She turned into a pillar of salt. He fathered Moab and Ammon by his daughters (incest).

2. The term *lot* is also mentioned in a process called casting the lot. The process of determining an outcome or reaching a decision over an issue, by the throwing of almost identical dice.

LOVE TEST: A test that ascertains the presence or absence of the love of God. The ultimate love test is the respect for human life.

LUCIFER: *Meaning: light bearer.*
Contemporary/Symbolic Connotation: The devil; satan; corrupt angel.

LUKE: *Meaning: luminous.* The name of the writer of Gospel according to Luke and the Book of Acts of the apostles. He was a medical doctor by profession, and worked and traveled with Paul.

LUST: Any overwhelming desire or craving. Commonly used within the context of excessive or unrestrained sexual desire.

LYDIA: Seller of clothes from Thyatira who responded to Paul's preaching and invited Paul to stay at her house in Philippi; the church also met in her house.

LYING: Misrepresenting or falsifying the truth.

MACHPELAH: *Meaning: Hebrew for "double."*

The cave purchased by Abraham from Ephron, where Sarah and Abraham were buried. Isaac, Rebekah, Leah, and Jacob were also buried there.

MAGDALA: *Meaning: a place of tower.* A town on the shore of the Sea of Galilee.

MAGIC, WITCHCRAFT, AND SORCERY: The art that purports to control or forecast natural events or forces by invoking the supernatural realm. The practice of using charms/spells or rituals to manipulate or control events of nature. Magician means in Hebrew "engraver" or a "writer." Magicians are believed to have occult knowledge and power. Magic is the means by which power is transferred from gods to humans. Also, magicians are people versed in the art of trickery and illusions. The power of magic is, however, highly limited; only God is omnipotent. Purpose of magic and sorcery is to determine the future and to control the future.

MAGOG: Hebrew for "land of God."
Means all the ungodly nations of the earth who oppose the people of God.

MALACHI: *Meaning: Hebrew for "messenger."*
This is the name of the last Book of the Old Testament and the name of one of the minor prophets in the Bible. Malachi was a prophet to the Jews who had returned from exile. He ministered to the people to take their spiritual life seriously.

MANASSEH: *Meaning: Hebrew for "God makes to forget."*

Key people with this name were:

1. This is the name of the firstborn of Joseph. His name means "forget" because Joseph said God has made him to get pains of his father's household. Jacob did not bless him as the first son.

2. Descendants of Manasseh who were blessed by Moses and allotted land east of the Jordan and allotted land west of the Jordan. One of the tribes of the 144,000.

3. Son of Hezekiah who was king of Judah. Unlike his father, he was Judah's most wicked king. Assyrians captured him, and later he repented of his sins and cleared the land of idols.

MANGER: The place in Bethlehem where Jesus was born.

MANNA: *Meaning: What is this?* A special food provided for the Israelites during their exodus from Egypt. It was white and resembled seed of coriander (see Exod. 16:14-21). It was described as "grain of heaven" (Ps. 78:24) and as "bread of heaven" (Ps. 105:40).

Contemporary/Symbolic Connotation:

God's provision, supernatural supply; rescue package.

MANOAH: *Meaning: Hebrew for "rest."*

He was the father of Samson. He and his wife were barren until the angel of God brought the promise of a son, Samson.

MARAH: *Meaning: Hebrew for "bitterness."*

This was the place where Israelites found bitter water. It was about three days' journey from the Red Sea crossing.

MARK: *Meaning: Greek for Markos and Latin for Marcus; a large hammer; polite/shining.*

One of the disciples of Jesus whose Jewish name is also John. He was a cousin of Barnabas and a close friend of Peter. He went to Antioch and did mission work with Barnabas and Saul, but deserted Paul in Pamphylia. He returned with Barnabas to Cyprus. He later became a fellow worker with Paul again. The writer of the Gospel according to Mark.

MARTHA: *Meaning: lady or mistress.* The name of the sister of Mary and Lazarus. She kept busy in the kitchen and was rebuked by Jesus for complaining about Mary, who chose to listen to Jesus instead. She went to meet Jesus after Lazarus died and confessed the resurrection of the dead. She saw the resurrection of Lazarus.

MARY: *Meaning: Greek form of Mariam; rebellion.*

Key people with this name were:

1. One of the people with this name was the mother of Jesus; the angel Gabriel announced her pregnancy and she later visited her cousin Elizabeth. Her virgin birth was announced to Joseph in a dream by an angel who assured him that Mary's pregnancy

was by the Holy Spirit. She gave birth to Jesus in a manger in Bethlehem, and she fled with Joseph and the baby to Egypt when Jesus' life was in danger, but returned and settled in Nazareth. She observed Jesus' crucifixion, and was entrusted to the apostle John at the cross; she was among the disciples at the ascension.

2. Another person with this name was Mary Magdalene, a woman who was a former demoniac. She helped to support Jesus' ministry and was present at Jesus' burial. She went to the tomb early on Easter Sunday and saw an angel after the resurrection. One of the first people to announce that Jesus had risen.

3. The name of the sister of Martha and Lazarus. Jesus visited them. She listened to Jesus' teaching and washed Jesus' feet. She was commended by Jesus as one who has chosen the better path that could not be taken from her.

MATTHEW: *Meaning: gift of God.* He was a former tax collector who became a disciple of Jesus and also an apostle of Christ. He was also the writer of the Gospel according to Matthew.

MATTHIAS: *Meaning: Greek for "gift of God."*

He was an apostle who was chosen to replace Judas by casting of lots.

MEANING OF A DREAM: The true meaning as to why God sent the dream.

MEAT: Something deep or of maturity. Something of value, or worthy of protection

MEDES AND PERSIANS: Two related nations. Refer to the people who live in the land of Medes and those who live in the land of Persia. Defeated the Babylonians and allowed Jews to rebuild Palestine.

MEDIATOR: Someone who helps bring reconciliation between two parties. Examples of mediation in the bible include: Moses spoke to Pharaoh for the Israelites; Abigail spoke to David for her husband; Esther spoke to the king for her people.

MEDITATION: Reflecting on God and His Word. To gain a sense of peace and develop close relationship with God. Meditation prepares us for important decisions and gives us strength for Christian living. It helps give us direction for life.

MEDIUMS/SPIRITISTS: People who believe that they can communicate with the dead, and claim (by trickery) to find out things about the future through consultation with the dead or other spirit from the realm of the dead.

MEEKNESS: The quality of a gentle spirit.

MEGIDDO: *Meaning: a place of troops.* This was the name of a city that was allotted to Manasseh, but they did not conquer it. Deborah and Barak fought there, but Solomon built it up. This is where Josiah was killed. Intrinsically,

M

the first battle at Armageddon ("hill of Megiddo") will take place in Megiddo.

MELCHIZEDEK: He was a mysterious personality in the Scriptures; he did not have a beginning or an end. A king of Salem, priest of God Most High who blessed Abram and was called a high priest forever.

Contemporary/Symbolic Connotation:

His priesthood was prophetic of Jesus.

MENAHEM: *Meaning: Hebrew for "comforted."*

He was a king of Israel who assassinated Shallum to become king. He was extremely cruel.

MENTAL PICTURES: Images present in your mind.

MEPHIBOSHETH: The name of the son of Jonathan who was lame, but he was shown kindness by David. He was accused of deserting King David during Absalom conspiracy by Ziba. He later explained his story to David, and he was spared from death.

Contemporary/Symbolic Connotation:

Restoration; favor; blessings from parents.

MERCY: Undeserved kindness and compassion.

MERIBAH: *Meaning: contention.* A place near Sinai where Moses struck the rock and water came out. Because of the quarreling of the Israelites, Moses called Meribah.

MESHACH: *Meaning: Hebrew for "tall."*

A man of Jewish nobility who was deported to Babylon, and his name was name changed from Mishael. He refused to be defiled by the king's food and later was an appointed administrator in Babylon. He refused to worship idols and was miraculously saved from the fiery furnace.

MESSIAH: *Meaning: Hebrew for "the anointed one."*

Ascribed to the Savior whose coming was promised by the Hebrew prophets. The Greek word *Christ* has the same meaning.

METAPHOR: A symbol with implied comparison, for example, Jesus is the lion of the tribe of Judah.

METHUSELAH: *Meaning: Hebrew for "man of Javelin."*

Son of Enoch, father of Lamech who lived 969 years and died in the very year of the flood.

MICAIAH: *Meaning: Hebrew for "who is like Jehovah."*

A prophet of the Lord; warned Ahab of disaster, but King Ahab had him under care of a governor in a house arrest. His prediction came true, and Ahab died as he has prophesied.

MICAH: Micah directed his message to Jerusalem and Samaria condemning the oppression, pride, greed, and corruption rampant among them. He warned that everyone would be held responsible for his action. He also encouraged them by predicting the coming of the Messiah.

MICHAEL: *Meaning: Hebrew for "who is like God."*

An archangel who stood against the forces of evil; conducted war in Heaven against satan.

MICHAL: *Meaning: Hebrew for "contraction of Michael" or "who is like God."*

The name of one daughter of Saul who became wife of David. She warned David of Saul's plot to spite David, and she was later given by Saul to Paltiel. David retrieved her, but in a twist of fortune, she criticized David for dancing before the ark in the public. For this, she was barren all her life.

MIDIANITES: Descendants of Abraham through Keturah. They were very wealthy people. They oppressed Israelites. Gideon was appointed to deliver Israelites from the Midianites oppression. Important Midianites include Jethro, the priest of Midian, and Zipporah, Moses' wife.

MILK: Special nutritional food, particularly suitable for feeding immediately after birth and early life until weaned.

Contemporary/Symbolic Connotation:

A special blessing from God; whiteness; spiritual blessings; instruction for the immature; pure doctrine.

MIND-SET: Preconceived ideas, or prejudiced point of view.

MIRIAM: *Meaning: rebellion or bitterness.* The name of the daughter of Amram and Jochebed who was the sister of Moses and Aaron. She watched over baby Moses and arranged for Moses'

mother to care for Moses. She led dancing at the Red Sea after successfully crossing into the Promised Land, but she later criticized Moses for marrying Zipporah. She was struck with leprosy, but was restored by Moses' prayers.

MISSION: Being sent out on a task.

MOABITES: *Meaning of Moab: "of his father."*

Of his father. Descendants of Moab, son of Lot who were related to Ammonites and held land east of the Jordan, and they served the god Chemosh. Grandson of Lot by incest with his eldest daughter.

MOLECH: The God of Ammonites, worshiped with orgies and child sacrifice.

MONEY: The means, established as an exchangeable equivalent of all commodities, and as a measure of their comparative value, such as gold, silver, or currency.

MONTH: One of the twelve time segments per year, based on the lunar system.

MOON: Created by God and controlled by God to govern the night and mark off the seasons.

MORDECAI: *Meaning: Hebrew for "chief god of Babylon."*

A Jewish gentleman of the tribe of Benjamin, an exile that brought up Esther; he exposed plot to kill Ahasueru/Xerxes and refused to honor Haman who maliciously made gallows for him. He begged Esther to foil

M

Haman's plot to exterminate the Jews. First, Haman was forced to honor him. He was later exalted by the king and, with Esther, established Purim. Haman was executed in the gallows, and Mordecai became prime minister in Haman's place.

Contemporary/Symbolic Connotation:

Lover of the Jews; fearlessness; determination; victory of enemy.

When Esther's words were reported to Mordecai, he sent back this answer: "Do not think that because you are in the king's house you alone of all the Jews will escape. For if you remain silent at this time, relief and deliverance for the Jews will arise from another place, but you and your father's family will perish. And who knows but that you have come to royal position for such a time as this?" (Esther 4:12-14).

MORIAH: Region where Abraham went to sacrifice Isaac; also refers to the mountain of God's provision and the place on which the temple of Solomon was built.

MOSES: *Meaning: drawn out of water.* He was a man from the tribe of Levi and brother of Aaron. He married Zipporah. He and Elijah appeared to Jesus Christ at the transfiguration. He was a special prophet, and Jesus is regarded as prophet like unto Moses. His parents were Amram and Jochebed.

Contemporary/Symbolic Connotation:

Deliverer of the people of God; a prophet.

MOST HOLY PLACE: The innermost room of the tent of the Lord's presence or the temple. The Ark of the Covenant was kept in the Most Holy Place. Only the high priest could enter the Most Holy Place, and he did so only once a year and on the Day of Atonement.

MOUNT EBAL & MOUNT GERIZIM: Mount Ebal was situated north of Mount Gerizim. The city of Shechem lies between the two mountains and roughly at the centre of Canaan. As the Israelites entered the Promised Land, curses and blessings were pronounced on top of these mountains to serve as symbolic reminder that God has code of conduct and a strict standards of rights and wrongs that nobody can escape from. Curses were pronounced on Mount Ebal and blessings on Mount Gerizim. Mount Ebal has a topographical and climatic condition that is normally barren at the peak, an ideal place to pronounce curses. Mount Gerizim was usually covered with vegetation and suitable as a place to pronounce the blessings.

MOUTH: The part of the body used for speaking and eating. The mouth is used for many other functions: to praise God, to testify concerning God, to speak words, to laugh with joy, to eat, to drink, and to kiss.

MULTIPLE DREAMS: More than two dreams in a single night. Each dream may refer to an aspect of the same message. This is a common occurrence in the life of a high-volume dreamer.

MURDER: The deliberate killing of another human. The sixth commandment is the commandment against murder.

MUSTARD: A large plant which grows from a very small seed. The seeds are ground into powder and used as spice on food.

MYRRH: A sweet-smelling resin that was very valuable. It served as a medicine.

MYRTLE: A kind of evergreen tree.

MYSTERIES OF GOD: Unexplained, inexplicable, or secret truth divinely revealed, which one could not know through reasoning.

MYSTERY: Secret truths revealed only by God. God discloses mysteries to His prophets; to His apostles. Only believers understand mysteries.

NAAMAN: *Meaning: Hebrew for "pleasant."*

A commander of the army of Syria who was afflicted with leprosy. He was cured at the hands of Elisha, by God's miracle. He took Israelite soil back to Damascus.

Contemporary/Symbolic Connotation:

Restoration; healing; outstanding person or performance

NABAL: *Meaning: Hebrew for "fool."*

The name of a wealthy Carmelite who was the husband of Abigail. His name means "foolishness." He refused and insulted David, in spite of previous kindness shown to him by David. His wife Abigail pleaded for his life.

NABI: *Meaning: Hebrew for prophetic spokesman or the official prophets.* Plural form is "Nabilim" as occurred in the days of Samuel (meaning the company of prophets).

NABOTH: This is the name of a man who owned a vineyard in Jezreel that was beside the palace of King Ahab. He refused to sell his inherited vineyard to the king, but later Jezebel killed him so that Ahab can acquire the vineyard. Ahab's family was destroyed for this.

NABU: The name of the Babylonian god of oratory prowess and literature, a source of false spirit of prophecy.

NADAB: Key people with this name were:

1. The name of the firstborn of Aaron. Moses consecrated him as priest. He was killed for offering unauthorized fire. God called the fire "strange fire."

2. Son of Jeroboam I, king of Israel who killed all his brothers, but was himself killed by Baash.

NAHUM: *Meaning: comforter.* The prophet Nahum prophesized concerning destruction of Nineveh, the capital city of Assyrians, and the city was eventually destroyed in 612 B.C.

NAOMI: *Meaning: Hebrew for "pleasantness."*

She was the wife of Elimelech and mother-in-law of Ruth who left Bethlehem for Moab during famine. She returned as a widow with Ruth when she said that she should be Mara (bitterness) instead of Naomi (pleasantness). She advised Ruth to seek marriage with Boaz and cared for Ruth's son Obed.

Contemporary/Symbolic Connotation:

Caring; considerate; good adviser.

M
N

So the two women went on until they came to Bethlehem. When they arrived in Bethlehem, the whole town was stirred because of them, and the women exclaimed, "Can this be Naomi?" "Don't call me Naomi," she told them. "Call me Mara, because the Almighty has made my life very bitter. I went away full, but the Lord has brought me back empty. Why call me Naomi? The Lord has afflicted me; the Almighty has brought misfortune upon me" (Ruth 1:19-21).

NAPHTALI: *Meaning: Hebrew for "fight" or "struggle" or "wrestling."*

Key people with this name were:

1. Son of Jacob by Bilhah whose name means "struggled." He was the second son of Bilhah.

Then Rachel said, "I have had a great struggle with my sister, and I have won." So she named him Naphtali (Genesis 30:8).

2. Tribe descended from Naphtali. They were blessed by Moses and allotted land, but they failed to fully possess the land. The tribe of Naphtali was one of the tribes of the 144,000.

NARD: An expensive perfume made from a plant.

NATHAN: *Meaning: Hebrew "God has given."*

He was a prophet at the royal palace during the reign of King David. He denounced David's sin with Bathsheba and revealed Adonijah plot to David. He participated in Solomon's coronation.

NATHANIEL: *Meaning: Hebrew for "God has given."*

One of Jesus' disciples who was probably also called Bartholomew. One of the disciples introduced by Philip. Jesus praised his integrity at their initial encounter.

NATURAL CONSCIOUSNESS: A critical awareness of one's own natural identity and situations.

NAZARENE: Someone from the town of Nazareth. Derived from the word of Nazareth, the hometown of Jesus Christ. Jesus was called of Nazarene (see Matt. 2:23). For most part, it was used as insulting designation, because the Jewish never thought that Messiah could come from Nazareth, a small town in Galilee. It was a region that was populated by many Gentiles and was held in contempt by orthodox Jews. Early Christians were stigmatized with the same name (see Acts 24:5).

NAZARETH: *Meaning: separated.* A Galilean town which had a poor reputation. Angel Gabriel appeared to Mary in Nazareth. This is the place where Jesus grew up, and He was called "Jesus of Nazareth." Jesus was rejected by the town, and He could not perform many miracles in Nazareth.

NAZIRITE: *Meaning: Hebrew for "people of vow" or "dedicated or consecrated person."*

A person who took a special vow to serve God. Such a person was not to drink beer or wine, cut his hair, or touch a dead body (see Num. 6:1-21). An Israelite who consecrated himself or herself and took a vow of separation and self-imposed abstinence for the purpose of some special service.

NEBO: The Babylonian god of education.

Bel bows down, Nebo stoops low; their idols are borne by beasts of burden. The images that are carried about are burdensome, a burden for the weary. They stoop and bow down together; unable to rescue the burden, they themselves go off into captivity (Isaiah 46:1-2).

NEBUCHADNEZZAR: *Meaning: Nebo protects the crown.* He was a Babylonian king who campaigned against Judah and destroyed Jerusalem and the temple. He was kind to Jeremiah and was impressed with Daniel and his friends. Daniel interpreted his dreams. He put Daniel's three friends in the fiery furnace in which they were divinely rescued. He lived seven years like an animal until he worshiped God.

Contemporary/Symbolic Connotation:

Wickedness; evil conqueror; erratic judgment.

NECRO: *Meaning: the dead.*

NECROMACY: The art of conjuring up the spirits of the dead in order to influence events.

NEHEMIAH: *Meaning: Hebrew for "Jehovah has confirmed" or "God comforts."*

He was a cupbearer for Artaxerxes. He became sad over condition of the exiles who had returned to Jerusalem. He later became governor of Jews. He rebuilt the walls of Jerusalem, showed concern for the poor, re-established

true worship with Ezra's help, and dedicated walls of Jerusalem.

Contemporary/Symbolic Connotation:

Righteous governor; considerate and kind person; restoration; builder of the city.

NEHUSHTAN: Bronze serpent that the people worshiped in the wilderness, which was condemned and destroyed by King Hezekiah.

NEIGHBOR: Anyone near you or any fellow human being.

NEPHILIM: *Meaning: those who cause others to fall; giants.* The Bible mentions Nephilim three times in the Scriptures. Bible gives account of God's displeasure with men in the days of Noah.

The Nephilim were on the earth in those days—and also afterward—when the sons of God went to the daughters of men and had children by them. They were the heroes of old, men of renown (Genesis 6:1-4).

They were giant beings who were believed to be the result of the unholy marriage of the fallen angels and the daughters of men. They were very wicked, cruel, and ruthless, and they sought to procreate themselves before the flood of Noah's time. They have been arrested by God and put away until the day of their final judgment.

NICODEMUS: *Meaning: Greek for "victor over the people" or "conqueror of the people."*

Pharisee who visited Jesus at night, and he also argued for fair treatment of Jesus. With Joseph, he prepared Jesus for burial.

N

Contemporary/Symbolic Connotation:

Secret disciple; a just person; considerate person.

NICOLAS: *Meaning: the people's victor or victor of the people.* One of the twelve apostles, a proselyte from Antioch, an earlier convert to Judaism.

NIGHT SEASONS: Related to night time, or periods in life full of difficulties.

Contemporary/Symbolic Connotation:

See under Dream Symbols.

NIGHTMARE: A dream arousing feelings of acute fear, dread, or anguish. Nightmare is a subjective term depending on the dreamer's perception.

NILE: *Meaning: dark blue.*

NIMROD: *Meaning: Hebrew for "rebel."* He was the son of Cush and the founder and king of the first empire after the flood. A mighty hunter. The empire included city of Babel in the land of Shinar.

Cush was the father of Nimrod, who grew to be a mighty warrior on the earth. He was a mighty hunter before the Lord; that is why it is said, "Like Nimrod, a mighty hunter before the Lord." The first centers of his kingdom were Babylon, Erech, Akkad and Calneh, in Shinar. From that land he went to Assyria, where he built Nineveh, Rehoboth Ir, Calah and Resen, which is between Nineveh and Calah; that is the great city" (Genesis 10:8-12).

NINEVEH: *Meaning: the dwelling of Ninus.* A city founded by Nimrod; the capital of Assyria. Jonah was told by

God to preach against it. The people of Nineveh repented, following Jonah's preaching. The people of Nineveh condemn believers because they repented when Jonah rebuked them.

NOAH: *Meaning: Hebrew for "rest" or "consolations."*

He was a righteous man and the son of Lamech.

When Lamech had lived 182 years, he had a son. He named him Noah and said, "He will comfort us in the labor and painful toil of our hands caused by the ground the Lord has cursed" (Genesis 5:29).

In the days of Noah, God was displeased with men on earth, but He found Noah righteous and saved him from the destruction of the flood.

OBADIAH: *Meaning: servant of Jehovah or worshiper of God.* Key people with this name were:

1. Servant of King Ahab who sheltered one hundred prophets from Jezebel and notified Ahab of Elijah's return.

2. Obadiah was a prophet in Israel who prophesized the destruction of Edom for their participation and jubilation during the destruction and plunder of Israel.

OBED: *Meaning: servant or one serving.* The son of Boaz by his wife Ruth, the father of Jesse. David was his grandson and was an ancestor of Jesus Christ.

OBED-EDOM: *Meaning: servant of Edom.* The name of a man of tribe of Hittites in whose house the ark of God was kept for three months. His household was blessed during this period.

OCCULT: Belief in ungodly supernatural power and to bring them under human control.

OFFERINGS: A presentation made to God as an act of worship or a sacrifice.

OG: King of Bashan who was destroyed by Israelites.

OLIVES, MOUNT OF: This is a key place of great importance in Christian history.

Located on a hill east of Jerusalem. David climbed it while fleeing from Absalom; Jesus often went there. The starting place of Jesus' triumphal entry. Where Jesus predicted destruction of Jerusalem. Where Gethsemane is located and the place where Jesus ascended into Heaven.

OMRI: King of Israel and father of Ahab.

OPEN HEAVEN: Access between the earth and the third heaven.

OPEN VISION: Vision received with natural eyes wide open, though the vision is perceived with spiritual eyes.

OPPRESSION: The oppression of a person by an evil and unclean spirit.

ORPAH: *Meaning: Hebrew for "stubbornness."*

Moabite daughter-in-law of Naomi who remained in Moab, while mate Ruth chose to follow Naomi.

OTHNIEL: *Meaning: powerful man of God.* Nephew of Caleb who married Caleb's daughter and became a judge. He freed Israelites from Syrians. The name of first judge of Israel after Joshua.

OUTCASTS: In Bible terms, it refers to Jews who were not allowed to attend synagogue worship because they had broken rules about foods that should not be eaten, and about being friendly with people who were not Jews. Such outcasts were looked down on by many of their fellow Jews, and Jesus was criticized for being friendly with them.

OUTER DREAM: A dream that contains another dream within it.

PALESTINE: *Meaning: land of sojourners or land of strangers.*

PANORAMIC VISION: A vision in motion (as in a movie).

PARABLE: Stories told with symbols that illustrate some truth or lesson. A story illustrating a lesson by using one element to represent another element.

PASSOVER: A Jewish religious festival, around April, which celebrates the freeing of the Hebrews from their captivity in Egypt.

PATRIARCH: The founder or head of a tribe or family. The Israelites regarded Abraham as their patriarch; they trace their ancestry to him. Also, Isaac and Jacob are regarded as part of the first three patriarchs of the Israelites. The twelve sons of Jacob are also regarded as patriarchs of the Israelites.

PAUL: *Meaning: Latin for "little or small."*

O
P

Originally called Saul of Tarsus, he was from the tribe of Benjamin, a Pharisee and was writer of many books of the New Testament. The apostle to the Gentiles, trained by Gamaliel. He remained unmarried all his life by the special grace of God.

PEKAH: *Meaning: Hebrew for "to open."*
King of Israel who assassinated Pekahiah to become king. He allied with Syria against Judah and inflicted much destruction on Judah. He failed in attempt to take Jerusalem.

PEKAHIAH: *Meaning: Hebrew for "Jehovah has opened."*
A king of Israel in Samaria, son of Menahem who reigned for two years Pekah assassinated him.

PENTECOST: *Meaning: the fiftieth day.* Literally refers to the Greek name for the Israelite festival of wheat harvest. The name Pentecost, which means "fiftieth," comes from the fact that the feast was held fifty days after Passover. The outpouring of the Holy Spirit and the spirit baptism of the Jesus' disciples also occurred on fiftieth day after His resurrection.

PERFECTION: Complete and without sin or error.

PERSECUTION: Oppression because of one's faith, or to harass or subject to persistent and severe ill treatment because of religion or affiliation.

PERSEVERANCE: Remaining firm in our faith.

PERSONAL TRAITS: Attributes specific to a person.

PETER: *Meaning: Greek for a "piece of rock."*
Peter's father's name was John. He was given the name Simon, and he was a brother of Andrew, a native of Bethsaida. He was originally an uneducated fisherman. He became one of the apostles. The teacher and head of early church.

PETITION: Asking God for personal things in prayers.

PHARAOH: *Meaning: sun king.* The title given to the king of Egypt. It was probably derived from an Egyptian word for "great house."

PHARISEES: *Meaning: separated ones.* A Jewish party, prominent at the time of Jesus. There were three prominent parties of Judaism during the time of Jesus: Pharisees, Sadducees, and Essenes. The Pharisees were by far the most influential of all the parties.

PHILIP: *Meaning: Greek for "lover of horses."*
Key people with this name were:

1. Disciple of Jesus who brought Nathaniel to Jesus and who introduced Greeks to Jesus. He was one of the apostles.

2. One of the seven deacons, he became an evangelist in Samaria and witnessed to and baptized Ethiopian eunuch. He had four daughters who prophesied.

P

PHILISTINES: The name given to the inhabitants of the plain of Palestine. Descendants of Mizraim, son of Ham. Though they were advanced in culture and war techniques, Joshua still failed to completely take over the land of Philistines. Notable Philistines include Goliath, who was killed by David, and Achish, the king of Gath.

PHINEHAS: *Meaning: Hebrew for "mouth of brass."*

Key people with this name were:

1. Son of Eleazar and grandson of Aaron who was noted for killing Zimri and Cozbi to end plague.

2. Son of Eli and the brother of Hophini. He was a wicked priest who scorned his father's rebuke. He brought the ark into battle, but he was killed in the battle and the enemy captured the ark of God.

PHOEBE: *Meaning: Greek for "bright/pure/radiant."*

Christian from Cenchreae who received commendation from the apostle Paul.

PHOENICIA: *Meaning: land of the palm trees* (see Acts 21:2).

PHYSICAL REALM: The sphere of the natural existence.

PICTORIAL DEPOSITORY: Center in the mind where issues relating to imagery and pictures are processed.

PICTORIAL VISION: A vision of pictures without motion.

PIETY: Devotion and reverence to God.

PILATE: *Meaning: spearhead.* Governor of Judea who presided over Jesus' trial.

PITY: Compassion for another's suffering or misfortune.

PLANT DREAM IN THE SPIRIT: Handling a dream's message in accordance with dictates of the Spirit of God, and in line with His Word and His manifest presence.

POSSESSION: The capture, control, and influence of a person by an invisible, wicked spirit.

POTENTIAL EVENT: Events likely to occur in the future.

POTIPHAR: *Meaning: Hebrew for "whom the God has given."*

Egyptian official who bought Joseph and put Joseph in charge of his household. He later sent Joseph to prison, unjustly, following his wife's false accusation.

POVERTY: State of lacking the means of providing material needs for life.

POWER: The art of being able to act and perform effectively.

PRAISE: Warm approval or strong commendation or glorification of a deity.

PRAYER: Communication with God, or addressing God through mediation or praise; a petition, favor, request.

PRISCILLA: *Meaning: Greek for "little old woman."*

Wife of Aquila, a tentmaker who invited Paul to live with them. She traveled with Paul to Ephesus and instructed Apollos. Paul considered her a fellow worker and the church met in their house.

PROGRESSIVE REVELATION: Revelation received in bits and pieces, in an increasingly unfolding manner.

PROMISE: God's pledge for the future.

PROPHET: A person who speaks by divine inspiration or as the interpreter through who divine will is expressed.

PROPHETIC DECLARATION: A proclamation under divine inspiration that is supernaturally revealed.

PROPHETIC PERFECT: Speaking of a future event as if it were already done because it is certain that God will do it.

PROPHETIC TAUNT: The use of sarcasm in prophetic speech. For example, the prophet Habakkuk used sarcasm in the forum of five woes (see Hab. 2:6-30). Sarcasm is using statements pointedly opposite the meaning of what the speaker wishes to convey. The prophet Habakkuk's purpose in this prophetic taunt is that God will judge greed and oppression, and that He will intervene on behalf of the righteous and establish His glorious kingdom.

1. The folly of extortion and plunder (see Hab. 2:6-8)

2. The folly of exploitation and injustice (see Hab. 2:9-10)

3. The folly of murder (see Hab. 2:11-14)

4. The folly of drunkenness and immortality (see Hab. 2:15-17)

5. The folly of idolatry (see Hab. 2:18-20)

PROVIDENCE: God's care and control over creation.

PSALMS: *Meaning: play a string instrument.*

PURE DREAM: A dream without a visionary component; dreams without involvement of the natural realm, as compared to a true dream, which is a dream sent by God.

PURIM: The Jewish religious holiday celebrating the deliverance of the Jews from Haman by Esther and Mordecai. The story is told in the Book of Esther.

RACHEL: *Meaning: Greek and Hebrew for "female sheep."*

Younger daughter of Laban who became the second wife of Jacob. Jacob loved her more than he loved Leah. She bore two sons and was the one who stole Laban's god.

RAHAB: *Meaning: Hebrew for "wide, spacious."*

Harlot at Jericho who hid spies and was spared when Jericho was destroyed. She was the mother of Boaz and became an example of true faith.

REALM OF THE SPIRIT: The sphere or arena of the spirit.

REBEKAH: *Meaning: Greek and Hebrew for "cow."*

Sister of Laban who became a bride for Isaac. She became the mother of Esau and Jacob. She helped Jacob deceitfully get Isaac's blessing, but she died without having set her eyes on Jacob again, after that incident.

P
Q
R

RECONCILIATION: Establishing harmony between conflicting parties.

RECURRING DREAMS: Dreams repeated more than twice over a long period of time. They may indicate issues that need to be resolved or are in the process of being resolved.

REDEMPTION: Freedom obtained through a price paid.

REHOBOAM: *Meaning: Hebrew for "widen or make spacious."*

Son of Solomon, who became a king of Judah and had various wives. He was asked to lighten Israelites' yoke, but refused to ease the Israelites' burden. This caused division in the kingdom. He was told not to fight to regain ten tribes. He then built up defenses of Judah.

REMNANTS: A small but faithful number of God's people preserved.

REPEATED DREAMS: Dreams repeated more than once within a short time, often in one single night. There may be minor variations in elements or symbolic action, but the dream's storylines are essentially the same.

REUBEN: *Meaning: Hebrew for "See, a son!"*

He was the firstborn of Jacob. He slept with his father's concubine, so forfeited the rights of the firstborn.

So Leah became pregnant and had a son, Reuben (meaning "God has noticed my trouble), for she said, Jehovah has noticed my trouble—now my husband will love me (Genesis 29:32 TLB).

REVELATION: God's disclosure of Himself and His truth.

Contemporary/Symbolic Connotation:

Curtain drawn back or veil removed.

REWARD: What God has in store for humans or good or bad consequences of our actions.

RIGHTEOUSNESS: The state of being perfect and without sin, right-standing with God.

RUTH: She was a Moabite, a widowed daughter-in-law of Naomi who decided to follow her back to Bethlehem. At the beginning, she gleaned in field of Boaz, but married him. She became the mother of Obed, an ancestor of David and ancestor of Jesus.

SABBATH: *Meaning: Hebrew for "rest."*

The seventh day of the week, a holy day on which no work was permitted.

SACKCLOTH: A coarse cloth made of goats hair, which was worn as a sign of mourning or distress.

SADDUCEES: *Meaning: disciples of Zadok.* A Jewish party, they were prominent in the time of Jesus. A sect of Judaism associated with priesthood whose beliefs centered mainly on the first five books of the Old Testament. They did not believe in resurrection or angels.

But that same day some of the Sadducees who say there is no resurrection after death came to Him and asked (Matthew 22:23 TLB).

SALOME: *Meaning: Greek for "peace."*

The mother of James and John, the sons of Zebedee. She asked for high

R
S

positions for her sons. She was one of those who watched Jesus die on the cross and went to the empty tomb. She was among the first to learn of Jesus' resurrection.

SAMARIA: *Meaning: belonging to the clan of Shamer.*

Samaria was a city built by Omri, king of Israel. It became capital of northern kingdom. Sometimes used as synonymous with the northern kingdom.

SAMARITANS: Natives of Samaria; the region between Judea and Galilee. The Jews—because of the differences in politics, race, customs, and religion—disliked them. People of a mixed race who resettled in Samaria and had a polytheistic religion. They wanted to help rebuild the temple, but their offer to rebuild the temple was refused. They tried to frustrate rebuilding of the temple and tried to frustrate rebuilding of Jerusalem.

SAMSON: *Meaning: Greek for "little sun" or "like the sun."*

Judge from the tribe of Dan whose birth was promised to the Manoah family by an angel. He married a Philistine woman and took revenge on Philistines. He was betrayed by Delilah and was later captured and had his eyes gouged out. Among his notable acts: killing of a lion, killing of thirty Philistines, killing of a thousand Philistines with a jawbone, the carrying off gates of Gaza, and pushing down temple of Dagon. He was an example of faith.

Contemporary/Symbolic Connotation:
Lack of self-control; lust; spirit of might; anointed of God.

SAMUEL: *Meaning: Hebrew for "name of God" or "God has heard."*

The son of Hannah who prayed that God would give her a son and that she would dedicate him to God's service. He was raised by Eli and was called by God to be a prophet. He was a judge and a prophet in Israel.

Contemporary/Symbolic Connotation:
Prophet; judge; king maker; teacher.

SANBALLAT: *Meaning: Hebrew for "the god Sin (moon god) has given life or made well."*

He was a chief political opponent of Nehemiah who ridiculed the rebuilding of Jerusalem and opposed rebuilding of Jerusalem. He schemed to harm Nehemiah, and his daughter married the high priest's son.

SANCTIFICATION: Being holy and becoming holy, or the process of separating or setting apart for the service of God; the state of being holy sanctified.

SANCTUARY: The part of a building dedicated to the worship of God. Sometimes the word refers to the central place of worship and not to the whole building. The part of the building set apart for divine communion.

SANHEDRIN: *Meaning: Hebrew for "a council" or "seated together."*

This was the Jewish political and religious council. It was headed by the high priest, and membership included chief priests, Pharisees, and Sadducees.

SAPPHIRA: *Meaning: Greek for "beautiful" or "gem."*

She was the wife of Ananias who deceitfully kept back part of their money and died for lying to God. They sold a field in their possession and pretended to bring the full amount sold to the apostles.

SARAH: *Meaning: Hebrew for "princess." Variation Sarai means "being contentious."*

Original name was Sarai, wife of Abram. She was barren and went with Abram to Canaan, taken by Pharaoh to be Abram's sister. She gave Hagar to Abram as concubine, but later mistreated Hagar so that Hagar ran away. Her name was changed to Sarah when birth of Isaac was promised. She laughed about a possible pregnancy. The prophecy was fulfilled, and Isaac was born. Abraham sent Hagar and Ishmael away at her request.

Contemporary/Symbolic Connotation:

Faithful wife, a mother figure; princess; fulfillment of promise.

But what does the Scripture say? "Get rid of the slave woman and her son, for the slave woman's son will never share in the inheritance with the free woman's son." Therefore, brothers, we are not children of the slave woman, but of the free woman (Galatians 4:30-31).

SAUL: *Meaning: wished or asked for.*

Contemporary/Symbolic Connotation:

Vindictive; jealous person; disobedient to the command of God; dislike subordinates.

SCEPTRE: A short rod held by kings.

A baton or staff (rod) carried by a ruler as a symbol of the authority (see Esther 4:11; Ps. 2:2,6,9; Heb. 1:8,9).

Contemporary/Symbolic Connotation:

As a sign of their authority; sign of favor or approval.

SCEVA: He was a Jewish chief priest. He had seven sons who the bible records were practicing casting out demons, but one day the demons beat them (see Acts 19:13-20).

SCHOOL OF PROPHETS: An organization of those who were true prophets. In the Old Testament, they went to school at Gibeah and Maioth, and were supervised by Samuel (see 1 Sam. 10:10; 19:20). Obadiah later hid a group of one hundred members of such school from execution by Jezebel (see 1 Kings 18:4).

A collegiate residential school seems to have been set up in Gilgal (see 2 Kings 4:38-44). Elisha was also the leader of another collegiate building (see 2 Kings 4:38-44).

SCORPION: A small creature, which has eight legs and a long tail with a poisonous sting. It can inflict a very painful and sometimes fatal wound. Scorpion is a symbol of evil. Jesus Christ gave believers power over the power of evil scorpions.

Contemporary/Symbolic Connotation:

See under Dream Symbols.

SCRIBE: A person who writes documents for others or copies written material. Some scribes were employed by ancient kings to prepare official documents, and so became important officials.

SECOND HEAVEN: The abode of spiritual warfare—the zone of conflict between good and evil forces. A place from which satan exerts his influence

SECURITY CONTENT OF A DREAM: The measure of sensitivity of information in a dream, coupled with its ability to cause damage if not maturely handled.

SEER: One who sees and receives insights by divine inspiration through pictures, dreams, and visions on a constant basis. Seers use the known to describe the unknown (see Ezek. 1; Rev. 1:12-16). Though many of Ezekiel's images are paralleled in the Book of Revelation, they are somewhat given in vocabulary familiar to Ezekiel.

SELF-DENIAL: Rejection of a self-centered life.

SELF-CONTROL: Control of one's body and emotions.

SENNACHERIB: *Meaning: Hebrew for "the moon god has taken the place of brothers to me."*

He was an Assyrian king who attempted siege of Jerusalem, but the angel of the Lord destroyed his army.

That night the angel of the Lord went out and put to death a hundred and eighty-five thousand men in the Assyrian camp. When the people got up the next morning—there were all the dead bodies! (2 Kings 19:35).

SERPENT: A name given to the dragon, which appears in the New Testament as a picture of the devil (see Rev. 12:3-17; 20:2-3).

Contemporary/Symbolic Connotation:

The devil; satan; the deceiver of brethren.

SETH: *Meaning: Hebrew for "appointed, put or set."*

He was the third son of Adam and Eve. He was made in Adam's image and is mentioned as an ancestor of Jesus.

SHADRACH: *Meaning: decree of the moon god.* One of the Hebrews deported to Babylon, whose name was changed from Hananiah. He refused to be defiled by food. He was appointed as one of the administrators in Babylon and refused to worship an image of a large statue set by the king, but God rescued him from the fiery furnace.

SHALLUM: *Meaning: Hebrew for "make peace or recompense or repay or retribution."*

One of the kings of Israel. Menahem assassinated him.

SHAMGAR: *Meaning: destroyer.* One of the judges who ruled in Israel; he was noted for killing six hundred Philistines. He judged Israel between Ehud and Barak.

S

SHAPHAN: *Meaning: Hebrew for "rock badger."*

He was the secretary during Josiah's reign. He supervised finances for temple repairs. He read the Book of Law to Josiah and visited prophetess Huldah to authenticate the discovered Book of Law.

SHEBA: *Meaning: oath.* Son of Bichin rebelled against David. He was beheaded. A place—the kingdom of Sheba where the queen visited Solomon (see 1 Kings 10:1-13; 2 Chron. 1:9).

SHECHEM: *Meaning: Hebrew for "shoulder of land" or "back."*

Key people/places with this name were:

1. This is the name of the man who raped Jacob's daughter, Dinah. In his plan to make amends, he agreed to circumcision and marriage, but was killed by Simeon and Levi.

2. The name of a city in Canaan, where the Lord appeared to Abram. It became one of the cities of refuge. This is where Gideon's son Abimelech was crowned king. Shechem was an ancient city situated between mountains Ebal and Gerizim. It was an important religious city in the history of Israel. God appeared to Abraham in Shechem (see Gen. 12:6), and after the conquest of the Promised Land, Joshua built an altar in Shechem.

SHEM: *Meaning: Hebrew and Greek for "fame."*

He was one of the sons of Noah. He covered his father with a garment and was blessed by Noah. Abram is a descendant of Shem.

SHEPHERD: A herder of sheep.

Contemporary/Symbolic Connotation:

The pastor; the leader or king.

SHILOH: *Meaning: Hebrew for "he to whom it belongs" or "rest."*

Shiloh is located in Ephraim, near Bethel. It was a notable religious center and became Joshua's political center. It was in Shiloh where Hannah asked the Lord for a son. Eli and sons ministered and God appeared to Samuel at Shiloh. Also, at Shiloh, the ark of God was taken to battle and captured by the enemy. A land in ruins in Jeremiah's day.

SHIMEI: *Meaning: Hebrew for "Jehovah has heard or listened" or "famous."*

Was the Benjamite who cursed David when he fled from Absalom's rebellion. When David returned, he spared him from execution, but later he was killed on Solomon's orders.

Contemporary/Symbolic Connotation:

See under Dream Symbols.

SIDON: *Meaning: a place of fishing.* Sidon was a major seacoast city of Phoenicia, Canaan. Its people were descendants of Ham. They were a peaceful, prosperous people and skillful in felling timber, but they served the goddess Ashtoreth.

SIGN: An outward event with a spiritual significance.

S

SIHON: *Meaning: brush.* A king of Amorites at the time Israelites approached the Promised Land. Though the Israelites sent an offer of peace, he marched out against Israelites but was destroyed.

SILAS/SILVANUS: *Meaning: Latin for "forest or wood."*

Companion of Paul, and he traveled with Paul on second missionary journey. He was also in prison with Paul at Philippi, in Thessalonica, and Berea.

SIMEON: *Meaning: Greek for "hearing."*

Key people with this name were:

1. The second son of Jacob. He was called Simeon because at his birth, his mother Leah said Jehovah has listened. Together with Levi, his brother, they revenged their sister's violation by slaughtering the men of Shechem.

She soon became pregnant again and had another son and named him Simeon (meaning 'Jehovah heard'), for she said Jehovah heard I was unloved and so he has given me another son (Genesis 29:33 TLB).

2. Tribe descended from Simeon, also one of the tribes of the 144,000.

3. Simeon who was a righteous old man who prayed for the salvation of Israel, and he rejoiced and blessed Jesus at Jesus' dedication at the temple.

SIMILITUDE: An element that closely resembles another element.

SIMON: *Meaning: Hebrew for "hears or listens."*

Key people with this name were:

1. Simon who was one of Jesus' disciples and was also known as Peter.

2. Simon who was another disciple of Jesus (called the Zealot). He became one of the apostles.

3. Simon, a Samaritan magician, who was baptized as a Christian. He thought he could buy the gift of God and offered Peter money for the power to impart the Holy Spirit. He was severely rebuked by Peter.

SINAI: *Meaning: bushy or pointed.* A desert area and was a place where the Israelites temporarily camped. Mount Sinai was also called Mount Horeb or the mountain of God because God came down from Mount Sinai. The Israelites refer to God as the God of Mount Sinai. Moses received the law at Mount Sinai. It was also at Mount Sinai that the Israelites worshiped the golden calf, made by Aaron when Moses was away for forty days and forty nights.

SISERA: Canaanite commander who fought against Deborah and Barak and was killed by Jael.

SLEEP: A temporary suspension in the exercise of the power of body and soul.

SODOM AND GOMORRAH: These were wealthy cities in the Jordan plain, but its people were extremely wicked inhabitants. Lot lived there by choice. Angels of the Lord stopped by Abraham's house on their way to bring judgment on Sodom and Gomorrah, and

S

though Abraham interceded for the cities, God eventually destroyed Sodom and Gomorrah for their wickedness.

Contemporary/Symbolic Connotation:

Total wickedness; God's judgment or eternal punishment.

SOLOMON: *Meaning: Hebrew for "peace."*

The wisest king who ever lived; he was son of David by Bathsheba. He married Pharaoh's daughter, and later married numerous pagan women. He wrote 3,000 proverbs and 1,005 songs, but he was led into sin by his many wives.

Contemporary/Symbolic Connotation:

Extraordinary wisdom; corrupt wisdom; great king; builder of God's temple.

SORCERER: A person who works magic for evil purposes.

SOUL DREAM: Dream dominated by issues emanating from a dreamer's soul.

SOUL REALM: The sphere of the soul or the act of handling decisions in the realm of emotion, feeling, or will.

SPIRIT: *Meaning: breath.* An immaterial being.

SPIRITUAL ATMOSPHERE: Impact or influence of the spirit that envelopes surroundings of an event or occurrence.

SPIRITUAL CONNOTATIONS: The reason beyond the obvious, which could touch on deeper meanings from a supernatural point of view.

SPIRITUAL ENCOUNTER: An experience in the spirit.

SPIRITUAL IMPARTATION: To bestow spiritual equipping from God upon a person.

STEPHEN: *Meaning: Greek for "crown" or "wealth."*

One of the seven deacons to assist the apostles in administration. Together with the others, they were considered filled with Holy Spirit and wisdom. Stephen was particularly knowledgeable and spoke eloquently. He was arrested by the Jews, which afforded him the opportunity to give a powerful speech to the Sanhedrin. He was, however, stoned to death for his courage and devotion to Christ.

Contemporary/Symbolic Connotation:

Boldness or fearless devotion to God; wise and knowledgeable person; eloquent speaker; martyrdom.

STEWARDSHIP: How one handles what God has given.

STONE: Something hard and unyielding. Not having a heart, unwilling to learn; a heart far from God.

SUPERIMPOSITION: When one object or person is superimposed upon another, such as when a known person gets superimposed upon an unknown person.

SYMBOL: An element that represents, stands for, or is thought to typify another element by association, resemblance, or convention. A material object used to represent a concept, such as a dove being a symbol of peace.

SYNAGOGUE: *Meaning: Greek for "a place where people gather together" or "led together."*

The word *synagogue* came into use after the Babylonians destroyed the Jewish temple during Babylonian captivity. It was later extended gradually throughout many Jewish towns as places of worship and as schools for teaching the Torah.

Contemporary/Symbolic Connotation:

Other functions include:

- As a local court of justice
- A grammar school
- For social activities
- As a council for elders' meetings

TAMAR: *Meaning: Hebrew for "palm tree."*

Key people with this name were:

1. Tamar, the wife of Judah's sons Er and Onan, who tricked Judah into fathering her children. She gave birth to twins, Peres and Zerah. Peres became an ancestor of Jesus.

2. Tamar, the daughter of David. She was the sister of Absalom who was raped by half-brother Amnon. Absalom later avenged this rape.

TASSEL: A group of threads or cords fastened together at one end and loose at the other. The Israelites were ordered to wear these on their clothes (see Num. 15:37-41).

TEMPTATION: Enticing one to sin against God. Pressure to give in to influences that may lead one away from God and into sin. God does not tempt us into sin. Satan entices us to sin. Situations tempt us to sin.

TEN COMMANDMENTS: Given by God to Moses for Israelites on Mount Sinai. They were written on stone tablets and later stored in the Ark of the testimony.

THADDAEUS: Disciple of Jesus and probably also known as Judas, son of James and one of the apostles.

THEOPHANIC DREAMS: Appearance of God in a dream.

THEOPHILUS: *Meaning: he who loved God or lover of God.* Friend of God; one to whom the Book of Acts of apostles was addressed.

THIRD HEAVEN: This is name of the highest Heaven, and the abode of God and the departed saints. The place of the highest revelations.

THOMAS: *Meaning: Aramaic for "twin."*

Disciple of Jesus who said he was ready to die with Christ and was willing to accompany Him to Jerusalem. However, he doubted Jesus' resurrection, but confessed Jesus as Lord and God when he saw the wounds on Jesus' hand.

TIMOTHY: *Meaning: Greek for "honoring God" or "honor to God."*

He was a faithful follower of apostle Paul. Paul called him his spiritual son.

He came from Lystra and was born of a mixed marriage. Therefore, he was uncircumcised and brought up as a good Jewish boy. Taught by faithful mother and grandmother, he became a believer through Paul.

TITHES: *Meaning: Hebrew for "ten."*

Coined from Abraham's gesture in the Book of Genesis. Abraham gave the priest of Salem, Mechizedek, one-tenth of his plunder. This gesture was the precedence for what was considered appropriate portion of one's wealth to give to God. The Bible says in the Book of Deuteronomy that one-tenth of annual produce is for God. It is to be used to support the ministry of the priests and the Levites, and God is to rebuke the devourer and open the window of Heaven and pour out blessings (see Num. 18:21).

TITUS: *Meaning: pleasant or protected.* The epistle that bears his name was letter of Paul to him. He was a spiritual son to Paul and was led to the Lord by Paul. Paul described him as a gentle co-worker.

TRINITY: One God in three persons—Father, Son, and Holy Spirit; there is only one God.

TRUE DREAM: A dream sent by God.

TRUST: Confidence put in someone or something, as in trust in God.

TRUTH: That which is accurate and agrees with reality.

URIAH: *Meaning: Hebrew for "my light is Jehovah" or "God is light."*

Hittite man who was the husband of Bathsheba and one of David's brave warriors. He was devoted to duty, but was killed on David's orders when David tried to cover his adulterous relationship with his wife.

URIM AND THUMMIM: *Meaning: light and perfect knowledge.* Like the casting of lots, was a means of deciding on an issue and consisted of two stones—one marked with "Yes" and the other with "No." They were stones carried by the high priest of Israel and used for determining the will of God.

USURY: *Meaning: Hebrew for "to lend on interest."*

UZZIAH: *Meaning: my strength is Jehovah or God is strength or the "might of God."* He was a son of Amaziah, king of Judah. He is also called Azariah. He was an effective and powerful king. He became proud and unlawfully burnt incense for which he was punished with leprosy.

VASHTI: *Meaning: Hebrew for "beautiful woman."*

The disobedient wife of Ahasuerus/Xerxes who was the queen of Persia. She refused to display her beauty when the king asked her to. For this, she was deposed as queen and replaced by Esther.

Contemporary/Symbolic Connotation:

Beautiful and stubborn; deposed queen; disobedient wife.

T
U
V

VISION: Supernatural sight perceptible by spiritual eyes, which has variable degrees of involvement of the mind, body, and natural realm.

VISIONARY ENCOUNTER: Spiritual experience in a vision.

VOICE OF AGREEMENT: Verbal proclamation as a form of agreeing with Heaven's decrees on earth.

VOICE OF AN ANGEL: The voice of proclamation of truth from an angel of God.

VOW: A solemn promise made to God. Notable biblical vows include: Jacob's vow at Bethel, Japheth's vow, Nazirite vow required for Samson, Hannah's vow regarding Samuel. Vows often arose in time of distress.

WARRING WITH A PROMISE: To confront your life challenges with prophetic promises received from God.

WHEEL IN THE MIDDLE OF A WHEEL: A pictorial representation of God's omnipresence. A wheel symbolizes movement. The wheels represent the flexibility and mobility of the living creatures, as reflection of the attributes of God.

WISDOM KEYS: Divine insight or solution into a given situation.

WISDOM TEST: A test that ascertains whether or not wisdom is of God.

WOE: An oracle of judgment consisting of two parts: a declaration of the wrong and a notice of impending judgment. The judgment usually applies the princi-ple of law of retaliations, a wrong would come back to haunt the wrongdoer.

WORD DEPOSITORY: Part of the mind that handles issues of the past.

WORD OF KNOWLEDGE: Knowing information beyond what one can know by natural means.

WORLD: Entire created universe, natural life as opposed to spiritual life.

WORLDLY IMAGES: Images of worldly nature, or those that evoke worldly desires.

XERXES/AHASUERUS: A king of Persia who deposed Queen Vashti and made Esther queen. He initially signed edict to annihilate the Jews. He was gracious toward Esther and received her without having summoned her into his royal presence or courtyard. He honored Mordecai when he discovered the noble role Mordecai had played in the past, and he was furious at Haman when he realized Haman's malice toward Esther and the Jews. He ordered Haman to be hanged and signed edict allowing Jews to defend themselves.

YEAR OF JUBILEE: A year when special indulgence may be granted after performing special religious acts.

YEAST/LEAVEN: A leavening substance for bread. Yeast is allowed in bread for offerings but not in others. Unleavened bread, also known as "the bread of affliction," was symbolic of the hardship and hasty departure from Egypt when there was no time to leaven the dough (see Deut. 16:3).

V
W
X
Y

Jesus also spoke of corrupt doctrines as "the yeast of Pharisees" when He said to His disciples, *"Beware of the yeast of the Pharisees."*

Contemporary/Symbolic Connotation:

A symbol of corruption and evil; a symbol of the penetrating influence of the kingdom.

YOKE: Something connects two or forms a bond between two to bring them together.

Contemporary/Symbolic Connotation:

A symbol of service to God's law; discipleship; oppression; bondage to sin; legalism; union with unbelievers.

ZACCHAEUS: *Meaning: Hebrew for "clean and pure" or "just."*

He was originally a man who corruptly enriched himself as a tax collector, but he later became eager to see Jesus and climbed a tree to see Jesus. He was privileged to host Jesus at his house and was led to God by Jesus.

ZADOK: *Meaning: Hebrew for "being righteous" or "being just."*

He was a priest in the time of David who ministered in Hebron after Saul's death. He helped bring the ark to Jerusalem and became David's priest. He was loyal to David during Absalom's rebellion and also loyal to David during Adonijah rebellion. He became the ancestor of a lineage of faithful priesthood.

Contemporary/Symbolic Connotation:

Faithful and loyal priesthood; committed to righteousness.

ZEAL: Fervent adherence to a commitment; enthusiastic and diligent devotion in pursuit of a case, goal or ideal.

ZEBEDE: *Meaning: God's portion.*

ZEBULUN: *Meaning: Hebrew for "toleration or habitation."*

Key people with this name were:

1. Son of Jacob by Leah whose name means "dwelling." He was the father of three sons.

She named him Zebulum (meaning Gift), for she said "God has given me good gifts for my husband for I have given him six sons" (Genesis 30:20 TLB).

2. Tribe descended from Zebulum.

ZECHARIAH/ZACHARIAH: *Meaning: Hebrew for "God has remembered."*

Key people with this name were:

1. Son of Jeroboam II; king of Israel who was assassinated by Shallum.

2. A postexilic prophet who encouraged rebuilding of temple and received various visions and prophesies from God on behalf of the people of Israel. He also prophesied the coming of the Messiah.

3. Father of John the Baptist who took his turn as priest in temple. He received announcement of the birth of a son, but because he questioned the archangel Gabriel, he could not speak for nine months. He gave the name "John" to his son.

ZEDEKIAH: *Meaning: Hebrew for "God is righteousness."*

Y
Z

Key people with this name were:

1. A false prophet who slapped true prophet Micaiah in the face during the reign of Ahab.

2. Son of Josiah who was also called Mattaniah. Nebuchadnezzar made him king of Judah. He asked Jeremiah to pray for Jerusalem and consulted with Jeremiah, but he later rebelled against Nebuchadnezzar and Jerusalem destroyed during his time.

ZELOPHEHAD: A son of Hepher, descendant of Manasseh, son of Joseph. He had five daughters but no son. The five daughters of Zelophehad approached Moses and the elders of Israel for equal rights for women in a godly spirit, trusting the Lord for justice. God granted their request for inheritance.

The daughters of Zelophehad son of Hepher, the son of Gilead, the son of Makir, the son of Manasseh, belonged to the clans of Manasseh son of Joseph. The names of the daughters were Mahlah, Noah, Hoglah, Milcah and Tirzah. They approached the entrance to the Tent of Meeting and stood before Moses, Eleazar the priest, the leaders and the whole assembly, and said, "Our father died in the desert. He was not among Korah's followers, who banded together against the Lord, but he died for his own sin and left no sons. Why should our father's name disappear from his clan because he had no son? Give us property among our father's relatives." So Moses brought their case before the Lord (Numbers 27:1-5).

The meanings of their names were:

- Mahlan meaning sickness or disease
- Noah meaning rest or comfort or consolation
- Hoglah meaning boxer or partridge
- Milcah meaning queen or counsel
- Tirzah meaning pleasantness

ZEPHANIAH: Zephaniah was a prophet in Judah. His preaching stirred King Josiah to institute major reforms in the kingdom.

ZERUBBABEL: *Meaning: Hebrew for "seed or offspring of Babylon or Babel" or "shoot of Babylon."*

Descendant of David who led a group of Jews from exile. He helped restore worship in Judah, helped rebuild temples, and tactfully handled opposition to rebuilding.

ZILPAH: Servant of Leah and mother of Gad and Asher.

ZIMRI: King of Israel who gained throne by assassination of King Elah, his master. He committed suicide.

ZION: *Meaning: mount sunny.* This was the Jebusite city captured by David; the place where David built his palace and the temple of the Lord. Zion also referred to as the holy mountain of God in Jerusalem; the whole city of Jerusalem or the whole nation of Judah.

Contemporary/Symbolic Connotation:

The heavenly throne of God; the prophetic kingdom of Jesus; the heavenly Jerusalem; the place from which Christ rules.

Z

ZIPPORAH: *Meaning: Hebrew for "bird" or "small bird."*

She was the daughter of Reuel, the priest of Midian. She became the wife of Moses and moved with Moses back to Egypt. She had two sons and later circumcised her son. Moses was ostracized by Aaron and Mariam because he was married to Zipporah.

ZOPHAR: One of Job's friends who tried to comfort him. He made his two speeches but was eventually compelled to offer sacrifices to God after Job's restoration.

Z

PART IV

OTHER SYMBOLIC OVERTONES

ACTIONS AND FEELINGS

Feelings or Emotions: Feelings in dreams are expressions of what the truest situation is in the life of the dreamer. They come without the moderating effect of social norms, mindsets, prejudices, or pretenses. Sometimes, the feeling expressed by the dreamer may be incongruous with what the dreamer thinks he or she is. If this happens, it is often because there are suppressed desires or hidden hurts, wounds, or scars in the life of the dreamer. By and large, most feelings in dreams are usually the reflection of the degree or intensity with which an actual event will eventually happen. However, in my experience, in over 80 percent of cases, the following feelings are symbolized as indicated in the following:

Anger: Anger.

Bitterness: Bitterness.

Hatred: Hatred.

Joy: Happiness.

Love: Love.

Sadness: Lack of joy.

Tears: Deep emotional move, could either be for a pleasant or unpleasant reason.

"Emotion, pains, joy, fear, etc. in the dream; in most cases they are often literal but what is usually more important is the degree or the intensity of the expression. For instance, crying in a dream may just help to indicate the deep emotional involvement when the events eventually occur in real life."

More information about feelings and emotions is found in my book, *Dreams and Visions Volume 2.*[9]

FLYING: The dreamer has the potential to soar high in the things of the Spirit. Divine miraculous intervention, especially the provision of escape from danger or acceleration toward destiny.

HUNGRY: Inspiration to desire spiritual food. Lack of adequate spiritual nourishment.

INABILITY TO MOVE: This may indicate hindrances to the divine purposes in the life of the dreamer. Call for intensification of spiritual warfare.

INDIFFERENT: Not considerate. Resistant. Perseverance. Carefree.

RUNNING: Depends on the context of the dream. Accelerated pace of events is approaching—either toward or away from something.

SLEEP: To be overtaken by something beyond your control.

HUNGRY: Inspiration to desire spiritual food. Death.

THINKING: A time of study, reflection, meditation, and intellectual exercise.

WALKING: The normal routine or run of life events; the expected pace of progression.

Walking, on gravel, on stones: Hard times.

Walking, on sand: May indicate not having sound foundation on the aspect of life the dream addresses.

Walking, on swampy, moldy path: May indicate sticky situation, hard times, or hindrances.

Walking, on clear waters: Moving in the Spirit and grace of God.

Walking, on dirty waters: Dabbling in wrong doctrines.

Walking, on a straight path with near infinite view: Many places to go in life.

WORRYING: Uncertain times, insecurity. Consider the context of its occurrence.

SCHOOLS AND SCHOOLING

*Note the level of education in the dream.

School building: May indicate a place of learning, church, or professional institute.

Primary (elementary) school: Indicates the fundamental things of life.

Secondary (junior/senior high) school: Indicates the equipping period of life.

Tertiary (college/university) school: Indicates the definite place of specialized call in the dreamer's life.

High school: Moving into a higher level of walk with God. Capable of giving same to others.

Delay/hindrances or disturbances during examinations: May be indications of negative influences that are at play in deciding the desired placement. It could represent personal weaknesses that are standing in the way of the dreamer.

End-of-school season: Indicates the completion of the equipping season.

Examination: On the verge of a promotion.

Failing examinations: May mean one is not meeting the requirement for the desired placement.

Inability to get to the school premises: Indicates you are not in the right place for the required equipping. Extraneous hindrances to the dreamer's drive to achieve required equipping.

Inability to locate a classroom: May indicate inner uncertainty about definite vocation or call of God in the dreamer.

Lateness: May indicate inadequate preparation for a time of equipping.

Old school time or place: May indicate similar time or season of experience, and importance is at hand or imminent.

Not finishing a test: Could mean inadequate preparation.

Passing examinations: Confirms divine approval for the promotion.

Preparing for examination: A season preceding a promotion.

Receiving or giving a lecture: The theme of the lecture is the message for the dreamer, or for the people or occasion.

Running out of paper, ink, or pen: Could indicate inadequate knowledge for the desired placement.

PARTS OF THE HUMAN BODY

BEARD: To have respect for authority.

So Hanun seized David's men, shaved off half of each man's beard, cut off their garments in the middle at the buttocks, and sent them away. When David was told about this, he sent messengers to meet the men, for they were greatly humiliated. The king said, "Stay at Jericho till your beards have grown, and then come back" (2 Samuel 10:4-5).

Beard, messy: Insanity.

Beard, trimmed: Respectable or sane.

BELLY: Feelings, desires. Spiritual well-being. Sentiment. Humiliation.

They conceive trouble and give birth to evil; their womb [belly] fashions deceit (Job 15:35).

Whoever believes in Me, as the Scripture has said, streams of living water will flow from within [from his belly] him (John 7:38).

For such people are not serving our Lord Christ, but their own [belly] appetites. By smooth talk and flattery they deceive the minds of naive people (Romans 16:18).

BONES: The substance of something. The main issue. Long-lasting.

Moses took the bones of Joseph with him because Joseph had made the sons of Israel swear an oath. He had said, "God will surely come to your aid, and then you must carry my bones up with you from this place" (Exodus 13:19).

Once while some Israelites were burying a man, suddenly they saw a band of raiders; so they threw the man's body into Elisha's tomb. When the

body touched Elisha's bones, the man came to life and stood up on his feet (2 Kings 13:21).

Bones, skeleton: Something without substance or flesh. Something without details.

EYES: The means of seeing. To want something. The seer's anointing.

Eyes, closed eyes: Spiritual blindness. Ignorance, mostly self-imposed.

Eyes, winking: Concealed intention or cunning person.

FACE: Who the person is. The identity of the person. The reflection of the heart of the person. Identity or characteristics. Image expression.

FEET: Symbol of the heart or thought pattern. The part of the body that comes in contact with the earth. The lower members of the Church. Not to be ignored. Have tendency to be ignored.

And with your feet fitted with the readiness that comes from the gospel of peace (Ephesians 6:15).

"Do not come any closer," God said. "Take off your sandals, for the place where you are standing is holy ground" (Exodus 3:5).

If the foot should say, "Because I am not a hand, I do not belong to the body," it would not for that reason cease to be part of the body (1 Corinthians 12:15).

Feet, bare foot: Humble before the presence of God. Lack of studying the Word of God. Lack of preparation.

Feet, diseased: Spirit of offense.

Feet, lame feet: Crippled with unbelief, mindset. Negative stronghold.

Feet, kicking: Not under authority or working against authority.

Feet, overgrown nails: Lack of care or not in proper order.

Feet, washing: Humility or Christian duty.

FINGERS: Image of activity, whether human or divine. Image of sensitivity. Denoting power or authority. Assigning blame. Unit of measure. For battle.

Then Pharaoh took his signet ring from his finger and put it on Joseph's finger. He dressed him in robes of fine linen and put a gold chain around his neck (Genesis 41:42).

The magicians said to Pharaoh, "This is the finger of God." But Pharaoh's heart was hard and he would not listen, just as the Lord had said (Exodus 8:19).

Then you will call, and the Lord will answer; you will cry for help, and He will say: Here am I. If you do away with the yoke of oppression, with the pointing finger and malicious talk (Isaiah 58:9).

For your hands are stained with blood, your fingers with guilt. Your lips have spoken lies, and your tongue mutters wicked things (Isaiah 59:3).

Each of the pillars was eighteen cubits high and twelve cubits in circumference; each was four fingers thick, and hollow (Jeremiah 52:21).

The young men who had grown up with him replied, "Tell these people who have said to you, 'Your father put a heavy yoke on us, but make our yoke lighter'—tell them, 'My little finger is thicker than my father's waist'"(1 Kings 12:10).

Praise be to the Lord my Rock, who trains my hands for war, my fingers for battle (Psalm 144:1).

Fingers, clenched: Pride or boastfulness.

Fingers, finger of God: Work of God or authority of God.

Fingers, fourth: Teacher.

Fingers, index: Prophet.

Fingers, little: Pastor.

Fingers, middle: Evangelist.

Fingers, pointed finger: Accusations or persecutions. Instruction or direction.

Fingers, thumb: Apostle.

FOREHEAD: That which is prominent and determines the identity of something or someone.

Therefore the showers have been withheld, and there has been no latter rain. You have had a harlot's forehead; you refuse to be ashamed (Jeremiah 3:3 NKJV).

They will see His face, and His name will be on their foreheads (Revelation 22:4).

HAIR: Cover, or something numerous, or man's glory. Protection, beauty, and identification. Mark of beauty or pride. Uncut hair is symbol of covenant. Long hair is a shame for men but glory for women. Sign of good age or dignity.

Whenever he cut the hair of his head— he used to cut his hair from time to time when it became too heavy for him—he would weigh it, and its weight was two hundred shekels by the royal standard (2 Samuel 14:26).

PARTS OF THE HUMAN BODY

Because you will conceive and give birth to a son. No razor may be used on his head, because the boy is to be a Nazirite, set apart to God from birth, and he will begin the deliverance of Israel from the hands of the Philistines (Judges 13:5).

Does not the very nature of things teach you that if a man has long hair, it is a disgrace to him, but that if a woman has long hair, it is her glory? For long hair is given to her as a covering. If anyone wants to be contentious about this, we have no other practice—nor do the churches of God (1 Corinthians 11:14-16).

As I looked, thrones were set in place, and the Ancient of Days took His seat. His clothing was as white as snow; the Hair of his head was white like wool. His throne was flaming with fire, and its wheels were all ablaze (Daniel 7:9).

Grey hair is a crown of splendor; it is attained by a righteous life (Proverbs 16:31).

Hair, baldness: Grief and shame or lacking in wisdom.

Hair, haircut: Getting something in correct shape or cutting off evil or bad habit or tradition.

Hair, long and well-maintained: Covenant and strength.

Hair, long on a man: Probably rebellious behavior or covenant relationship.

Hair, long on a woman: Glory of womanhood. Wife or submissive church.

Hair, long and unkempt: Out of control.

Hair, losing hair: Loss of wisdom or glory.

Hair, out of shape: Not in order.

Hair, shaving: Getting rid of things that hinder or things that are dirty.

Hair, short on a woman: Probably lack of submission or manliness.

HANDS: Power. Personal service, taking action on behalf of someone. A person in action. Means of service. Means of expressing strength.

The fear and dread of you will fall upon all the beasts of the earth and all the birds of the air, upon every creature that moves along the ground, and upon all the fish of the sea; they are given into your hands (Genesis 9:2).

So they called together all the rulers of the Philistines and said, "Send the ark of the god of Israel away; let it go back to its own place, or it will kill us and our people." For death had filled the city with panic; God's hand was very heavy upon it (1 Samuel 5:11).

My Father, who has given them to Me, is greater than all; no one can snatch them out of My Father's hand (John 10:29).

Stretch out your hand to heal and perform miraculous signs and wonders through the name of your holy servant Jesus (Acts 4:30).

The Lord rewards every man for his righteousness and faithfulness. The Lord delivered you into my hands today, but I would not lay a hand on the Lord's anointed (1 Samuel 26:23).

The Lord says to my Lord: "Sit at my right hand until I make your enemies a footstool for your feet" (Psalm 110:1).

But Israel reached out his right hand and put it on Ephraim's head, though he was the younger, and crossing his arms, he put his left hand on

Manasseh's head, even though Manasseh was the firstborn (Genesis 48:14).

Do not neglect your gift, which was given you through a prophetic message when the body of elders laid their hands on you (1 Timothy 4:14).

For this reason I remind you to fan into flame the gift of God, which is in you through the laying on of my hands (2 Timothy 1:6).

Hands, clapping: Joy and worship.

Hands, fist: Pride in one's strength.

Hands, covering face: Anger. Guilt or shame.

Hands, holding: In agreement.

Hands, left hand: Something spiritual.

Hands, place on the right hand: Position of honor.

Hands, put hand on the head: Blessings. Ordination.

Hands, raised: Surrender or worshiping.

Hands, right hand: Oath of allegiance; means of power of honor, natural strengths.

Hands, shaking hands: Coming to an agreement. Surrender.

Hands, stretched out hands: In security or anger.

Hands, striking: Demonstrating strength or anger.

Hands, trembling: To fear; spirit of fear; anxiety/awe at God's presence.

Hands, under thighs: In oaths.

Hands, washing: Declaring innocence or to dissociate oneself.

HEAD: Leader. To take responsibility. Be proud of something. God-ordained authority—husband. Christ. Christ as head of all people. God as the Father and head of Christ.

And Moses chose able men out of all Israel, and made them heads over the people: rulers of thousands, rulers of hundreds, rulers of fifties, and rulers of tens (Exodus 18:25 NKJV).

If anyone goes outside your house into the street, his blood will be on his own head; we will not be responsible. As for anyone who is in the house with you, his blood will be on our head if a hand is laid on him (Joshua 2:19).

Now I want you to realize that the head of every man is Christ, and the head of the woman is man, and the head of Christ is God (1 Corinthians 11:3).

For the husband is the head of the wife as Christ is the head of the church, His body, of which He is the Savior (Ephesians 5:23).

Instead, speaking the truth in love, we will in all things grow up into Him who is the Head, that is, Christ (Ephesians 4:15).

And He is the head of the body, the church; He is the beginning and the firstborn from among the dead, so that in everything He might have the supremacy (Colossians 1:18).

He has lost connection with the Head, from whom the whole body, supported and held together by its ligaments and sinews, grows as God causes it to grow (Colossians 2:19).

And you have been given fullness in Christ, who is the head over every power and authority (Colossians 2:10).

PARTS OF THE HUMAN BODY

Head, anointed: Set apart for God's service.

Head, covered with the hand: Signifying sorrow.

HEART: Most mentioning of the heart in Scripture is almost never in literal terms. The seat of affection. The seat of intellect. Innermost being.

Do not trust in extortion or take pride in stolen goods; though your riches increase, do not set your heart on them (Psalm 62:10).

The Lord saw how great man's wickedness on the earth had become, and that every inclination of the thoughts of his heart was only evil all the time (Genesis: 6:5).

Blessed are they who keep His statutes and seek Him with all their heart (Psalm 119:2).

The Lord was grieved that He had made man on the earth, and His heart was filled with pain (Genesis 6:6).

HEEL: The crushing power.

HIPS: Reproduction. Relating to reproduction or supporting structure.

KNEES: Sign of expression of relationship. Submission, blessing, or fear. Submission to Christ. Blessing. A measure of faith.

Then, at the evening sacrifice, I rose from my self-abasement, with my tunic and cloak torn, and fell on my knees with my hands spread out to the Lord my God (Ezra 9:5).

That at the name of Jesus every knee should bow, in heaven and on earth and under the earth, and every tongue confess that Jesus Christ is Lord, to the glory of God the Father (Philippians 2:10-11).

Why were there knees to receive me and breasts that I might be nursed? (Job 3:12)

Your words have supported those who stumbled; you have strengthened faltering knees (Job 4:4).

They are brought to their knees and fall, but we rise up and stand firm (Psalm 20:8).

Strengthen the feeble hands, steady the knees that give way (Isaiah 35:3).

Knees, trembling: Weakness or fear.

LEGS: Means of support. Spiritual strength to walk in life. Symbol of strength. Object of beauty. Something you stand on—your foundational principles.

His pleasure is not in the strength of the horse, nor His delight in the legs of a man (Psalm 147:10).

Then I saw another mighty angel coming down from heaven. He was robed in a cloud, with a rainbow above his head; his face was like the sun, and his legs were like fiery pillars (Revelation 10:1).

His legs are pillars of marble set on bases of pure gold. His appearance is like Lebanon, choice as its cedars (Song of Solomon 5:15).

How beautiful your sandaled feet, O prince's daughter! Your graceful legs are like jewels, the work of a craftsman's hands (Song of Solomon 7:1).

His face turned pale and he was so frightened that his knees knocked together and his legs gave way (Daniel 5:6).

I heard and my heart pounded, my lips quivered at the sound; decay crept into my bones, and my legs trembled. Yet I will wait patiently for the day of calam-

ity to come on the nation invading us (Habakkuk 3:16).

Legs, legs giving way: Giving up on the issue.

Legs, female: Power to entice.

LIPS: Reflects the quality of the heart. Lying lips. Can determine outcome in life. Issuing deception. Object of seduction.

Let their lying lips be silenced, for with pride and contempt they speak arrogantly against the righteous (Psalm 31:18).

He who guards his lips guards his life, but he who speaks rashly will come to ruin (Proverbs 13:3).

Words from a wise man's mouth are gracious, but a fool is consumed by his own lips (Ecclesiastes 10:12)

The Lord says: "These people come near to Me with their mouth and honor Me with their lips, but their hearts are far from Me. Their worship of Me is made up only of rules taught by men (Isaiah 29:13).

His cheeks are like beds of spice yielding perfume. His lips are like lilies dripping with myrrh (Song of Solomon 5:13).

MOUTH: Instrument of witnessing. Speaking evil or good words. Something from which comes the issues of life. Words coming against you.

NECK: Associated with beauty. A place to secure something valuable. Capture and subjection. Cut off or break.

Neck, outstretched: Arrogance.

Neck, long neck: Noisy.

Neck, risk the neck: To take risk.

Neck, stiff-necked: Stubbornness.

Are they not finding and dividing the spoils: a girl or two for each man, colorful garments as plunder for Sisera, colorful garments embroidered, highly embroidered garments for my neck— all this as plunder? (Judges 5:30)

They will be a garland to grace your head and a chain to adorn your neck (Proverbs 1:9).

Let love and faithfulness never leave you; bind them around your neck, write them on the tablet of your heart (Proverbs 3:3).

In His great power God becomes like clothing to me; He binds me like the neck of my garment (Job 30:18).

The Lord has appointed you priest in place of Jehoiada to be in charge of the house of the Lord ; you should put any madman who acts like a prophet into the stocks and neck-irons (Jeremiah 29:26).

Therefore in hunger and thirst, in nakedness and dire poverty, you will serve the enemies the Lord sends against you. He will put an iron yoke on your neck until He has destroyed you (Deuteronomy 28:48).

Who risked their own necks for my life, to whom not only I give thanks, but also all the churches of the Gentiles (Romans 16:4 NKJV).

NOSE: Discerning spirit. Discernment, good or bad. Intruding into people's privacy. Gossiper.

SHOULDERS: The responsibility, the authority. Something, person or animal on which burden or load is laid or can be placed. Something that can be of good for work. Governmental responsibility. Sign of unity—shoulder to shoulder. Captivity.

For as in the day of Midian's defeat, you have shattered the yoke that burdens them, the bar across their shoulders, the rod of their oppressor (Isaiah 9:4).

For to us a child is born, to us a son is given, and the government will be on His shoulders. And He will be called Wonderful Counselor, Mighty God, Everlasting Father, Prince of Peace (Isaiah 9:6).

Then will I purify the lips of the peoples, that all of them may call on the name of the Lord and serve Him shoulder to shoulder (Zephaniah 3:9).

He says, "I removed the burden from their shoulders; their hands were set free from the basket" (Psalm 81:6).

They tie up heavy loads and put them on men's shoulders, but they themselves are not willing to lift a finger to move them (Matthew 23:4).

Shoulders, bare female shoulders: Enticement.

Shoulders, broad: Capable of handling much responsibility.

Shoulders, drooped: Defeated attitude, overworked, overtired, burnt-out.

TEETH: Primary symbol of strength. Image of good consumption by breaking down into tiny bits. To simplify into its smallest bits for easy processing for wisdom. Power.

And there before me was a second beast, which looked like a bear. It was raised up on one of its sides, and it had three ribs in its mouth between its teeth. It was told, "Get up and eat your fill of flesh!" (Daniel 7:5)

Like the ungodly they maliciously mocked; they gnashed their teeth at me (Psalm 35:16).

But the subjects of the kingdom will be thrown outside, into the darkness, where there will be weeping and gnashing of teeth (Matthew 8:12).

Teeth, baby teeth: Immaturity.

Teeth, breaking of teeth: Defeat and/or losing wisdom.

Teeth, brushing teeth: Gaining understanding.

Teeth, false teeth: Wisdom of this world.

Teeth, gnashing of teeth: Sign of taunt, division or regret and sorrow.

Teeth, toothache: Trial, problems.

BUILDINGS

Personalities or Structure of an Organization

I will show you what he is like who comes to Me and hears My words and puts them into practice. He is like a man building a house, who dug down deep and laid the foundation on rock. When the flood came, the torrent struck that house but could not shake it, because it was well built (Luke 6:47-48).

CHURCH BUILDING: Pertaining to church, ministry, or the call of God.

COURTROOM: Being judged. Under scrutiny. Persecution, trial.

CURRENT HOUSE: The dreamer's make-up.

FACTORY: A place of putting things together. A place of protection. A church.

Factory, foundation: Something on which the person or object stands on.

Factory, idle: Not put into proper use.

Factory, in good state: Good standing.

Factory, ruins: Needing attention.

FAMILY HOME: Related to the past. Something from the past influencing the present. Something from the bloodline.

House, high-rise: Multi-talented ministry; multiple ministries in one place.

House, mobile home: A transitory situation. Character in transition. Temporary place.

House, moving home: Changes in personality.

House, new: New personality, either natural or spiritual.

House, old: Past or something inherited. If in good state, then it is righteous or good from the past. If in bad state, then it is sin or weakness that runs in a family.

House, shop: A place of choices. Business related venue.

House, under construction: In process of formation.

LIBRARY: Time or place of knowledge; education.

OFFICE BUILDING: Relates to circular jobs, the dreamer's office life.

Parts of a Building

BACK: Something in the past or unexpected.

BATHROOM: A period of cleansing; entering a time of repentance. A place of voluntary nakedness. Facing reality in individual life.

BEDROOM: A place of intimacy. A place of rest or where you sleep and dream. A place of covenant or a place of revelation.

FRONT: Something in the future.

KITCHEN: A plea of nourishment; heart. The mind or intellect, where ideas are muted in the natural realm. The heart (Spirit). Where revelations are received and nurtured for the equipping of others.

ROOF: The covering.

SITTING ROOM: That which is easily noticed by the public. The revealed part.

States of a Building

CRACKED WALL: Faulty protective measures. Not adequately protected.

LEAKING ROOF: Inadequate spiritual cover.

MODERN: Current doctrine up-to-date.

NEGLECTED: Lack of maintenance.

OLD-FASHIONED: Tradition or old belief.

BUILDINGS

NUMBERS

Spiritual Significance of Numbers

God speaks through numbers a great deal, and the Bible is full of evidence of God's arithmetic. Numbers are high-level forms of symbolism. I have put together some numbers and their generally accepted scriptural relevance or meaning. The spiritual significance of numbers given here is based on the Word of God, and I have found it very useful in my personal experience.

ONE: Unity. The number of God. The beginning, the first. Precious.

There is one body and one Spirit—just as you were called to one hope when you were called—one Lord, one faith, one baptism; one God and Father of all, who is over all and through all and in all (Ephesians 4:4-6).

I and the Father are one (John 10:30).

That all of them may be one, Father, just as You are in Me and I am in You. May they also be in Us so that the world may believe that You have sent Me. I have given them the glory that You gave Me, that they may be one as We are one (John 17:21-22).

Make every effort to keep the unity of the Spirit through the bond of peace (Ephesians 4:3).

And I will pour out on the house of David and the inhabitants of Jerusalem a spirit of grace and supplication. They will look on Me, the one they have pierced, and they will mourn for Him as one mourns for an only child, and grieve bitterly for Him as one grieves for a firstborn son (Zechariah 12:10).

A mediator, however, does not represent just one party; but God is one (Galatians 3:20).

TWO: Union, witnessing or confirmation. It could also mean division depending on the general context of the events or revelation.

The man said, "This is now bone of my bones and flesh of my flesh; she shall be called 'woman,' for she was taken out of man." For this reason a man will leave his father and mother and be united to his wife, and they will become one flesh (Genesis 2:23-24).

But if he will not listen, take one or two others along, so that every matter may be established by the testimony of two or three witnesses (Matthew 18:16).

He is a double-minded man, unstable in all he does (James 1:8).

So God made the expanse and separated the water under the expanse from the water above it. And it was so. God called the expanse "sky." And there was evening, and there was morning—the second day (Genesis 1:7-8).

Then the king said, "Bring me a sword." So they brought a sword for the king. He then gave an order: "Cut the living child in two and give half to one and half to the other" (1 Kings 3:24-25).

THREE: Resurrection, divine completeness and perfection. Confirmation. The trinity of Godhead. Restoration.

Therefore go and make disciples of all nations, baptizing them in the name of the Father and of the Son and of the Holy Spirit (Matthew 28:19).

For as Jonah was three days and three nights in the belly of a huge fish, so the Son of Man will be three days and three nights in the heart of the earth (Matthew 12:40).

Jesus answered them, "Destroy this temple, and I will raise it again in three days" (John 2:19).

FOUR: Creation or to rule or to reign. On the fourth day of creation, God made two great lights—the sun and the moon—to rule the day and the night.

And God said, "Let there be lights in the expanse of the sky to separate the day from the night, and let them serve as signs to mark seasons and days and years, and let them be lights in the expanse of the sky to give light on the earth." And it was so. God made two great lights—the greater light to govern the day and the lesser light to govern the night. He also made the stars. God set them in the expanse of the sky to give light on the earth, to govern the day and the night, and to separate light from darkness. And God saw that it was good. And there was evening, and there was morning—the fourth day (Genesis 1:14-19).

Also before the throne there was what looked like a sea of glass, clear as crystal. In the center, around the throne, were four living creatures, and they were covered with eyes, in front and in back. The first living creature was like a lion, the second was like an ox, the third had a face like a man, the fourth was like a flying eagle. Each of the four living creatures had six wings and was covered with eyes all around, even under his wings. Day and night they never stop saying: "Holy, holy, holy is the Lord God Almighty, who was, and is, and is to come" (Revelation 4:6-8).

FIVE: Grace or the goodness of God. Fivefold ministry.

It was He who gave some to be apostles, some to be prophets, some to be evangelists, and some to be pastors and teachers (Ephesians 4:11).

SIX: The number of man. Weakness of humanity or the flesh. Can mean evil or satan. God created man on the sixth day.

Then God said, "Let us make man in Our image, in Our likeness, and let them rule over the fish of the sea and the birds of the air, over the livestock, over all the earth, and over all the creatures that move along the ground." So God created man in His own image, in the image of God He created him; male and female He created them (Genesis 1:26-27).

Nebuchadnezzar the king made an image of gold, whose height was sixty cubits and its width six cubits. He set it up in the plain of Dura, in the province of Babylon (Daniel 3:1 NKJ).

"Scenes of restricted liberty or movement in a dream or vision may indicate demonic presence or influences because as the Bible says, where the spirit of God is there is liberty. Restriction or inability to speak or move any part of the body in the dream indicates that the chance of demonic influence is very high. Also, the presence of undue fear or confusion should cause you to suspect the influence of the demonic."

More information about discerning evil and natural influences is found in my book, *Dreams and Visions Volume 2.*[10]

SEVEN: Completeness or spiritual perfection. Rest. Blessing. Redemption.

Thus the heavens and the earth were completed in all their vast array. By the seventh day God had finished the work

He had been doing; so on the seventh day He rested from all His work. And God blessed the seventh day and made it holy, because on it He rested from all the work of creating that He had done (Genesis 2:1-3).

But in the days when the seventh angel is about to sound his trumpet, the mystery of God will be accomplished, just as He announced to His servants the prophets (Revelation 10:7).

The seventh angel poured out his bowl into the air, and out of the temple came a loud voice from the throne, saying, "It is done!" (Revelation 16:17)

At the end of every seven years you must cancel debts. This is how it is to be done: Every creditor shall cancel the loan he has made to his fellow Israelite. He shall not require payment from his fellow Israelite or brother, because the Lord's time for cancelling debts has been proclaimed (Deuteronomy 15:1-2).

EIGHT: New birth or new beginning. The circumcision of male children of Israel on the eighth day is a type of new birth.

On the eighth day, when it was time to circumcise Him, He was named Jesus, the name the angel had given Him before He had been conceived. When the time of their purification according to the Law of Moses had been completed, Joseph and Mary took Him to Jerusalem to present Him to the Lord (as it is written in the Law of the Lord, "Every firstborn male is to be consecrated to the Lord") (Luke 2:21-23).

For the generations to come every male among you who is eight days old must be circumcised, including those born in your household or bought with money from a foreigner—those who are not your offspring (Genesis 17:12).

NINE: Fruit of the Spirit. Harvest or the fruit of your labor. Nine gifts of the Spirit.

But the fruit of the Spirit is love, joy, peace, patience, kindness, goodness, faithfulness, gentleness and self-control. Against such things there is no law (Galatians 5:22-23).

To one there is given through the Spirit the message of wisdom, to another the message of knowledge by means of the same Spirit, to another faith by the same Spirit, to another gifts of healing by that one Spirit, to another miraculous powers, to another prophecy, to another distinguishing between spirits, to another speaking in different kinds of tongues, and to still another the interpretation of tongues (1 Corinthians 12:8-10).

TEN: Law and responsibility. Tithe is a tenth of our earning, which belongs to God. It is also the number for the pastoral. Judgment. Ten plagues upon Egypt.

ELEVEN: Confusion, judgment, or disorder.

TWELVE: Government. The number of apostleship.

One of those days Jesus went out to a mountainside to pray, and spent the night praying to God. When morning came, He called His disciples to Him and chose twelve of them, whom He also designated apostles (Luke 6:12-13).

Jesus said to them, "I tell you the truth, at the renewal of all things, when the Son of Man sits on His glorious throne, you who have followed Me will also sit on twelve thrones, judging the twelve tribes of Israel" (Matthew 19:28).

THIRTEEN: Thirteen evil thoughts from the heart listed. Rebellion or spiritual depravity.

For from within, out of men's hearts, come evil thoughts, sexual immorality, theft, murder, adultery, greed, malice, deceit, lewdness, envy, slander, arrogance and folly (Mark 7:21-22).

FOURTEEN: Deliverance or salvation. The number of double anointing.

Thus there were fourteen generations in all from Abraham to David, fourteen from David to the exile to Babylon, and fourteen from the exile to the Christ (Matthew 1:17).

FIFTEEN: Rest, mercy.

Mordecai recorded these events, and he sent letters to all the Jews throughout the provinces of King Xerxes, near and far, to have them celebrate annually the fourteenth and fifteenth days of the month of Adar as the time when the Jews got relief from their enemies, and as the month when their sorrow was turned into joy and their mourning into a day of celebration. He wrote them to observe the days as days of feasting and joy and giving presents of food to one another and gifts to the poor (Esther 9:20-22).

Say to the Israelites: "On the fifteenth day of the seventh month the Lord's Feast of Tabernacles begins, and it lasts for seven days. The first day is a sacred assembly; do no regular work" (Leviticus 23:34-35).

SIXTEEN: Love—sixteen things are said of love.

Love is patient, love is kind. It does not envy, it does not boast, it is not proud.

It is not rude, it is not self-seeking, it is not easily angered, it keeps no record of wrongs. Love does not delight in evil but rejoices with the truth. It always protects, always trusts, always hopes, always perseveres. Love never fails. But where there are prophecies, they will cease; where there are tongues, they will be stilled; where there is knowledge, it will pass away (1 Corinthians 13:4-8).

SEVENTEEN: Immaturity. Transition. Victory.

Joseph, a young man of seventeen, was tending the flocks with his brothers, the sons of Bilhah and the sons of Zilpah, his father's wives, and he brought their father a bad report about them (Genesis 37:2).

Jacob lived in Egypt seventeen years, and the years of his life were a hundred and forty-seven (Genesis 47:28).

And on the seventeenth day of the seventh month the ark came to rest on the mountains of Ararat (Genesis 8:4).

EIGHTEEN: Bondage.

Then should not this woman, a daughter of Abraham, whom satan has kept bound for eighteen long years, be set free on the Sabbath day from what bound her? (Luke 13:16)

The Israelites were subject to Eglon king of Moab for eighteen years (Judges 3:14).

He became angry with them. He sold them into the hands of the Philistines and the Ammonites, who that year shattered and crushed them. For eighteen years they oppressed all the Israelites on the east side of the Jordan in Gilead, the land of the Amorites (Judges 10:7-8).

NUMBERS

NINETEEN: Faith. Nineteen persons mentioned in Hebrews chapter 11.

Now faith is being sure of what we hope for and certain of what we do not see. This is what the ancients were commended for... (Hebrews 11:1-32).

TWENTY: Redemption (silver money in the Bible).

THIRTY: Blood of Jesus. Dedication. The beginning of service. Salvation.

Then one of the Twelve—the one called Judas Iscariot—went to the chief priests and asked, "What are you willing to give me if I hand Him over to you?" So they counted out for him thirty silver coins (Matthew 26:14-15).

Count all the men from thirty to fifty years of age who come to serve in the work in the Tent of Meeting. This is the work of the Kohathites in the Tent of Meeting: the care of the most holy things (Numbers 4:3-4).

Joseph was thirty years old when he entered the service of Pharaoh king of Egypt. And Joseph went out from Pharaoh's presence and traveled throughout Egypt (Genesis 41:46).

David was thirty years old when he became king, and he reigned forty years (2 Samuel 5:4).

FORTY: Trial. Probation. Testing or temptation.

Remember how the Lord your God led you all the way in the desert these forty years, to humble you and to test you in order to know what was in your heart, whether or not you would keep His commands. He humbled you, causing you to hunger and then feeding you with manna, which neither you nor your fathers had known, to teach you that man does not live on bread alone but on every word that comes from the mouth of the Lord. Your clothes did not wear out and your feet did not swell during these forty years. Know then in your heart that as a man disciplines his son, so the Lord your God disciplines you (Deuteronomy 8:2-5).

Jesus, full of the Holy Spirit, returned from the Jordan and was led by the Spirit in the desert, where for forty days He was tempted by the devil. He ate nothing during those days, and at the end of them He was hungry (Luke 4:1-2).

So he got up and ate and drank. Strengthened by that food, he traveled forty days and forty nights until he reached Horeb, the mountain of God (1 Kings 19:8).

On the first day, Jonah started into the city. He proclaimed: "Forty more days and Nineveh will be overturned" (Jonah 3:4).

FIFTY: Number of the Holy Spirit. Jubilee, liberty. The number for the Holy Spirit: He was poured out on the day of Pentecost which was fifty days after the resurrection of Christ.

Consecrate the fiftieth year and proclaim liberty throughout the land to all its inhabitants. It shall be a jubilee for you; each one of you is to return to his family property and each to his own clan (Leviticus 25:10).

SIXTY: Pride or arrogance. The image that Nebuchadnezzar set up was sixty cubits high.

Nebuchadnezzar the king made an image of gold, whose height was sixty cubits and its width six cubits. He set it up in the plain of Dura, in the province of Babylon (Daniel 3:1 NKJV).

SEVENTY: Universality or restoration. Israel lived in exile for seventy years after which they were restored.

In the first year of his reign, I, Daniel, understood from the Scriptures, according to the word of the Lord given to Jeremiah the prophet, that the desolation of Jerusalem would last seventy years (Daniel 9:2).

EIGHTY: Beginning of a high calling or becoming spiritually acceptable.

Moses was eighty years old when he started his ministry to deliver the Israelites.

NINETY: Fruits are ripe and ready. Abraham was ninety-nine years old when God appeared to him.

When Abram was ninety-nine years old, the Lord appeared to him and said, "I am God Almighty; walk before Me and be blameless" (Genesis 17:1).

ONE HUNDRED: God's election of grace. Children of promise. Full reward. Abraham was one hundred years old when his son Isaac (child of promise) was born.

Abraham was a hundred years old when his son Isaac was born to him (Genesis 21:5).

ONE THOUSAND: The beginning of maturity; mature service or full status.

Multiples or Complex Numbers

For these numbers, the meaning lies in the way it is pronounced rather than as it is written.

Example: *2872* is pronounced "Two thousand, eight hundred, seventy-two."

Two thousand = confirmed spiritual maturity or mature judgment.

Eight hundred = new beginning into the promises.

Seventy-two = confirmed, completed, and restored.

ENDNOTES

1. Dr. Joe Ibojie, *The Final Frontiers* (Aberdeen, UK: Cross House Books), 2010.
2. Ibid.
3. Dr. Joe Ibojie, *The Watchman,* (Pescara, Italy: Destiny Image Europe), 2009.
4. Ibid.
5. Ibid.
6. Dr. Joe Ibojie, *The Justice of of God: Victory in Everyday Living* (Aberdeen, UK: Cross House Books), 2009.
7. Ibid.
8. Dr. Joe Ibojie, *Dreams and Visions Volume 2* (Aberdeen, UK: Cross House Books), 2009.
9. Ibid.
10. Ibid.

ABOUT THE AUTHOR

D R. JOE IBOJIE, founder and senior pastor of The Father's House, travels nationally and internationally as a Bible and prophetic teacher. He combines a unique prophetic gifting with rare insight into the mysteries of God and the ancient biblical methods of understanding dreams and visions. His ministry has blessed thousands by bringing down-to-earth clarity to the prophetic ministry. He is a popular speaker worldwide. He and his wife, Cynthia, live in Aberdeen, Scotland.

MINISTRY INFORMATION

DR. JOE IBOJIE IS THE SENIOR PASTOR OF
THE FATHER'S HOUSE

A family church and a vibrant community of Christians located in Aberdeen Scotland, UK. The Father's House seeks to build a bridge of hope across generations, racial divides, and gender biases through the ministry of the Word.

You are invited to come and worship if you are in the area.

For location, please visit the church's Website:

www.the-fathers-house.org.uk

For inquiries:

info@the-fathers-house.org.uk

Call 44 1224 701343

HOW TO LIVE THE SUPERNATURAL LIFE IN THE HERE AND NOW

Are you ready to stop living an ordinary life? You were meant to live a supernatural life! God intends us to experience His power every day! In *How to Live the Supernatural Life in the Here and Now* you will learn how to bring the supernatural power of God into everyday living. Finding the proper balance for your life allows you to step into the supernatural and to move in power and authority over everything around you. Dr. Joe Ibojie, an experienced pastor and prolific writer, provides practical steps and instruction that will help you to:

- Step out of the things that hold you back in life.
- Understand that all life is spiritual.
- Experience the supernatural life that God has planned for you!
- Find balance between the natural and the spiritual.
- Release God's power to change and empower your circumstances.

Are you ready to live a life of spiritual harmony? Then you are ready to learn *How to Live the Supernatural Life in the Here and Now!*

DREAMS AND VISIONS VOLUME 1

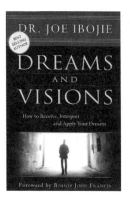

Dreams and Visions presents sound scriptural principles and practical instructions to help you understand dreams and visions. The book provides readers with the necessary understanding to approach dreams and visions by the Holy Spirit, through biblical illustrations, understanding of the meaning of dreams and prophetic symbolism, and by exploring the art of dream interpretation according to ancient methods of the Bible.

ILLUSTRATED BIBLE-BASED DICTIONARY OF DREAM SYMBOLS

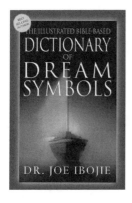

This book is a companion to *Dreams & Visions: How to Receive, Interpret and Apply Your Dreams* and will help today's believers understand what dream symbols mean. When used through the Holy Spirit, it can help the reader take away the frustration of not knowing what dreams mean and avoid the dangers of misinterpretation.

—Joseph Ewen
Founder and Leader of Riverside Church Network
Banff, Scotland, UK

This book is a treasure chest, loaded down with revelation and the hidden mysteries of God that have been waiting since before the foundation of the earth to be uncovered. *Illustrated Bible-Based Dictionary of Dream Symbols* shall bless, strengthen, and guide any believer who is in search for the purpose, promise, and destiny of God for their lives.

—Bishop Ron Scott Jr.
President, Kingdom Coalition International
Hagerstown, Maryland

Illustrated Bible-Based Dictionary of Dream Symbols is much more than a book of dream symbols; it has also added richness to our reading of God's Word. Whether you use this book to assist in interpreting your dreams or as an additional resource for your study of the Word of God, you will find it a welcome companion.

—Robert and Joyce Ricciardelli
Directors, Visionary Advancement Strategies
Seattle, Washington

DREAMS AND VISIONS 2

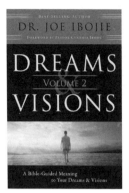

God speaks to you through dreams and visions. Do you want to know the meaning of your dreams? Do you want to know what He is telling and showing you? Now you can know!

Dreams and Visions Volume 2 is packed full of exciting and bible-guided ways to discover the meaning of your God-inspired, dreamy nighttime adventures and your wide-awake supernatural experiences!

Dr. Joe Ibojie reveals why and how God wants to communicate with you through dreams and visions. In this *second volume*, the teaching emphasizes how to gain clearer understanding of your dreams and visions in a new, in-depth, and user-friendly way.

THE JUSTICE OF GOD
VICTORY IN EVERYDAY LIVING

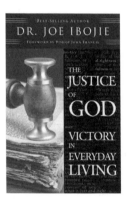

Only once in awhile does a book bring rare insight and godly illumination to a globally crucial subject. This book is one of them! A seminal work from a true practitioner, best-selling author, and leader of a vibrant church, Dr. Joe Ibojie brings clarity and a hands-on perspective to the Justice of God.

The Justice of God reveals:

- How to pull down your blessings.
- How to regain your inheritance.
- The heavenly courts of God.
- How to work with angels.
- The power and dangers of prophetic acts and drama.

THE WATCHMAN
THE MINISTRY OF THE SEER IN A LOCAL CHURCH

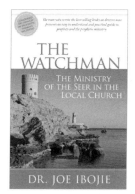

The ministry of the watchman in a local church is possibly one of the most common and yet one of the most misunderstood ministries in the Body of Christ. Over time, the majority of these gifted people have been driven into reclusive lives because of relational issues and confusion surrounding their very vital ministry in the local church.

Through the pages of *The Watchman* you will learn:

- Who these watchmen are.
- How they can be recognized, trained, appreciated, and integrated into the Body of Christ.
- About their potential and how they can be channelled as valuable resources to the local leadership.
- How to avoid prophetic and pastoral pitfalls.
- How to receive these gifted folks as the oracles of God they really are.

The 21st century watchman ministry needs a broader and clearer definition. It is time that the conservative, narrow, and restrictive perspectives of the watchman's ministry be enlarged into the reality of its great potential and value God has intended.

THE FINAL FRONTIERS
COUNTDOWN TO THE FINAL SHOWDOWN

The maladies that define the focal feature of our existence are that we face a continuous threat from the challenges of the earth in a fallen state. Every now and again, we witness the eruptions of nature against man with catastrophic consequences, but these are only miniature representations of an immense cosmic cataclysm that could occur. Gradually the things that make the earth precious to us are disappearing with few taking notice. *The Final Frontiers* is a peep into the future and a call to action. It provides you with a practical approach to the changing struggles that confront humanity now and in your future and reveals through Scriptures and modern-day experiences:

- What was lost at the Fall
- The elements of nature in God's service
- How to defeat the devil at the mind game
- Invisible realms of hell
- Spiritual weaponry
- Peace and the ultimate redemption

"In writing this book, I feel like the prophet Jeremiah, calling humanity to be alert to the ploy of the enemy, to break the secret bubble, and reveal the shapes of warfare to come." —Dr. Joe Ibojie

DREAM COURSES

DREAMS ARE THE PARABLE LANGUAGE of God in a world that is spiritually distancing itself from experiencing the reality of His Presence. They are personalized, coded messages from God. Through dreams, God breaks through our thought processes, mindsets, prejudices and emotions to connect with the spirit of man. In this way He shows us what we might have missed or not heard or what our natural mind was incapable of comprehending. We all dream. He speaks to us at our individual levels and leads us further in Christ. God's ultimate purpose in dreams and visions is to align us to His plan and purposes in our lives!

The purpose of these courses is to equip the saints for the end-time move of God by learning the art of hearing Him and understanding how He speaks through dreams at an individual level.

Each dream course builds on the knowledge gained in the previous course. Attendees are strongly encouraged to take the courses in order for maximum effectiveness.

Topics covered include:

COURSE 1

- Introduction to dreams and visions.
- Biblical history of dreams and visions.
- How dreams are received.

- Hindrances to receiving and remembering your dreams.
- How to respond to your dreams.
- Differences between dreams and visions.
- Introduction to interpreting your dreams.
- Understanding the ministry of angels.

COURSE 2

- Introduction to the language of symbols (the language of the spirit).
- Different levels of interpretation of dreams.
- Why we seek the meaning of our dreams.
- What to do with dreams you do not immediately understand.
- Maintaining and developing your dream-life.
- Expanding the scope of your dreams.
- Improving your interpretative skill.
- Visions and the Third Heaven.

COURSE 3

- Responding to revelations.
- Interpreting the dreams of others.
- Guidelines for setting up a corporate dream group.
- Prophetic symbolism.
- How to organize Dream Workshops.
- The Seer's anointing.
- The ministry of a Watchman.
- Spiritual warfare (fighting the good fight).
- Understanding the roles of angels and the different categories of angelic forces.
- How to work with angels.

COURSE 4

- Living the supernatural in the natural.
- Understanding the spiritual senses.
- Maintaining balance while blending the natural and the spiritual senses.
- Security and information management in revelatory ministry.
- Understanding the anointing.
- Dialoguing with God.
- An anatomy of scriptural dreams.

WEEKEND COURSES

Friday

- Registration begins at 5:00 P.M.
- Teaching begins at 6:00 P.M.

Saturday

- Registration begins at 9:00 A.M.
- Sessions begin at 10:30 A.M., 1:30 P.M. and 7:00 P.M.

One Week Course (Monday through Friday)

Courses begin Monday morning and conclude Friday evening.
- Registration begins each day at 9:00 A.M.
- Sessions begin at 10:00 A.M. and end at 5:00 P.M.

There are breaks for lunch and tea.

The contents of each Dream Course will be covered in two weekend courses or a single one-week course (Monday through Friday).

To Request a DREAM COURSE in your area of the world, please call to arrange a program to fit your needs:

Dr. Joe Ibojie
info@the-fathers-house.org.uk
44-1224-701343
44-7765-834253